TRANSFORMATIONAL CHANGE IN ENVIRONMENTAL AND NATURAL RESOURCE MANAGEMENT

The aim of this book is to catalyse global interest in the pursuit of transformational changes in natural resource and environmental management. Transformational policy reforms involve fundamental shifts in strategy with far-reaching consequences for the structure of industries, the way people behave and the resources they use.

Transformational reforms typically involve a decision to change a suite of institutional arrangements that will result, within a short period of time, in a paradigm shift and the emergence of an approach that will be recognised as being totally different to the arrangements that were previously in place.

Transformational change is well established in business and can deliver outstanding results. In the world of policy development, however, many transformational policy reforms flounder. Unlike incremental policy reforms, they are often seen to be politically risky and prone to failure.

Using examples of success and failure, coupled with insights from practitioners and academics who have succeeded in getting transformational reforms implemented, this book presents a set of guidelines for excellence in the pursuit of transformational policy reforms. It includes detailed case studies from Australia, China, Europe, New Zealand, Southeast Asia and the USA.

Mike Young was the Gough Whitlam and Malcolm Fraser Chair in Australian Studies at Harvard University, USA. He holds a Professorial Chair in Water and Environmental Policy at Adelaide University, Australia, and is an Honorary Professor at University College London, UK, and a Research Fellow at Duke University's Nicholas Institute for Sustainable Environmental Policy Solutions, USA.

Christine Esau is a journalist and research editor based in Australia, with a particular interest in compelling environmental dialogues.

Earthscan Studies in Natural Resource Management

Transformational Change in Environmental and Natural Resource Management
Guidelines for policy excellence
Edited by Michael D. Young and Christine Esau

Community Innovations in Sustainable Land Management
Lessons from the field in Africa
Edited by Maxwell Mudhara, Saa Dittoh, Mohamed Sessay, William Critchley and Sabina Di Prima

The Water, Food, Energy and Climate Nexus
Challenges and an agenda for action
Edited by Felix Dodds and Jamie Bartram

Mitigating Land Degradation and Improving Livelihoods
An integrated watershed approach
Edited by Feras Ziadat and Wondimu Bayu

Adaptive Cross-scalar Governance of Natural Resources
Edited by Grenville Barnes and Brian Child

The Water, Energy and Food Security Nexus
Lessons from India for development
Edited by M. Dinesh Kumar, Nitin Bassi, A. Narayanamoorthy and M.V.K. Sivamohan

Gender Research in Natural Resource Management
Building capacities in the Middle East and North Africa
Edited by Malika Abdelali-Martini, Aden Aw-Hassan

Contested Forms of Governance in Marine Protected Areas
A study of co-management and adaptive co-management
Natalie Bown, Tim S. Gray and Selina M. Stead

Adaptive Collaborative Approaches in Natural Resource Management
Rethinking participation, learning and innovation
Edited by Hemant R. Ojha, Andy Hall and Rasheed Sulaiman V

Integrated Natural Resource Management in the Highlands of Eastern Africa
From concept to practice
Edited by Laura Anne German, Jeremias Mowo, Tilahun Amede and Kenneth Masuki

For more information on books in the Earthscan Studies in Natural Resource Management series, please visit the series page on the Routledge website: www.routledge.com/books/series/ECNRM/

TRANSFORMATIONAL CHANGE IN ENVIRONMENTAL AND NATURAL RESOURCE MANAGEMENT

Guidelines for policy excellence

Edited by Michael D. Young and Christine Esau

First published 2016
by Routledge
2 Park Square, Milton Park, Abingdon, Oxon OX14 4RN

and by Routledge
711 Third Avenue, New York, NY 10017

Routledge is an imprint of the Taylor & Francis Group, an informa business

© 2016 Michael D. Young and Christine Esau, selection and editorial material; individual chapters, the contributors

The right of the editors to be identified as the authors of the editorial material, and of the authors for their individual chapters, has been asserted in accordance with sections 77 and 78 of the Copyright, Designs and Patents Act 1988.

All rights reserved. No part of this book may be reprinted or reproduced or utilised in any form or by any electronic, mechanical, or other means, now known or hereafter invented, including photocopying and recording, or in any information storage or retrieval system, without permission in writing from the publishers.

Trademark notice: Product or corporate names may be trademarks or registered trademarks, and are used only for identification and explanation without intent to infringe.

British Library Cataloguing-in-Publication Data
A catalogue record for this book is available from the British Library

Library of Congress Cataloging in Publication Data
Names: Young, M. D. (Michael Denis), 1952- author. | Esau, Christine., author.
Title: Transformational change in environmental and natural resource management : guidelines for policy excellence / edited by Michael D. Young and Christine Esau.
Description: London ; New York : Routledge is an imprint of the Taylor & Francis Group, an Informa Business, [2016] | Includes bibliographical references and index.
Identifiers: LCCN 2016013289 | ISBN 9781138884694 (hbk) | ISBN 9781138884748 (pbk) | ISBN 9781315715919 (ebk)
Subjects: LCSH: Environmental management. | Natural resources--Management. | Environmental policy.
Classification: LCC GE300 .T73 2016 | DDC 333.7--dc23
LC record available at https://lccn.loc.gov/2016013289

ISBN: 978-1-138-88469-4 (hbk)
ISBN: 978-1-138-88474-8 (pbk)
ISBN: 978-1-315-71591-9 (ebk)

Typeset in Bembo
by Saxon Graphics Ltd, Derby

Dedication

For Susie, Kate and Annabelle
Hawk, Alister and Olivier
Mia, Olivia, Emily and Henry

CONTENTS

List of figures		ix
List of tables		x
Contributors		xi
Preface		xiii
1	Transformational change: in search of excellence Mike Young	1
2	Significant, sustainable environmental reform is difficult in any democracy Kevin Rudd	14
3	Unpacking the dynamics of successful change: ten insights from the private sector Rebecca Henderson	21
4	An assessment framework for resilient public policy R. Quentin Grafton and Walter Reinhardt	38
5	Lessons from reforming fossil-fuel subsidy regimes Georgeta Vidican	61
6	Two steps forward, one step back: the ongoing failure to capture synergies in natural resource management (Australia) Andrew Campbell	80

7   Never waste a crisis: drought as an opportunity to bring
    robust water-policy reform to California   95
    Dustin Garrick

8   Development of water markets in China   109
    Scott M. Moore

9   Drought policy: lessons and strategies to change the
    transformational game   120
    Deborah C. Peterson

10 The collision of aspiration and reality in payments for
    ecosystem services   136
    James Salzman

11 Angling for a solution: fisheries management and the
    individual transferrable quota regime in Aotearoa
    (New Zealand)   147
    Adam Banasiak

12 New York City's payment for ecosystem services: providing
    clean water for millions   164
    Tim Purinton and Marina LeGree

13 Empowering consumers: Forest Stewardship Council
    leadership in internationally traded product certification   180
    Juliette Gundy and Julia Radice

14 The art of good governance: analysing water management
    success in Phnom Penh   194
    Timothy Grant

15 Guidelines for transformational change in environmental and
    natural resource management   207
    Mike Young and Christine Esau

    Index   221

FIGURES

3.1	Clay Christensen's explanation of the innovator's dilemma	26
3.2	Uniqueness and complementary assets over the life cycle	28
3.3	Scenario grid exploring alternative futures for higher education	30
4.1	Timeline for National Competition Policy reform	41
4.2	Water reform in the Murray–Darling Basin	45
4.3	Home Insulation Program	49
4.4	Timeline of Mineral Resources Rent Tax	54
4.5	Estimated and actual revenues of Mineral Resources Rent Tax	55
5.1	Stakeholder identification and salience based on three attributes	67
5.2	Model policy cycle showing strategic points for internal and external support building	70
5.3	The learning spiral concept	74
7.1	California's surface water system	99
7.2	Cumulative groundwater losses and surface water deliveries in California's Central Valley since 1962	101
8.1	Predicted changes in demand for water in China	110
11.1	New Zealand exclusive economic zone established in 1978	148
12.1	New York City water supply watersheds	165
14.1	Changes in PPWSA revenue, expenses and profit	200

TABLES

3.1	Forms of innovation	25
4.1	Assessment score of resilient public policy	43
4.2	Stakeholders engaged before and after announcement of the Home Insulation Program (HIP)	52
5.1	Negative and positive communication messages about fossil-fuel subsidy reform	72
6.1	Landcare and regional NRM policy in Australia assessed against 10 guidelines for durable environmental policy reform	92
8.1	Recent water trades in the Shiyang River Basin	114
13.1	Structure of the Forest Stewardship Council as at December 2009	187

CONTRIBUTORS

Adam Banasiak works as a consultant with the Cadmus Group, San Francisco, USA.

Andrew Campbell was Director of the Research Institute for the Environment and Livelihoods, Charles Darwin University, Australia, and is now Director of the Australian Centre for International Agricultural Research, Australia.

Christine Esau is a freelance journalist, writer and editor in Adelaide, Australia.

Dustin Garrick was Philomathia Chair in Water Policy, McMaster University, Hamilton, Ontario, Canada, and is now at the Smith School of Enterprise and the Environment, Oxford University, Oxford, UK.

R. Quentin Grafton is Professor of Economics, ANU Public Policy Fellow, Fellow of the Asia and the Pacific Policy Society, Director of the Centre for Water Economics, Environment and Policy at the Crawford School of Public Policy, and Editor in Chief of Policy Forum.net at The Australian National University, Australia.

Timothy Grant specialises in urban water policy research and is a dual masters student at the Fletcher School of Law and Diplomacy and Tufts School of Urban Environmental Policy and Planning at Tufts University in Medford, Massachusetts, USA.

Juliette Gundy is Senior Policy Analyst at the Privy Council Office, Ottawa, Canada.

Rebecca Henderson is the John and Natty McArthur University Professor at Harvard University, USA, where she has a joint appointment at the Harvard Business School in the General Management and Strategy Units in Cambridge, Massachusetts, USA.

Marina LeGree is Executive Director of Ascend: Leadership through Athletics in Norfolk, Virginia, USA.

Scott M. Moore was Giorgio Ruffolo Post-Doctoral Research Fellow at the Harvard University Kennedy School of Government, USA. He is currently a Young Professional with the World Bank Group Global Water Practice in Washington DC, USA.

Deborah C. Peterson is Director at Sapere Research Group, Melbourne, Australia. She is a Distinguished Fellow and past President of the Australian Agricultural and Resource Economics Society, and the founding co-editor of the *Australian Journal of Agricultural and Resource Economics*.

Tim Purinton is Director, Division of Ecological Restoration for the Commonwealth of Massachusetts, USA.

Julia Radice is Program Manager at the Association of Climate Change Officers, Washington, DC, USA.

Kevin Rudd is a former Prime Minister of Australia.

Walter Reinhardt is a visiting fellow at the Fenner School of Environment and Society, the Australian National University, Canberra, Australia.

James Salzman is the Donald Bren Distinguished Professor of Environmental Law with joint appointments at the UCLA School of Law and at the Bren School of the Environment at UC Santa Barbara, California, USA.

Georgeta Vidican is a professor at the Institute of Economics, University Erlangen-Nürnberg, Germany, and an Associate Researcher at the German Development Institute, Bonn, Germany.

Mike Young is Professor of Environmental and Water Policy at the University of Adelaide, Australia; a Research Fellow with the Nicholas Institute for Environmental Policy Solutions at Duke University, Durham, USA; and an Honorary Professor at University College London, UK. In 2013/14, he held the Gough Whitlam and Malcolm Fraser Chair in Australian Studies at Harvard University, Cambridge, Massachusetts, USA.

PREFACE

Successful transformational policy reform requires extraordinary skill from the earliest concept stages through to implementation and enduring performance. The primary goal of this book is to offer guidelines about the best way to catalyse interest, package proposals, recognize possible pitfalls and achieve ongoing support for such changes so that they do not flounder.

The book's concept was developed jointly by the editors during their time at Harvard University as we contemplated reasons why transformational changes are sometimes placed in the "too hard" basket in deference to incremental policy changes that involve less risk but restrict outcomes.

Established in 1977 through an Australian Government endowment, the Gough Whitlam and Malcolm Fraser Chair in Australian Studies seeks to bring unique Australian knowledge to Harvard University. This book arises from the appointment of Mike Young to this Chair and the opportunity to teach a course on this topic and for us organise a conference that brought together people with deep experience in the pursuit of transformative policy reforms.

Contributors to this book were asked to identify fundamental drivers for enabling successful reform, drawing on real life experiences of transformational policies. As is the case with books like this one, each chapter involves an overview of a specific example. Those interested in more detail are encouraged to delve deeper.

We benefited immensely from the opportunity to interact with the many talented minds in the Kennedy School of Government, the Business School and School of Engineering and Applied Sciences. Support for the conference was provided by the Harvard University Centre for the Environment. In particular, we would like to acknowledge contributions made by Peter Rogers and the late John Briscoe who opened doors for us at Harvard. We benefited immensely from the opportunity to interact with these two brilliant minded luminaries and many others including David Haig, Rebecca Henderson, Henry Lee, Nicholas Burns and Graham Allison.

We also benefited from our time at the Rockefeller Foundation's Bellagio Centre where we spent a month developing the guidelines that shaped this book.

In the pursuit of opportunities to take the concepts embedded in this book further, a course in Transformational Change is now being offered by Mike Young through the Global Food and Resource Studies Program at the University of Adelaide.

Christine Esau and Mike Young

1

TRANSFORMATIONAL CHANGE

In search of excellence

Mike Young

> Political survival depends on making quality decisions; compromised policies lead to voter dissatisfaction; letting things drift is political suicide.
>
> Roger Douglas

Using case studies, this book searches for guidelines to assist those interested in developing a proposal for a transformational policy reform and working to ensure its successful implementation.[1] This chapter digests the resultant guidelines. Most derive from experience associated with reforms that seek to make greater use of market mechanisms (see Guideline 13.7 in Chapter 13).

What do you have to do to get a proposal for a transformational policy reform seriously considered, accepted and implemented?

The idea of transformational change is well established in business and can deliver outstanding results. In the world of public policy, however, many transformational reforms flounder. The list of reasons for failure is long. Reasons include disagreement over objectives, difficulties gaining stakeholder and bureaucratic support, lack of legal precedent, insufficient comprehension of administrative complexities and lack of attention to scientific knowledge. As a result, political leaders often settle for incremental policy reforms, even though they recognise transformational change is needed.

Transformational policy reforms involve fundamental shifts in strategy with far reaching consequences for the structure of industries, the way people behave and the resources they use. Typically, they involve the creation of very different governance, administrative arrangements and incentives.

For ease of discussion, this book's guidelines are grouped into a logical sequence:

- Developing the case for change.
- Securing interest in the proposition.
- Careful design and refinement of the package to be implemented.
- Negotiating the reform package.
- Implementing the reform.
- Adaptation and ongoing improvement.
- Learning.

In practice, at least, the first four of these steps tend to occur in messy parallel processes. In the final chapter of this book, the various guidelines identified and listed in each chapter are classified into these seven groups.

Developing the case for change

What's the problem?

It may seem self-evident, but typically the case for a transformational reform begins with a realisation that a problem exists. Often, however, it is more useful to describe the problem as an opportunity. Whatever approach is taken, there is normally a need to begin by defining the issue in ways that the community, as well as specialists, can comprehend (see Guideline 2.1 in Chapter 2). The costs and benefits of inaction need to be transparent, estimated using methodologies that have broad scientific support (see Guidelines 4.4 and 7.9) and contestable (4.2). Use of multiple methodologies helps to bring about consensus. Almost without exception, the case for change needs to be compared with the status quo and, also, what is achievable via a simple incremental reform.

Not one but two discussions

When developing the case for change, it is insufficient to rely upon the presence of detailed reports. Both the general public and specialists need to be convinced that a problem exists and that the opportunity to fix it is real and realisable (2.3). Academics tend to focus on the detail. It is essential that the dialogue involves one or more policy entrepreneurs who, with credibility, can present an overview of what is proposed (12.2). To this end, simple narratives help. In Phnom Penh, Ek Sonn Chan, the General Director of the Phnom Penh Water Supply Authority, began fixing the city's water supply by making it clear that non-payment of bills and corrupt activities would have to stop. One of Ek Sonn Chan's early actions, fearlessly and protected by TV cameras, was to walk into the Cambodian Army's barracks and switch off their water supply until they paid their bill. The opportunity he identified was to make everyone pay for the water they used and, through this simple reform, collect the revenue needed to extend and improve the service offered to all, without fear or favour.

A simple unambiguous vision

When searching for a solution, it is useful to begin by developing a clear vision of the final outcome and options for its attainment (12.4). In the case of water reform in Australia's Murray–Darling Basin the vision was simple: if a formal limit was placed on the maximum amount of water that could be taken and low-cost opportunities to trade water established, the nation and its natural resources would be better off. It was understood that the detail on how best to implement this vision could be worked out subsequently. The gains would come from the improvements in water use efficiency, innovations that competitive market forces would bring and avoidance of serious environmental impacts.

If a transformational change is to occur, it is necessary to gain strong administrative and political support (3.1) and, if possible, a mandate for action (2.2). The narrative underpinning this mandate needs to be both simple and compelling (4.6; 9.3).

Comprehensive information campaigns tend to play an important part in gaining the necessary support for a transformational reform (5.7; 5.8). However, there is a strong case for encouraging independent people to act as policy entrepreneurs. Repeated messaging using different styles and ways of communication can be critical (8.7). Work hard to establish a strong relationship with the media that is built around a sense of trust.

Early design

As a general rule, most transformational reforms propose a sequence of policy and administrative changes that, if implemented, can be expected to enhance a community, sector or region. During the initial stages, it is common for public opinion to be a poor guide as to what is best (3.2). One of the prime reasons is that people tend to think only of incremental reforms. Without careful analysis it is difficult to think through all the implications of a complex, interdependent array of changes – especially when many of the responses are non-linear.

Furthermore, the past is often a poor guide to the future. In business, for example, existing products often appear better than ones still under development (3.3).

When a business sets about developing a new idea or new product, there is a need for strong support from the top of an organisation (3.10). Support from political leaders is equally important when developing a proposal for a transformational policy reform. During the early stages of development, it is important that leaders appear to be confident that a way to implement the proposed reform can be found (1.6). During this process, scenario analysis can be used to work through and refine the case for change (3.5). Scenario analysis can be particularly useful in helping to develop the narratives needed to garner interest in the proposed reform.

Investment in knowledge

During the process of developing the core proposition, there is a need for early investment in the science and data collection coupled with exploration of broad alternatives (12.12). Ultimately, the constellation of arrangements and predictions about likely outcomes needs to be contestable and will be contested by professional analysts and by stakeholders (4.2).

Learning from setbacks

Many draft proposals and countless stakeholder interactions may be needed to build the consensus needed to enable implementation and then sustain a new policy regime (13.1).

Sometimes, the search for the best way to begin a transformational policy is lengthy and can involve several false starts. Early failures can be opportunities to learn about what is achievable and, also, what is needed to implement a reform successfully (13.3). "Persistence and patience" can be particularly important in the development of detail (9.1). In the case of Australia's attempts to reform drought policy, for example, there have been many false starts and set-backs. Each of these attempts, however, produced lessons that made the next attempt easier.

Understanding risk

Sometimes, it is better to see a proposal for a transformational policy reform as the start of a journey which, when reviewed with the benefit of hindsight, will be seen to have been worthwhile. One should expect to be surprised by the extent of innovation and change that will result from a transformational change (10.6). It should neither be assumed that all benefits have been identified nor that all the identified benefits will eventuate (10.7).

In the lead-up to the decision to implement, many compromises may be made. As a result, the benefits of a transformational reform are easily overestimated (10.1). Be careful: never sell the public short (1.5).

Securing interest in the proposition

Chances of success can be improved if the policy development processes include a search for common goals using language that aligns with the interests of key stakeholders (12.3). Early investment in the ways to cast the proposition so that it can be advocated by a broad coalition of interests (6.8) can be expected to increase prospects for success. The broader the coalition of support, the greater the chances of success (13.4). During this search for the right language, it should not be assumed that stakeholders have a sophisticated understanding of their own best, long-term interests (6.8).

Supportive alliances

Early investment in the development of new alliances and narratives can be critical as, in many cultures, those likely to gain the most from a transformational reform often are reluctant to come forward. Search for those who are likely to benefit from such reform and recruit them into the policy development process (2.5).

When significant opposition is encountered, there is a strong case for examining the source of this opposition. Often views and biases are deeply entrenched. "Our current system is working. It ain't broke so don't try to fix it!" If an identifiable alliance is missing, map out stakeholder interests (5.2) and find a way to build one or more alliances that are likely to champion the case for change (10.3; 5.4). Often resistance is due to the fact that people don't like anyone attempting to fix a wheel that is not broken.

As soon as one or more of these new alliances have been established, support them by undertaking the work that enables the development of new narratives (5.6). Necessarily, some of this work will be empirical. It is important to ensure that the proposal is evidence-informed, derived using robust and accepted methods, and has been reviewed by qualified, capable and unbiased analysts (4.1). Ensure that this work is undertaken by people with a strong public standing. Once the

---

BOX 1.1

A selection of guidelines from a presentation by a renowned New Zealand reformer, Roger Douglas, written soon after he left politics:

Guideline 1.1
For quality policies, you need quality people.

Guideline 1.2
Speed is essential. It is impossible to go too fast.

Guideline 1.3
Once you start the momentum rolling, never let it stop.

Guideline 1.4
Let the dog see the rabbit.

Guideline 1.5
Never sell the public short.

Guideline 1.6
Don't blink, public confidence rests on your composure.

Guideline 1.7
Get the fundamentals right.

(Douglas, 1990)

empirical work has been completed, search for simple stories and examples of the benefits likely to flow from implementation of the reform.

When assembling the proposal, try to ensure that there is at least one influential group that is prepared to work tirelessly for the proposed reform. Think carefully about polycentric leadership models and, if possible, ensure that these leaders are well resourced (6.8).

One of the best ways to achieve broad support is to engage with as many different types of beneficiaries as possible and search for ways to turn them into parents, champions and sponsors of the reform (6.8). Remember to treat early protagonists with respect. With attention to detail and process, early detractors can become the biggest supporters of a proposed reform (11.5; 13.9).

Entrepreneurship

It is unusual for a transformational reform to get over the line unless there is a least one and preferably many policy entrepreneurs prepared to push for action (12.2). When a cadre of policy entrepreneurs is lacking, search for a way to create them. One of the prime roles of a policy entrepreneur is to search for ways to reveal the nature of the expected benefits and the consequences of inaction (3.6). In addition to presenting the case for change in a convincing manner, policy entrepreneurs can also play an important public role in explaining detail.

Careful design and refinement of the reform package

Once the broad case has been established, it is important to work on the design detail to instil confidence in a proposed reform. Stakeholders need to feel confident that the proposed reform will work. The old adage that "there can be devil in the detail" is worth considering. Often, there is considerable opportunity to learn from experience elsewhere (5.9).

When reading this book's case studies, you cannot help but conclude that it is important to pay attention to distributional implications. Search for astute ways to package the reform. If possible, find a way to organise the reform process so that no group can argue that the proposed reform is likely to make them worse off (12.8).

Early in the development of a transformative proposal, it is common for many people to perceive that the reform will make them worse off (6.9). Try to avoid talking about compensating losers (2.4). Instead, look for ways that will enable all involved to benefit (9.6). Remember that, if the case for a transformational change is strong, the reforms should produce a sizable net benefit to society. If this is truly the case, then there should be enough gains to make nearly all, if not all, people better off. There are a range of options to manage costs felt by some parties, including managing the pace of change, introducing transition arrangements, and, as a last resort, directly compensating losers (5.3).

Trials and pilots

Trials are often put forward as a way to test the validity of a proposition. Often trials are implemented to build knowledge and, by demonstrating benefits, draw more people into a position where they are prepared to support wider implementation. Trials, or pilots, as they are sometimes called, should be organised so as to demonstrate the extent of benefits (8.3) in a timely manner (12.3). Trials can be particularly important in building administrative capacity (9.5) and in resolving administrative tensions (8.4). Trials can also be used to identify winners and bring them into the public debate (2.5).

When choosing the location of a trial, it is strongly recommended that it involves institutions with a history of working together (8.2). During a trial, work hard to secure support from beneficiaries (14.3). Trials can also be used to "buy" the time necessary to bed down new institutional arrangements and build administrative capacity (8.1). In China, for example, administrators are using trials to build the databases and monitoring systems necessary to enable widespread development of water-trading arrangements (8.5). When implementing a trial, it is important to put in place arrangements to ensure rigorous testing of the proposed reform. If there is a chance that the policy will or may be subsequently abandoned, inadequate testing may occur (8.6).

Policy detail

This chapter is not the place for specifying the design details. Nevertheless, there are tricks to the trade. As already mentioned, seek ways to "grandfather in"[2] as many existing stakeholders as possible. Avoid creating losers. Find a way to build in arrangements that can be expected to increase the value of the new regime to each participant (11.5). If possible, search for a design that ensures that the costs and risks of unravelling or undermining the reform are more costly than the benefits of continuing with it (6.14).

As a general rule, pay attention to the fundamental structure of a proposed reform and make this structure as robust as possible. Some parts of the package should be non-negotiable. To this end, consider defining entitlements, administrative boundaries, etc., so that they are consistent with natural conditions and processes (7.4; 11.3). Be prepared to use more rather than fewer instruments so that it is administratively possible to change the weight given to different objectives (11.1) and, at the same time, keep use within limits (7.5). In particular, avoid mechanisms that lock in arrangements that cannot be sustained (11.4). Remember to consider carefully and account for the effects that the proposed policy reform will have on other programs and policy arrangements (6.3).

During this stage in the development pay particular attention to policy coherence (7.6; 7.7; 7.10) and the effects of the reforms on other policies. Never lose sight of the whole package. Think carefully about interactions and ensure that the package does not erode the benefits of previous policy gains (6.5).

When it comes to natural resource and environmental issues, broad stakeholder support is more likely if the mechanisms used align well with and reveal understanding of biophysical relationships and details (7.4). Climate change experts, for example, will be looking for arrangements that anticipate shifts in variability. Hydrologists can be expected to be concerned about return flows.

Once a policy reform has been implemented, high level political interest in it tends to wane. To this end, every effort should be made to lock in budgetary arrangements. Reforms that rely upon ongoing access to government budgets face much greater risks than reforms whose cash-flow is self-sustaining (10.4). Seek others ways to lock in ongoing support for change and make back-sliding difficult (9.7). As a result of the decision to make Australian water entitlements mortgageable, for example, a mechanism that locks in enduring support from the banking sector has been created.

Finally, design the package so that success can be demonstrated early and used to prevent undermining of the reform (12.3). Make sure, as Douglas argues, that the dog can see the rabbit (1.4). That is, ensure that benefits can be seen by those most affected by the reform.

Governance issues

Transformational reforms take time to implement and are easily hijacked. To this end, careful attention to governance arrangements is critical. As a general rule, the broader the structure of the proposed governance system, the more legitimacy it will have and the greater its capability will be (13.5). Legitimacy can be created by ensuring that all stakeholders believe that they have a voice and an equitable say (13.6). This does not necessarily mean that all stakeholders need to be represented on a governing body. Indeed, many robust administrative structures are led by small, independent, expertise-based boards (Young, 2014).

Robust governance systems often do not attempt to control all elements centrally (12.4). If the system is well-designed and administrators are accountable, then there is a strong case for delegation (7.11; 11.7; 12.14) or better still investment in subsidiarity arrangements that limit the role of a central authority to that needed to ensure policy coherence. Provide incentives for local innovation coupled with trans-boundary coordination. Clarify roles and responsibilities to ensure accountability (7.3).

Crises

Much can and has been said about the role of crises in opening up an opportunity to implement a transformational reform. Crises open up opportunities – critical junctures – that make consideration of the case for a reform possible (5.1; 6.4). During crises, people tend to look for new ideas and are prepared to consider them. Leaders need to be seen to act and, if the prior design work is in place, often are willing to introduce new legislation with far reaching consequences (12.1).

Leaders can act, however, only when the prior work has been done and its key elements kept fresh (4.3).

The high levels of public awareness and concern typically associated with a crisis establish a sense of urgency and help to create a burning platform (6.5) that can be seized by policy entrepreneurs (13.2). In particular, they create opportunities to overcome barriers proposed by vested interests (7.6) – especially those who otherwise are well placed to rort and game a proposed reform (10.8).

During a crisis, rapid shifts in community and political understanding of the real cause of systemic problems tend to emerge quickly (7.1; 7.2; 7.8). With water management, the case for limiting use and developing new sharing arrangements tends to become obvious only during a drought as was the case in the emergence of Australia's millennium drought (Chapter 4) and, more recently in the western USA (Chapter 7). When the true causes of systemic risks are not well understood, band-aid solutions can exacerbate systemic risks and worsen the situation (7.11).

Those interested in supporting a reform need to be aware that draft plans and proposals need information to be kept current so that when a crisis occurs they can move quickly (4.3). In particular, they should realise that, if the ground work has not been done, the opportunity can be lost quickly (9.2). Moreover, if the necessary background work has not been adequately prepared, there is a risk that other reforms will be put in place in ways that exacerbate underlying problems (7.11).

The success of Australia's compulsory gun buy-back program offers a classic example of the value of preparedness. It was announced immediately after 35 people were killed and 23 wounded in a mass shooting incident. Australians were shocked and, within two weeks, the Prime Minister had convinced all states and territories to participate in a national gun buy-back program and agree to very restrictive controls on ownership. Rapid implementation was possible because eight years earlier a National Committee on Violence had prepared a proposal for and recommended introduction of a compulsory gun buy-back program (Chapter 9).

Negotiating the reform package

Once high-level interest has been secured, attention moves to a focus on details and the suite of arrangements necessary to get a reform over the line.

Try to ensure secure engagement with and support from as many different kinds of beneficiaries as possible (6.8). Try to involve them in sorting out the detail and claiming ownership of the solution. Unfortunately, this style of engagement sits uncomfortably with researchers. In the case of a transformational reform, however, the more people who think that the proposed reform was either their idea or one that they reshaped into a form suitable for adoption, the better.

Remember the importance of building a strong evidence base (6.6). Marshall the facts (6.6) and cultivate as many policy entrepreneurs as possible (2.5). Never assume that the facts will speak for themselves. Expect those opposed to a reform to be well organised, well resourced and politically ruthless (6.6).

Stakeholder consultation

Much has been written about the importance of stakeholder negotiation. Early engagement with stakeholders enables attention to language and the development of ways to both increase acceptance of the case for reform and structure the reform program so as to avoid creating losers (2.6; 9.4; 12.7). Beware of the way that consultation occurs. Those involved in researching the case for reform can unintentionally raise expectations. If, for example, a researcher surveys a community about the question of how much compensation they think they should receive, then that community must be expected to start to think that:

- they are likely to be made worse off; and
- that they are entitled to compensation – even if this was not previously the case.

Getting to "Yes"

Getting from acceptance of a mandate to a position that enables implementation can be difficult. During the final stages of negotiation, it is necessary to bring people who are likely to gain from implementation into public discussions (2.5) and build stories around them. If possible, continuously search for and bring new people into the debate so that the case for change remains fresh (6.11).

Work hard to understand how implementation works and how success is interpreted in terms of dominant political theories of the day (6.11). Work on narratives and keep them fresh to ensure ongoing resonance and legitimacy with the current political context (6.11).

During the process of negotiating a transformational reform and getting approval to implement it, details can be changed. In particular, it is very easy to end up in a position where there is a wide gap between the original policy intent – the vision – and what is to be implemented (6.10). It is critically important to think hard about allocating responsibility and ensuring the right people and agencies have the necessary skills (6.10). Identify the fundamental concepts and core principles and don't compromise them. Get the fundamentals right (1.7). Stay true to them (6.13).

Implementing the reform

Don't begin a transformational reform until long-term arrangements are in place and, to the extent possible, bipartisan support has been secured (6.2; 12.9).

If possible, begin implementing the package in places where success can be demonstrated swiftly. Ensure that the data necessary to confirm success is collected and the resultant evidence distributed widely (12.13).

A large part of implementation is about the maintenance of relationships among stakeholders (6.10). To this end, ensure the teams involved in program delivery find the entire process socially rewarding (6.10). If possible, delay implementation in areas where there is strong opposition until effectiveness can be demonstrated elsewhere.

Administration

When beginning to implement a transformational reform, it can be advantageous to appoint a new leader who has not been associated with or responsible for the development of the policies and administrative arrangements that are about to be replaced (12.6; 14.1). Remember that, for quality policies, you need quality people (1.1). When negotiating the deal necessary to reduce run-off in the Catskill Mountains, which supply water to New York, an impasse was resolved via the simple act of changing the people responsible for leading negotiations. A fresh face and a new communication style was all that was needed to bring the program back on track (Chapter 12). Trust in those responsible for overseeing early implementation is critical to success.

Old habits die hard and during the early stages of implementation it is easy to fall back into old ways. To this end, it can be useful to nurture the reform by establishing a separate administrative structure (3.9; 11.6). Among other things, a separate administrative structure makes it easier to bring in new skills and appoint people with the appropriate expertise (12.10; 12.11). It also makes it easier to escape from the practices associated with prior policy arrangements (6.13) and build the sense of entrepreneurship needed to ensure that the reform is successful (3.4).

New administrative structures

In business, it is recognised that successful innovation – the commercial equivalent of a transformational reform – requires entrepreneurial energy that typically is lacking in structures known for their operational excellence (3.8). Prospects for success will be greater if the new administrative structure has an independent revenue base and/or whose members understand that their future is dependent upon ongoing access to an adequate budget (14.2; 10.2).

Speed

Once a decision has been made to begin implementation and the necessary legislation has been passed, typically, there is a need for rapid implementation; that is, the time between announcement and conversion to the new regime needs to be rapid. There are many reasons for speedy implementation. In particular, there is often a need to minimise opportunities for people to rort and game the reform process (10.8; 11.2). In the case of the conversion of fishing licences into shares, for example (Chapter 11), speedy implementation can be necessary to prevent people from fishing in ways that are designed to increase the number of shares they receive. Douglas (1990; see Box 1.1) argues that it is impossible to go too fast (1.2) and that once you start the momentum, you should never let it stop (1.3).

Sequencing

Attention to the sequence of a reform package is critical. In particular, try to ensure that the benefits arrive early (1.4). Ideally, realisation of benefits will either preceed or come with increased charges (14.4). Sequence implementation so as to consciously increase chances of ongoing success (5.5) and, in particular, ensure that dialogue with key stakeholders is ongoing and setbacks avoided (5.5).

Tracking and celebrating progress

During the early stages of implementation, a rolling report card needs to be established (2.8). To this end, it is critical to monitor progress systematically and celebrate and communicate even modest achievements (6.12). At the same time, be seen to be measuring impacts on those who might be expected to lose out as a result of the reform (6.11). Search for low-cost ways to use surrogate indicators (10.5). Cultivate a positive supportive relationship with the media.

If the early stages of implementation involve controversy, be careful to ensure that you have more and better data than anyone else – especially more than any opponents to a reform (6.11). Collect and organise data so that success can be demonstrated quickly (12.3). Never assume that the case for mobilised support is complete. Continuously restate the case for reform and, as implementation occurs, continue to refine it (6.11).

In addition, be very careful to deal quickly with any mal-administration (14.5). In Phnom Penh, for example, having announced that he intended to wipe out corruption, it was particularly important for Ek Sonn Chan to be seen to deal quickly and firmly with those who continued to pursue corrupt practices (Chapter 14).

Adaptation and ongoing improvements

It is common for all transformational reforms to need fine tuning and adaptation as innovations occur, administrative skills improve (13.8) and the reform begins to change behaviour. In business considerable effort is invested in the search for ways to ensure ongoing experimentation so as to increase the probability that a change will endure (3.7).

Adaptation should be encouraged, but you should ensure that this does not destroy the original vision. To this end, it is important to understand that during implementation it is normal for the policy entrepreneurs and administrators associated with the development of the proposal to move on. When this occurs, it can be relatively easy for a group of stakeholders to hijack the reform and take it in unintended directions. Former Australian Prime Minister Kevin Rudd observes that ideological and political opponents of a reform can be expected to be deeply obstructive (Chapter 2). For this reason alone, there is a strong case for ongoing, comprehensive oversight of implementation (2.7).

Those responsible for implementing a transformational reform sometimes make mistakes. When this occurs, there is a strong argument for acting quickly and replacing key people (12.5).

When the vision is supported by a majority of stakeholders but there is a lack of trust or a negotiation impasse, be prepared to appoint a new policy entrepreneur (12.5). In the case of the development of the ecosystem service payment system used to keep clean the water that supplies New York, an impasse was resolved by simply changing the personnel involved (Chapter 12).

Learning

It is common in a book like this one to close with advice about the importance of periodically reviewing progress (2.10). To this end, it can be advantageous to set a formal review date (2.9). Formal review dates enables criticisms to be "parked" for resolution at a later date. Reviews can be used to add the next level of detail and take advantage of administrative capacities that have been developed during the first stages of implementation. Remember that reviews often focus on the adequacy or otherwise of a program budget.

Those involved in setting a review date need to be aware, however, that the terms of reference for a review typically begin by examining the degree to which formally stated objectives have been achieved (6.1). To this end, you need to be careful to avoid the use of aspirational objectives that, during the process of review, will be found to have not been achieved (6.1).

If it is clear that a transformational reform is not working, and that failure is not due to poor implementation, then analyse why and be prepared to "disrupt yourself" rather than waiting for someone else to demolish your program (7.14).

Finally, ensure that the "three lenses of knowledge and influence" – political judgement, professional practice and scientific research – are all considered, mutually reinforcing and well-aligned with the reform agenda (6.7; Head, 2008).

Notes

1 Box 1.1 contains guidelines published by Roger Douglas (Douglas, 1990).
2 "Grandfathering" is jargon for the concept of defining a new regime which gives existing resource users, for example, a suite of opportunities that are similar to those that they currently enjoy. An initial exemption from a new regulation coupled with an incentive that makes transition to the regime affordable is an example of grandfathering.

References

Douglas, R. (1990) "The politics of successful structural reform". *Policy Magazine*, 6(1): 2–6.
Head, B. (2008) "Three lenses of evidence-based policy". *Australian Journal of Public Administration*, 67(1): 1–11.
Young, M. (2014) "Designing water abstraction regimes for an ever-changing and ever-varying future". *Agricultural Water Management*, 145: 32–8.

2

SIGNIFICANT, SUSTAINABLE ENVIRONMENTAL REFORM IS DIFFICULT IN ANY DEMOCRACY

Kevin Rudd

Background

In this chapter, I reflect on some core guidelines to develop sustainable environmental policies from the perspective of a politician who has sought to bring about change. They derive from my own experience as a practitioner, as opposed to an environmental scientist or a global activist. I focus particularly on Australian experience in transforming the way it manages water and plans to limit its impacts on climate change.

The message

Guideline 2.1
Define a problem in ways that people in the community, as well as specialists, can comprehend.

Whether it is in the carbon or the water-pricing space, defining the problem in the public mind makes the case for a transformational change. If the public either does not understand the problem or is not convinced of the need for a new approach, there is little chance of getting a reform adopted. I have discovered from my own experience that well-meaning social democrats and activists who carry a clear view of what the problem is in their own hearts tend to hold a considerable degree of contempt that the public doesn't get it. This does not work.

Therefore, the beginning of any transformational policy reform process is to define the problem, and frame it in terms the community can understand.

Take climate change, for example. If you simply go through the mantra of saying "climate change, climate change, climate change" like a medieval monk's chant, it is unlikely to have a huge effect.

Problems like these need to be defined by giving credibility to the risks being taken by society. This problem needs to be defined in the public's mind by observing, for example, that an international panel of scientists – the IPCC – has come to the conclusion that, if the world keeps on using fossil fuels, average global temperatures can be expected to rise by between three and four degrees before the end of the century and that this may have fundamentally adverse and irreversible consequences for future food and water supplies. Messages like these are concepts that the public can understand. They can also understand that climate change may bring about extreme changes in weather conditions that could adversely affect many people, including those within their community.

So my first Guideline is "Define the problem before you seek to solve it". Many people working in the public policy space and also in the political space, particularly on the progressive side of politics, don't do this.

A mandate

Guideline 2.2
Establish a mandate for action.

If there is a need for change, then the electoral process can be used to clearly define the mandate for action by the government of the day.

If you are approaching an election, make it very clear that, after the election, you intend to implement all elements of your mandate. In my case, during the campaign that led to my election as Prime Minister of Australia, I said to the Australian people, "If you elect me as Prime Minister, within the first month, I will ratify the Kyoto convention". I went on to say, "If you elect me as your Prime Minister, within the first term, I will legislate for a mandatory renewable energy target of 20% by 2020. If you elect me as Prime Minister, I will use an emissions trading scheme to seek to put a price on greenhouse gas emissions."

No one in the entire debate which unfolded in Australia after my election ever questioned the nature of the mandate for change we established because we had been explicit about the changes we would make. The mandate we established was clear, not just in general terms of promising to act on the climate change problem but rather in terms of the specific actions we were proposing to embrace.

Establishing mandates for change is about the legitimisation of the democratic process and the course of action you are going to follow. It also prevents subsequent de-legitimisation of the process you are about to implement.

The message

Guideline 2.3
Establish a simple message and document its complexity.

It is critical to simplify messages concerning what you are going to do, what it is going to cost and what benefit will be delivered from it. Again, what I find about the climate change debate, or, for that matter, a lot of the water policy debate in Australia, is that they have largely been dialogues of the deaf, dominated by highly informed, specialised interest groups on either side of the political divide. Communication of the message to others has not worked well. A large proportion of the general community, and even some elite community leaders and journalists, remain uninformed about the basic factual dimensions of the argument. The reason for this is that those involved in the debate have not been able to craft a simple message.

Simplicity in the explanation of any changes you are about to embrace, why you are pursuing them, what they will cost, what their benefits will be, and how these benefits will be measured over time is fundamental. Any message that seeks to substitute a simple description of the core realities with a broader, more attractive political or philosophical language, will fail.

Importantly, some elite groups will seek to de-legitimise the message. The simple public message must be supported by a much more detailed message for specialist constituencies so that they can't attack the case for reform on the grounds of technical incompetence at one level or another.

The simple message and the complex message must be mutually reinforcing. You cannot have one without the other. In my experience when it comes to Australian environmental policy debates, too much of the second is done in the absence of the first.

Compensate

Guideline 2.4
Identify potential economic losers and find a way to ameliorate impacts on people who otherwise would lose during the process of implementation.

When developing a case for a major reform, it is vital to find a way to compensate those who expect to lose. In the case of Australia's Murray–Darling Basin plan, for example, you cannot say to a community that has operated in a law-abiding way for the last, say, hundred years, "Sorry guys, you can't do it any more, goodbye, leave your farm and it's been nice knowing you". This is not a terribly good message in politics.

A more effective message is to recognise that a change must occur and explain why. In the case of the Murray–Darling Basin, we had to be very blunt in identifying what those changes would mean to local communities and irrigators and we had calculated a need to be ready to compensate for the loss of the entitlement and economic opportunities they had historically enjoyed. Changes, like these, need to be recognised as one-off adjustment processes.

That will not, by the way, eliminate opposition from these groups, but it will reduce some of the angst and enable engagement with them. In particular, it is important that others in the community can and do say "Look, they are losing but, yes, they are being compensated".

Recruiting winners

Guideline 2.5
Recruit economic winners, or what Gladwell would call "mavens",[1] to take their message to the general media.

Recruiting economic winners to the debate is critical. In the process of bringing about a transformational policy reform, economic winners need to be encouraged to become mavens in spreading a message around the community as well as in the general media. The public needs to hear the case for reform from those who they would expect to benefit. In the case of water policy reform or putting a price on carbon, for example, it is not sufficient for me in my position as Prime Minister or for the Environment Minister or the Minister for Water to state the case. Rolling third-party endorsement right across the body politic is essential to reinforce the legitimacy of the policy reforms being undertaken. Otherwise, those leading the reform will suffer a death from 1,000 cuts.

For those engaged in framing the decision, therefore, it is essential to identify not only the economic losers but also the winners. In the case of carbon pricing, the obvious winners are the renewable energy industry and the public at large.

In the case of water reform, the obvious winners were the people of Adelaide, downstream irrigators and those interested in the environment. A way needs to be found to bring these constituencies into the broad national debate. It is important that messaging is not simply the sound of one hand clapping by brave political leaders in the back of a car heading towards a rumble after a guillotine attack. There needs to be others out there, hopefully not in the car with you, saying that reform is necessary and useful for a range of reasons.

Third-party endorsement on a rolling basis is essential. This requires much more than noteworthy academic institutions issuing a press release and then believing that their hands have therefore been washed of responsibility because they have now done their bit. Academics, as well as the winners, have to engage in the blood and gore of the general media debate, the online social media debate and, as I've said before, if all this comes together, those who are mavens within their local community will help create a critical mass of opinion over time, so that people listen to what you tell them.

Identify opponents

Guideline 2.6
Identify the ideological or vested-interest opponents to a proposed reform and develop an offensive strategy to deal with them.

Often those of us concerned about local and global environmental public goods prefer not to be put in the front line of a fight against the vested interest groups who are trying to oppose a reform. Typically, those trying to push the debate in precisely the reverse direction do so for ideological reasons or pure vested interests. Often these vested interests are corporate but not always explicitly so.

So my message, reinforced by what I stated previously, is to be very careful to identify those likely to be opposed to a reform and to develop a strategy to deal with the arguments they are likely to put in the way of a reform. You need to expect a highly sophisticated campaign to come rolling at you that invariably will be privately funded and well developed. Nearly all of the guidelines developed earlier form part of the strategy needed. This is, quite simply, *not* something to be contracted out. The interests of the public will prevail only if the case for reform is well thought out and well communicated.

In summary, therefore, getting a transformational policy reform over the line is as much about identifying the economic losers and offering them sufficient incentives to diffuse their arguments as it is identifying the winners, both direct and indirect, so that they become champions of change. If this is done well, you can run an offensive campaign, not a defensive campaign, against those who otherwise would tear the reform apart.

Oversight

Guideline 2.7
Ensure that there is ongoing, comprehensive oversight of implementation.

This is where those responsible for developing a policy reform pass the baton and, as they do so, encounter a new set of risks. Comprehensive oversight over the implementation of the reform is as important as getting legislative and political permission to make a change. Unfortunately, this second, major phase is often regarded by policy entrepreneurs as inherently boring.

The grand policy entrepreneurship needed to bed down a legislative change is measurable but this is just the beginning. Actors in Parliament often lose interest in the details surrounding the operationalisation of legislative changes necessary to bring about the change. The detailed practice of implementation provides the most fertile ground for derailing a reform.

Ideological and political opponents of a reform can be expected to become deeply obstructive to it and continuously search for ways to destroy the political legitimacy that has been established; that is, de-legitimisation of a reform can occur through a second wave of attack. The first wave, the policy decision itself, may have been successful. In the second wave, however, attackers will observe "the policy decision itself may have been okay, but look at the way it is being implemented". They will then argue that "everyone will have to go back and think about it all once again, carefully and thoroughly". This is de facto language for saying "We're going to kill this thing slowly and thoroughly".

As an aside, this is precisely what happened when attempts to make Australia a leader in the management of greenhouse gas emissions came off the rails in 2013. The Australian Government set out to establish an emissions trading system, with the support of the Greens. Instead we ended up with a carbon tax that established a carbon price and a round of attacks from vested interest groups that eventually de-legitimised the reforms that had been put in place.

A report card

Guideline 2.8
Establish a rolling report card on implementation progress.

Rolling report cards are needed so that the benefits of a reform can be appreciated by the constituency and, importantly, also by elite opinion leaders. A new battle to gather empirical data emerges and is crucial in order to sustain the legitimacy of the reform over the long term. For example, during the mandate for lowering greenhouse gas emissions, we introduced a carbon tax. By measuring the effect of this tax over time, we were able to say confidently to the Australian public that Australia's aggregate greenhouse gas emissions diminished following the introduction of the tax. So the measurement of implementation, of environmental, economic and social advantages, is critical for reinforcing the legitimacy of the reform.

A formal review

Guideline 2.9
Set a formal date for review of the efficacy and effectiveness of the reform.

You cannot simply assume that reforms will be self-sustaining. Change induces further change including not anticipated at the time reforms were being some implemented. Even the most ardent supporters of a reform will have questions about new realities that emerge. So a periodic, preferably legislatively entrenched review offers a useful way to deal with changes in an efficient manner.

Whether it is a 5-, 7- or 10-year review, the dynamics of review processes require political attention. There is a danger that I implore you to note. If there is a change of government and you have set up a mandatory legislative review, then the review process can be manipulated politically to produce a negative outcome when measured against the long-term efficacy objective set. Mindful of that particular political shoal, however, it is necessary by one means or another to have a periodic review against the original ambitions established in the first place.

The next step

Guideline 2.10
Following the review, explore what further structural reform is needed.

Throughout all of the above, explore what is the next most essential structural reform.

The accumulated scar tissue and experience of a reform can be harnessed to advantage. In particular, the direct experience of policy entrepreneurs and those who supported them in the wider advocacy process can be used to develop new propositions for reform.

In Australia, we have not done this perfectly by any stretch of the imagination. Transformational proposals for change involve tough processes that are difficult to sell. That said, I believe their pursuit has been worthwhile and outstanding results have been achieved.

Note

1 Mavens are "information specialists", or "people we rely upon to connect us with new information". They accumulate knowledge, especially about the marketplace, and know how to share it with others. Gladwell cites Mark Alpert as a prototypical maven who is "almost pathologically helpful", further adding, "he can't help himself". In this vein, Alpert himself concedes, "A Maven is someone who wants to solve other people's problems, generally by solving his own." According to Gladwell, mavens start "word-of-mouth epidemics" due to their knowledge, social skills, and ability to communicate and "Mavens are really information brokers, sharing and trading what they know". Source: http://en.wikipedia.org/wiki/The_Tipping_Point (accessed 28 April 2016).

Reference

Gladwell, M. (2000) *The Tipping Point: How Little Things Can Make a Big Difference*. New York: Little, Brown.

3

UNPACKING THE DYNAMICS OF SUCCESSFUL CHANGE

Ten insights from the private sector

Rebecca Henderson

Introduction: change is hard

Change is hard. Several years ago a division of one of the world's leading telecommunications companies was evaluating a new product opportunity – something that was quite unlike anything that was then available and that had the potential to take the division into an entirely new market. The prototypes were impressive and, although no one was sure exactly who would use the new gizmo, most people in the organization were deeply enthusiastic about its future. Sales of the division's traditional products were declining, and there were rumours that the entire business would be shut down if it didn't come up with something new. An outside consultant was brought in to evaluate the idea, and recommended wholeheartedly that the new product be launched. The division's general manager, however, decided against making the investment. In explaining his decision he said:

> I see. You're suggesting that we invest millions of dollars in a market that may or may not exist but that is certainly smaller than our existing market, to develop a product that customers may or may not want, using a business model that will almost certainly give us lower margins than our existing product lines. You're warning us that we'll run into serious organizational problems as we make this investment, and our current business is screaming for resources. Tell me again just why we should do this?
> Divisional General Manager, Telecommunications Equipment Company (personal communication)

In hindsight it was a disastrous decision not to proceed. The company's traditional business collapsed, while the product it had rejected was commercialized by others – first as the Blackberry and later as the smart phone. The company had rejected one of the most important products of the twenty-first century – because they were captured by the organizational and strategic logic of their *current* business. Their most deeply held assumptions of how the world worked – of what their customers wanted and of how they were likely to make money – were derived from their current experience. Moreover, few people inside the company had either the entrepreneurial skills or the incentives required to exploit the new idea. They had been trained, and were rewarded, for managing the existing business – and between them they killed what could have been the salvation of the company.

Some firms, however, succeed in reinventing themselves again and again. Corning Glass is a classic example. Corning began life in the nineteenth century as a maker of light bulbs and signal glass for railroads. The firm set up a specialized research lab in 1908, and over the next 50 years generated a stream of important, and highly profitable, innovations, including Pyrex® and the revolutionary "ribbon machine" – the centre piece of a process to mass manufacture light bulbs. By 1945, Corning was producing 37,000 different items made from 450 different glasses, and accounted for 45 per cent of the United States' light bulb glass market. The firm was the leading provider of glass to the television industry in the fifties and sixties. By 2000, Corning had approximately 40 per cent of the worldwide market for optical fibre, and was one of the world's largest merchant manufacturers of optical modules and components. Its market value had skyrocketed to $50 billion and the firm was widely regarded as a runaway success (Henderson and Reavis, 2009). However, in 2002, the worldwide telecommunications crash cut Corning's revenues from $6.3 billion to $3.1 billion. The company's stock collapsed and Corning had to take a $5.4 billion loss and lay off over 12,000 people. Undeterred, the firm built an entirely new business in glass for large screen LCD televisions, and then reinvented itself again as the provider of "gorilla glass" – the glass used on the Apple iPhone. By 2014 the company had revenues of more than $9.7 billion and seemed poised for even further growth.

What made the difference? Why do some firms thrive when faced with the challenge of innovation while others remain trapped in old patterns and old ways of behaving? I have been studying this problem – as researcher, teacher and private consultant – for almost thirty years. This chapter summarizes what I have learned in the hope that, when it comes to innovation, lessons from the private sector may be useful to the public. Introducing innovative public policy is, of course, different from introducing innovative new products, but my sense is that both the factors that often make innovation so hard and the solutions that can make it easier are sufficiently similar across the two settings that there is much to be gained from focusing on the private sector. The chapter begins by exploring why change is so hard, and why it is so often the case that well-established organizations reject innovations that have the potential – at least in theory – to make everyone much better off. It can be easy to blame failure on the arrogance or incompetence of well-entrenched leaders or tradition-bound middle managers, but my work suggests that failure more often results from a multiplicity of factors, all of which must be addressed if the firm is to succeed. I then turn to a discussion of why some firms succeed before speculating as to how many of these solutions may be useful within the public sector.

Why is innovation so difficult?

Proposing to do things differently nearly always creates resistance. In general this resistance has four roots: the perception that "it's not happening", or that there's no need to change, the belief that the firm's customers are perfectly satisfied with existing solutions, the fear that any innovation will be much less profitable than the existing products and last – but by no means least – the fact that large, old, successful organizations are usually overwhelmingly focused on "operational excellence" – and hence have developed a set of skills that make them very successful at doing what has always been done, but much less effective at doing really new things.

"It won't happen"

Guideline 3.1
Strengths often become weaknesses. Old ways of seeing make it very difficult to understand that the world is changing.

Many significant innovations were initially dismissed as unlikely or impractical (main frame computers, cell phones, next day parcel delivery) and some innovations that were much heralded never take off (bubble memories, food pills). Even if one can be relatively certain that in the largest sense a particular technology or innovation will "work" – that, for example, nanotechnology will prove to be important, or that gene sequencing will revolutionize drug discovery – there is always uncertainty about how long it will take to develop something new and about whether anyone will want it, and this uncertainty often becomes an excuse for holding back, or for taking a "wait and see" position. The problem is rarely that any given firm is not aware that the world may change. Large, well-run organizations employ smart and thoughtful people, and these people notice new products, follow new firms and go to the kinds of conference where one learns about new opportunities. The problem is much more often that well-established, successful organizations don't "see" the potential of new ways of doing things or understand their potential because they interpreted them using their existing ways of looking at the world.

Sometimes this is because the new ways of doing things challenge the fundamental identity of the firm – the story it tells itself about what's important and what its customers value. From at least 2006 on, for example, many observers and friends of the firm tried to warn Nokia that the iPhone represented a serious threat to their core business. Nokia uniformly dismissed the idea. In 2006 Nokia was making around a million phones a day and represented a third of the valuation of the Finnish stock exchange. They "knew" that the iPhone was serving a niche market, that the growth would be in the developing markets and that what consumers wanted was cheap, reliable phones. But, they dismissed Apple as a serious competitor (Cheng, 2014).

This is famously a problem in the case of the military, who are often accused of preparing for the last war. Winston Churchill, for example, expended enormous energy in the 1930s trying to persuade the British Army to build tanks – a weapon that had first been deployed in the 1914–18 war, and that Churchill believed would prove to be immensely successful – but with only very limited success. The British Army appears to have found it very difficult to believe that horse-mounted cavalry was obsolete, given the central role that the cavalry had played in land based war for hundreds of years (Murray and Millett, 1998).

Sometimes existing systems of beliefs deprive firms of crucial data. An English pottery firm for which I once worked, for example, was puzzled by the fact that their sales were not increasing in what was apparently a booming market, despite the fact that according to their own statistics their market share was holding steady. It turned out that they had not asked their market research firm to gather information on the sales of their Japanese competitors – whose business, it turned out was rapidly growing – because they were "sure" that no one in the UK would buy Japanese china (personal communication).

Sometimes the problem is not the overall identity or system of beliefs inside the firm but the way in which knowledge is organized. In most large firms, for example, knowledge about particular problems becomes localized within particular groups. Knowledge can come to be organized by technological component. In the automobile industry, for example, there are engineers who spend their entire lives thinking about engines, or drive trains or brakes. Knowledge can also be organized by function. Those who work in marketing know all about marketing products, while those who work in production know all about making them. In these situations the firm develops two kinds of knowledge: "component knowledge", detailed knowledge about the pieces of the problem, and "architectural knowledge", knowledge about the ways in which the pieces fit together.

In the early days of an industry both kinds of knowledge tend to be relatively fluid and accessible: when there is no general sense of what a smart phone looks like, for example, or what it means for a building to be sustainable, it is critical that everyone talks to everyone else as new products or services are brought to market. Once the industry has stabilized, however, and it is clear what features customers value and which technologies are best suited to provide them, innovation becomes largely "incremental" – that is, they focus on improving the performance of particular components, rather than on thinking about the parameters of the system as a whole. Simultaneously, as organizations grow larger and the task of improving each component gets more complex, a focus on incremental innovation leads the firm to focus on the generation of "component knowledge", or detailed knowledge about each individual component or piece of the problem.

This kind of focus often means that "architectural knowledge" – the detailed understanding of how the components fit together – becomes embedded in technical specifications or in the procedures and routines that coordinate the work

TABLE 3.1 Forms of innovation

		Architectural knowledge	
		Preserved	*Destroyed*
Component knowledge	*Preserved*	Incremental Innovation (e.g. more fuel efficient conventional cars)	Architectural Innovation (e.g. Zipcar)
	Destroyed	Modular Innovation (e.g. Tesla, driverless cars)	Radical Innovation (e.g. light rail)

of various specialists. Any organization is constantly barraged with information. As the tasks that it faces stabilize, it develops filters that allow it to identify those pieces of information that are most critical to getting the work done. People talking to each other "know" what it is that they should talk about. As this process plays out the architectural knowledge of the organization becomes much less visible and – often – much harder to change. "Architectural innovation" – innovation in which the components of the firm remain more or less the same but the relationship between them changes – can then create great difficulties for established firms (Table 3.1).

One can see architectural innovation happening today in the world of publishing. Much of the "component knowledge" of the industry – how to find great authors, how to edit their texts and so on – is still very relevant. But the context in which this knowledge is being used is quite different. Written content is being distributed and paid for quite differently – and both publishers and many well-established journalists are struggling to adapt to a very different world.

"Our customers don't want it"

Guideline 3.2
New products and new offerings often meet emerging needs. Existing customer preferences may be poor guides to the structure of future demand.

The dynamics that I've outlined thus far often lead firms to ignore or misunderstand emerging customer needs. But Clay Christensen has compellingly argued that one of the most pervasive and important roots of organizational inertia is the insistence on staying *too* close to your existing customers – of understanding their needs too well and of mistaking these needs for those that characterize the entire market. He cites, as one example, the failure of the large integrated steel producers to understand the threat that the mini-mill producers represented to their core business. Mini-mill-produced steel was initially of such terrible quality that it could be used only in rebar, and the established steel producers dismissed it as a possible threat since their largest and most lucrative customers – the car companies – placed a huge premium on quality. They thus ceded the low end of the market to the mini-mill

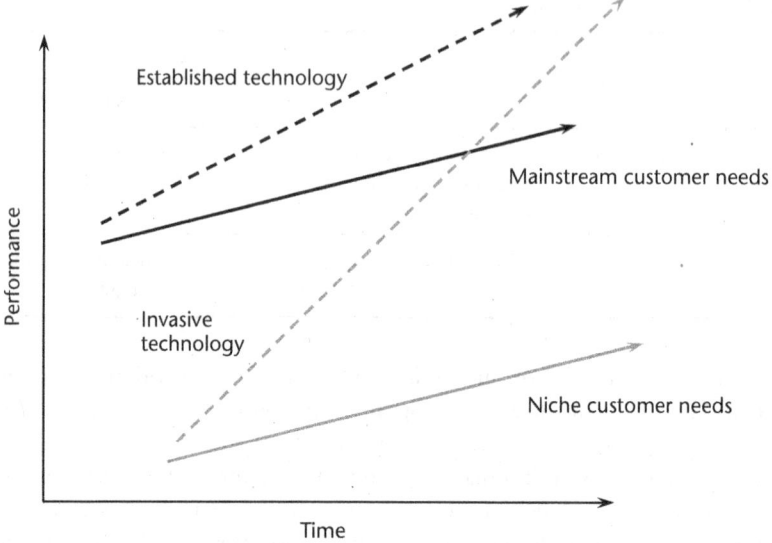

FIGURE 3.1 Clay Christensen's explanation of the innovator's dilemma

producers, allowing them a foothold that they eventually used to dominate the entire market (Christensen, 1997).

I've seen this dynamic at work in the context of the semiconductor photolithographic alignment equipment business (very large machines that draw very small lines on silicon wafers). Perkin Elmer, the firm that dominated the industry throughout the seventies did so by selling "scanning projection aligners". The aligners were beautiful machines and Perkin Elmer's core customer, IBM, loved them. In the late seventies, however, a firm called GCA introduced an aligner they called the "stepper". In theory the technology underlying the stepper was such that it would – eventually – allow the user to project much smaller lines onto wafers than the scanner ever would. But the first steppers were very, very slow. Perkin Elmer went to IBM and asked them if they would like Perkin Elmer to develop its own stepper, but IBM told them it was a crazy idea – that the scanner met all their needs and that no one would ever want anything so slow. But – just as Clay predicts – the stepper manufacturers had found a niche in the market that Perkin Elmer had missed. There were users in the industry who were happy to trade off speed for the increased accuracy they were able to obtain with the stepper, and scanner sales eventually collapsed (Henderson, 1988).

"We won't make any money"

Guideline 3.3
Existing products nearly always appear to be more profitable than new products: but investing in new products may nonetheless be essential to ensure that a firm continues to prosper.

The third major barrier to significant change is that new products or offerings nearly always look less profitable than the current business. (Indeed when this is not the case – medical equipment is the classic – the established firms usually show no hesitation in innovating rapidly.) Digital photography, for example, looked less profitable than conventional film-based photography, while online education looks much less profitable than residential education, and music publishers are still fighting to work out if there is any money in digital music at all.

This is not merely a perceptual problem. Significant innovations look less profitable – and often *are* less profitable, at least initially – both because there is significant uncertainty about whether they will succeed and because all the "complementary assets" that established firms have developed to support existing products (brand names, distribution channels, production facilities and so on) are often no longer a source of competitive advantage.

In general, the only way to ensure that something really new will make money (in the absence of cast-iron intellectual property protection, which is rare) is to ensure that it reaches the market first. When EMI first introduced the CAT scanner, for example, they found that their patents were relatively easy to invent around – but nevertheless the fact that it took their competitors nearly four years to deliver a competitive product gave them (at least initially) a tremendous opportunity to capture value. That year EMI made net profits of £26.6 million on sales of £207 million (approximately $146 million on sales of $1,134 million at today's prices and exchange rates) (Bartlett 2001).

If the market develops very quickly, and if competition is slow to enter, then speed can be a very effective method of capturing value, but if all the firms in an industry rely on moving quickly to make money, they may introduce products so quickly that all the available profits are consumed in rapid product development – the current cut-throat competition in several segments of the "app" market is an obvious example.

In most industries the dynamics of competitive advantage look something like the dynamics illustrated in Figure 3.2.

This framing yields immediate insights into why innovation so often looks less profitable for established firms than the existing business. The comparison is often between mature projects that take full advantage of the company's existing complementary assets, or between new, highly uncertain ventures that will be forced to rely on uniqueness to make money.

One large IT firm with which I worked, for example, had the good fortune to have 40 per cent+ gross margins on many of their product lines. They identified a market into which their technology could be deployed, but their early research suggested that it would not offer better than a 20 per cent gross margin. The disparity between the two prevented active investment in the second market for some time, despite the fact that their analysis suggested that the second market would definitely return more than the firm's cost of capital.

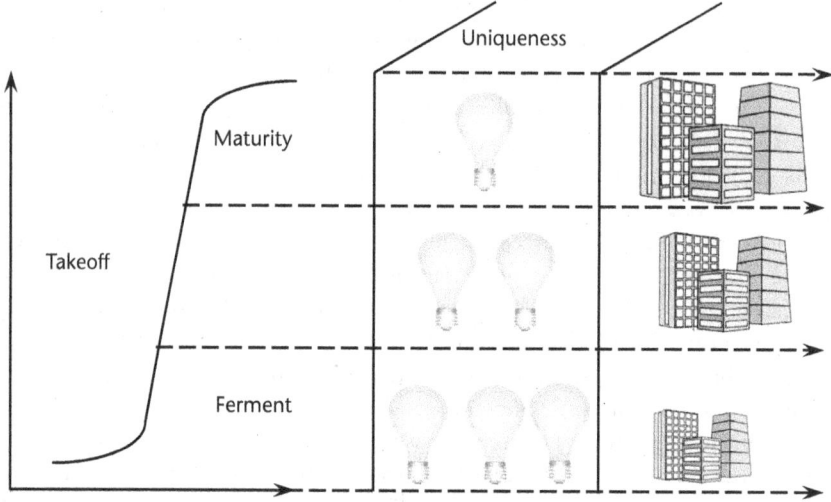

FIGURE 3.2 Uniqueness and complementary assets over the life cycle

"We'll never get it done"

Guideline 3.4
Successful innovation requires generating entrepreneurial energy – but most established organizations are optimized to deliver operational excellence.

Last but not least, many firms have trouble doing anything significantly new because the skills and capabilities they have developed in support of the current business are not well suited to doing new things. At the most basic level, firms are often subject to "capability traps". The manufacture of conventional photographic film, for example, requires the deposition of seven levels of material on top of each other, at micro-millimetre tolerances, on film that is moving at 20–30 miles an hour *in the dark*. One of the reasons that Kodak was so profitable for so many years was because it was one of the few firms that had mastered this skill. This was a powerful source of competitive advantage – but it was not transferable to digital photography.

In the case of Kodak this was so obvious that, in itself, it created few problems. However, the fact that Kodak's marketing skills and distribution channels were not well suited to selling digital products turned out to be much less obvious – and thus created many more problems. Firms often assume that their skills and capabilities can be transferred, often forcing those trying to do new things to grapple with assumptions and approaches that are inherited from the old business and may be ill suited to the new.

A more subtle manifestation of this problem – and one that is often even more destructive – is the fact that many well-established firms have focused deeply on the pursuit of operational excellence. Operational excellence is one of the great sources of competitive advantage. Recent work in the measurement of productivity, for example, suggests that, in many industries, the most productive firms are as much as 40–60 per cent more productive than the least, and this difference persists even after differences in capital and labour quality, product margins and geographic location, suggesting that operational excellence can be a hugely valuable skill (Syverson, 2011).

Unfortunately the kinds of people, skills, metrics and time horizons that are suited to the support of operational excellence are not, in general, conducive to the generation of significant innovation or the taking of risks. A manager whose entire career has been spent "making the numbers" and learning to fine tune an existing system is unlikely to be either temperamentally or otherwise equipped to design an entirely new businesses or to rethink the fundamentals of the existing operation. I have never forgotten meeting with the divisional general manager of a large chemical company whose CEO had publicly committed to an aggressive project of company reinvention. After a polite conversation about how interesting and important the new initiatives were likely to be, the manager looked me in the eye and said, "But you know, Fred [the CEO, not his real name] can give all the speeches he likes, but in the end I wake up with my [operating] number, I go to sleep with my number, I take my number on vacation." Left unsaid was the corollary – that the reinvention effort was very unlikely to succeed. Worst of all, the attempt to manage operational excellence and innovative flexibility within the same organization can create enormous tension unless it is explicitly addressed.

Doing new things in old organizations is thus difficult for at least four reasons:

- well-established, successful firms don't "see" new things because they are not looking for them;
- they pay too much attention to their current customers and thus miss the emergence of new needs;
- they underinvest because new things look less profitable than the existing business; and
- they have difficulty developing entrepreneurial energy because they are so deeply invested in operational excellence.

What can be done? The remainder of the chapter outlines some of the tools and approaches used by firms such as Corning that have succeeded in persistently reinventing themselves.

Seeing the world in new ways

Guideline 3.5
Scenario analysis offers a powerful way of identifying opportunities and addressing major uncertainties which otherwise might be missed.

Some years ago I was invited by the then President of MIT to go to New Orleans to take part in a meeting designed to explore the "future of higher education". The group was a diverse one that included college presidents, professors and senior administrators, and they came from a wide range of institutions including small liberal arts colleges, big public universities and community colleges. We spent the morning of the first day in small groups listing all of the major uncertainties that might affect our futures. We covered pages and pages of easel paper with ideas about things that might or could happen, and, if they did, would have a significant effect on higher education. The afternoon was then spent arguing about them. It was a lively discussion, but in the end we settled on two that we thought were likely to be particularly critical:

- whether support for public education would continue to stay strong; and
- whether distance learning technologies would work.

Following Schwartz (1991), we used these two uncertainties to put together a two by two, and labelled each of the quadrants (Figure 3.3). The top right quadrant was "the official future" – the state of the world that at the time all of our institutions were implicitly counting on. We were acting as if we were sure that public support for education was going to remain rock solid, and even increase. And we were assuming that distance learning would always be a poor second best to direct, face-to-face experience in a classroom. When we asked ourselves, what were the odds of each scenario coming true, however, we realized that there was a very real chance that some of the other scenarios might well materialize.

For me, the experience was a revelation. I had just been tenured, and I was wholly caught up in my own research, secure in the knowledge that I had a great job in one of the oldest and most successful industries in the country. Listening to the others in the room, however, I realized that there was a very good chance that

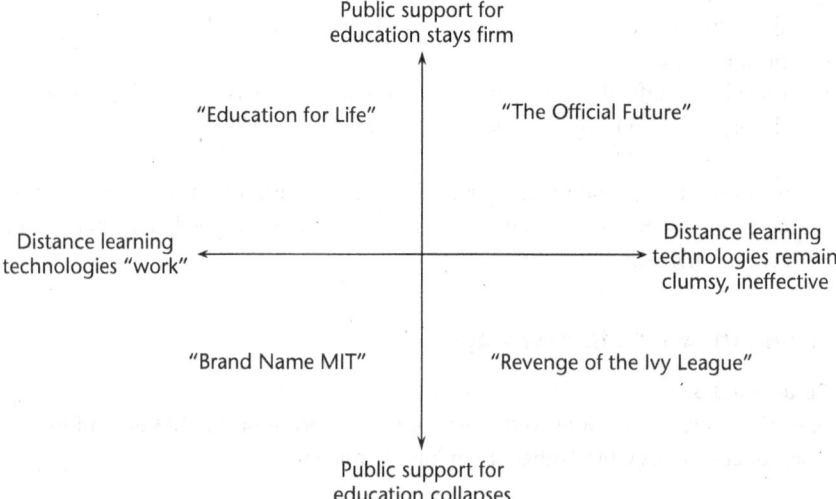

FIGURE 3.3 Scenario grid exploring alternative futures for higher education

public support would – if not collapse – at least become much harder to sustain. And, being a professor at MIT, I was easily persuaded that distance learning technologies might be a powerful educational tool. I just hadn't thought about the implications of the idea for my day-to-day life. Moreover, I knew just how many resources MIT had allocated to exploring ways of positioning the university if the world changed, and it wasn't very many, rather a very, very small fraction of the resources that were happily employed in supporting business as usual.

I came back to MIT and debriefed the President, and a couple of years later MIT announced an Open Courseware initiative – a commitment to put every MIT course up on the net for everyone to see. It was a path-breaking idea, and it positioned MIT on the front lines of the debate about the future of education. Our President at the time, Charles Vest, was a visionary leader whom I believe sent me to New Orleans precisely because he was thinking deeply about these issues – and I like to think that this analysis helped him both make and communicate his decision to go ahead with Open Courseware. And the experience converted me to the use of this technique – a variant of "scenario analysis". I've been using it ever since.

As the discussion above suggests, one of the reasons that many organizations have difficulty responding to significant shifts in the world around them is that they don't "see" them. Both individuals and firms develop maps of the world – expectations about what is likely to happen and ways of interpreting news – that tend to reinforce the firm's sense of itself. Up to a certain point this is a great source of strength: a strong, shared identity can be a powerful source of focus and an underpinning of a coherent culture. But, when it acts as a blindfold to important shifts in the environment that may dramatically impact the firm, it becomes a problem.

Scenario analysis is particularly helpful in overcoming these kinds of tendency. It pulls senior managers away from day-to-day business to talk explicitly about the ways in which the world might change in uncomfortable and unpredictable ways. It doesn't pretend to lead to a right answer or a definite forecast, but generates instead a set of scenarios that may or may not come true with probabilities that can be discussed. And it allows for a much richer discussion about how – if the world may indeed change – the firm should respond.

Making money from innovation

Guideline 3.6
Work hard during the early stages of change to understand why innovation will benefit customers and how the organization can charge enough for these benefits to pay for the change.

One of the most important means that firms use to build the organizational will to explore new ways of doing things is to be very clear as to how the firm might make money pursuing them. It's difficult to make major investments in quite different kinds of businesses when the existing business is both profitable and well understood.

As suggested above, new opportunities often look less profitable than incremental opportunities in the existing business. Failing to address this issue convincingly and relying on "vision" without offering a thoughtful answer to this question runs the risk of creating significant organizational resistance as employees who have invested years of their lives in the current business come to resent what is too often seen as someone else's pet project. This resistance may appear to be "cultural" or "organizational" – as in "the operating managers just don't understand how vital these new initiatives are to our health" – but it is also often the result of a diffuse unease amongst existing operational managers as to whether this new initiative is strategically sensible.

A fundamental prerequisite for a successful move into a new area is thus a carefully worked out and aggressively communicated strategic rationale. This need not look like a fully articulated, every "t" crossed strategic "plan". Indeed, a focus on the development of such a plan is usually disastrous in the kinds of rapidly changing situation in which these kinds of new efforts find themselves. But it should include some broad brush answers to the three central questions of strategy:

- How will our innovation create value for our customers? (Why do we believe there may be demand for this offering? From what kind of customers?)
- How will we be able to capture some of this value for ourselves? (How can we imagine differentiating ourselves from possible competitors and creating some kind of sustainable competitive advantage?)
- How will we deliver this value? (Do we have the skills and capabilities required to execute?)

Strategy development as a process of experimentation

Guideline 3.7
The probability of a transformational change enduring will be greater if it is introduced through a process of ongoing experimentation.

Any firm attempting to move through a discontinuity has to balance the predictability and routine of the operational excellence that characterizes business as usual with the uncertainty of doing something new. We understand intuitively that the discovery of new products or services requires leaving space and setting aside time for experimentation, whether it's in an R&D group, a new product development space or an entrepreneurial firm. Successful firms allow for experimentation and creativity *in the development of strategy, or in the development of new business models*. The story of how Apple came to do well through not only creative and beautiful design but also through pioneering development of the App Store and iTunes Store has highlighted the importance of this issue, but examples such as Zipcar and AirBnB are current examples of firms where innovation is in the business model.

In the early 2000s, for example, Eli Lilly's senior team came to believe that the development of "targeted therapeutics" – drugs that respond to particular features of a patient's profile, which can only be prescribed after a diagnostic test – was going to be central to their future. They thought long and hard about what this implied for their corporate strategy. If diagnostics was going to be central to developing and selling these drugs, should they buy a diagnostics company? If physicians needed to be educated as to when and how such drugs should be prescribed, did they need a new sales force? How should targeted therapeutics be priced? By definition, targeted therapeutics command smaller markets than conventional blockbuster drugs because they are sold only to those segments of the patient population to which they are suited. For example, Herceptin, a treatment for breast cancer, is prescribed only for those patients who have a particular gene mutation. But if one can identify patients who are likely to respond to a particular drug, in principle, it should be possible to conduct smaller and more focused clinical trials, saving money – and to charge more for them, since physicians can be more confident that the drugs will work (Henderson and Reavis, 2009b).

One approach to these issues might have been to pick one model and to decide to make it work – but instead Lilly embarked on a process of analytic and actual experimentation. Experienced staff working closely with experienced operating managers ran detailed simulations of alternate cost and revenue scenarios – not in the belief that any of them were "right" but to give the operating managers a sense of the parameter space within which it might be profitable and the key trade-offs that it implied. The approach paid off.

One particularly important tool is exploring potential demand in new ways. Christensen and his collaborators, for example, have suggested focusing on "jobs to be done" as a powerful way to open pathways to experimentation (Christensen and Raynor, 2003). Von Hippel suggests working with users, who are the source of a surprising fraction of new ideas, as a source of insight (Von Hippel, 1994). The Corning Corporation uses a "deep dive" process to really understand customer needs (Henderson and Reavis, 2009). All three approaches share a commitment to breaking out of the existing patterns of customer/consumer understanding to support thinking about the market in new ways and to low cost, rapid experimentation. Just as Ideo has pioneered rapid prototyping of physical products, so these firms are experimenting with ways to prototype new business models.

Organizing for discontinuous innovation

Guideline 3.8
Success requires balancing entrepreneurial energy and operational excellence.

As I outlined above, managing discontinuous innovation is hard because it asks the organization to do two things at once: to be simultaneously creative and experimental *and, also,* to be totally focused on operational excellence. It's easy to dismiss the problems large firms experience in doing this as simply the results of "culture" or "bad management" but, as argued above, the roots of the issue run far more deeply than any single explanation. Moving an organization through these kinds of transition requires action on many fronts and careful attention. Managing significant innovation in established organizations thus requires not only building the space and capabilities to generate and support innovation – in itself a difficult enough task – but also holding these capabilities in tension with the structures and systems that support the continued pursuit of operational excellence within the main body of the firm.

One commonly cited solution to this dilemma is to set up a separate organizational unit to pursue innovation. But such an organizational move – however handled – is never sufficient if the purpose is to transform the core of the established firm. Such a transformation is critically dependent on the ability of the senior management team to manage "ambidextrously", to use the phrase coined by Michael Tushman and Charles O'Reilly (1997). Ambidextrous management requires the senior team to have the strategic vision to understand the potential of the new opportunity, the skills to manage the existing organization and the ability to hold the two in tension. This is often achieved by building respect for these two ways of working within the firm.

Creating space for innovation – choosing a structural solution

Guideline 3.9
Sheltering new ideas in a separate organization can be a powerful route to innovation but these units must be managed with care.

Faced with the need to build new patterns of behaviour and to define a distinctly different strategy, many firms have found it helpful to structure the attempt to move into a discontinuity using a distinctly different entity. The most famous example of this strategy is IBM's development of the PC using a small group sent off to Florida. As it happens, this was the second time that IBM had used a carefully sheltered separate organization to launch the company into an entirely new area. They had used the same strategy, with huge success, in the development of the IBM 360 main frame family of computers in the 1960s and 1970s (by some measures the most profitable new product ever launched), and it has become the fashionable route to discontinuous innovation.

However, while setting up a separate unit is often the best way of tackling the problem of carrying an organization through a discontinuity, it is critical to be aware of two things:

- such a move only works when the separate unit is appropriately supported by the host organization – or when the right strategy, people, incentives and procedures are in place;
- it is *not* always the best solution. For some firms and some kinds of project, working within the confines of the existing business may greatly increase the

odds of success. For others, using a "pseudo" venture capital approach, working through a joint venture, or even using an acquisition may be most appropriate.

The goal of any structural solution is to enable the firm to access *both* operational excellence *and* entrepreneurial energy. Going outside the firm – for example by making an acquisition or by setting up a new unit staffed with new people that is geographically remote from the main body of the firm – ensures that the new venture will have lots of entrepreneurial energy but increases the risk that it will not be adequately connected to the current business. Similarly using an internal team to tackle discontinuous innovation ensures that the innovation will be closely coordinated with the existing business, but also raises the risk that it will be difficult to get the team to think truly creatively about the new opportunity.

One critical consideration is the health and flexibility of the organization's existing culture. Firms in fast-moving industries who have a history of reinventing themselves typically find it relatively straightforward to set up new units inside the existing structure. They then manage them by having clearly defined executive sponsors, by putting the right people into clearly defined leadership roles and by carefully managing the relationship with the core business.

It is also important to think deeply about the incentive structure surrounding any new effort. Often a firm will set up a new unit, charge it with going to market in quite different ways, and then ask those in the unit to work extraordinarily hard building the new business while using the existing incentive regime to compensate them. This rarely works!

Ambidextrous senior managers

Guideline 3.10
Transformative changes require strong administrative and political support from the very top of the organization.

Senior management involvement is also critical if the firm is to manage the organizational problems inherent in doing really new things. Without engaged, persistent CEO involvement, discontinuous projects often seemed fated to fail.

Michael Tushman and Charles O'Reilly (1997) describe the ideal senior team during times of change as one that is "ambidextrous" – or as one that is able to manage simultaneously *both* the demands of the core, mature business *and* the needs of the new, growth business. Ambidextrous teams understand that growth businesses often require new kinds of people to run them, new financial targets and, of course, new strategies. These same teams understand how to manage the core business successfully without insisting that the new businesses "look like" the core.

Since senior managers often gain their seniority through their success in managing the existing business, building ambidexterity can be a challenge. Andy Grove, then CEO of Intel, once famously asked Gorden Moore, the company's founder and then Chairman of his board, "What would new management do if they came to Intel now?" and on hearing the answer asked, "Why don't we go out through the revolving door, come back in and do it ourselves?" (Burgelman, 1994). But this level of self-consciousness is not always present. Many companies that move successfully into discontinuities either see a change in a significant fraction of their senior team, or invest significantly in building ambidexterity at the senior level.

In conclusion

Creating discontinuous innovation within the boundaries of established firms is difficult but not impossible. Those who succeed open up the organization to the possibility of change using techniques such as scenario analysis, carefully explore the ways in which innovation can be profitably introduced, and experiment extensively with alternative approaches. They pay a great deal of attention to the need to balance entrepreneurial energy and innovative drive with operational excellence. Often, initially, they use a separate unit to shelter new ideas but always pay careful attention to the allocation of resources and the structure of incentives. They rely throughout on a committed, attentive, "ambidextrous" senior team. Since in many ways these guidelines reflect the fundamental human and strategic dynamics of change in any organization I would be surprised if many of them do not also hold true within the public sector.

References

Bartlett, Christopher (2001) "EMI and the CAT Scanner". Harvard Business School Case No 383194, Revised November 2001.

Burgelman, Robert (1994) "Fading memories: A Process Study of Strategic Business Exit in Dynamic Environments". *Administrative Science Quarterly* 39(1): March.

Cheng, Roger (2014) "Farewell Nokia: The rise and fall of a mobile pioneer." CNET, April 25, 2014. Available at: www.cnet.com/news/farewell-nokia-the-rise-and-fall-of-a-mobile-pioneer/

Christensen, Clayton (1997) *The Innovator's Dilemma*. Boston, MA: Harvard Business School Press.

Christensen, Clayton and Michael Raynor (2003) *The Innovator's Solution*. Boston, MA: Harvard Business School Press.

Henderson, Rebecca (1988) "The Failure of Established Firms in the Face of Technological Change: A Study of Photolithographic Alignment Equipment". phD Thesis submitted to the Harvard Economic Department.

Henderson, Rebecca (2009) "Eli Lilly's Project Resilience: Anticipating the future of the pharmaceutical industry". MIT Case No 07-043, January 2009b. Available at: https://mitsloan.mit.edu/LearningEdge/strategy/Resilience/Pages/default.aspx (accessed 29 April 2016).

Henderson, Rebecca and Cate Reavis (2009) "Corning Incorporated: The Growth and Strategy Council". MIT Case No 08-056, January 2009a. Available at: https://mitsloan.mit.edu/LearningEdge/strategy/CorningIncorporated/Pages/Corning-Incorporated-The-Growth-and-Strategy-Council.aspx (accessed 29 April 2016).

Murray, Williamson and Allan Millett (eds) (1998) *Military innovation in the interwar period*. Cambridge: Cambridge University Press.
Schwartz, Peter (1991) *The Art of the Long View*. New York: Doubleday.
Syverson, Chad (2011) "What Determines Productivity?" *Journal of Economic Literature* 49: 326–65.
Tushman, Michael and Charles O'Reilly (1997) *Winning through innovation*. Boston, MA: Harvard Business School Press.
von Hippel, Eric (1994) "Sticky Information and the Locus of Problem Solving: Implications for Innovation". *Management Science* 40(4): 429–39.

4

AN ASSESSMENT FRAMEWORK FOR RESILIENT PUBLIC POLICY

R. Quentin Grafton and Walter Reinhardt

> Intelligence is not to make no mistakes, but quickly to see how to make them good.
>
> Bertolt Brecht

Introduction

This chapter explores, through four case studies in Australian public policy, the factors that support resilient transformational public policy. We define resilient public policy as policy that is both durable and beneficial from a broad socio-economic perspective. The four case studies encompass a period of more than 30 years and different federal governments:

- Australia's National Competition Policy (NCP) of the 1990s, which saw real price reductions in electricity, water, rail transport, port charges, telecommunications and milk.
- Water reform in the Murray–Darling Basin during a major drought in the first decade of this Millennium, which generated some beneficial outcomes despite being very poor value for the A$13bn expenditure and having substantial deficiencies in design and implementation.
- Mineral Resources Rent Tax (MRRT) initiated in 2010 with the stated intent to increase revenues to the Australian government but which has delivered barely a fraction of the revenues proposed and could be characterised as a complete failure in design, implementation and communication.
- A Home Insulation Program (HIP) that began in 2009 and was intended to provide economic stimulus in response to the Global Financial Crisis and reduce residential energy costs for heating and cooling. Widespread failures in

design and implementation, including inadequate consideration of risks, inadvertently led to the loss of lives and hundreds of house fires.

Our purpose is not to be critical of a particular government or of individuals, but rather to learn from what transpired so as to give insights for policy makers to promote resilient transformational changes to public policy in the future. In other words, through assessment of what worked and what failed, we provide informed and evidence-based insights about what to do, and what to avoid in the public policy-making process.

An assessment framework for resilient public policy

Public policy making is frequently defined as a process (Colebatch, 2005) that, ideally, follows a policy cycle (Althaus et al., 2013) involving:

- problem identification;
- policy formulation;
- policy adoption;
- policy implementation; and
- policy evaluation.

Whether or not public policy is developed sequentially through these steps, it must at least include a defined goal and series of instruments (Dovers and Hussey, 2013) intended to achieve the stated objective(s).

Our contribution is to provide an assessment framework that can be used in all stages of the policy cycle and not just in terms of policy evaluation. Thus, while our chapter represents an ex-post assessment of four Australia public policy processes, the framework can equally be used in the preparation and delivery of almost all changes to public policy.

Our assessment framework complements rather than substitutes for existing descriptions and prescriptions of how to undertake effective public policy (Bardach, 2011). The framework uses six key guidelines to evaluate public policy decision making:

Guideline 4.1
Evidence-informed, or whether the best available data is used and analysed with robust and accepted methods and with qualified, capable and unbiased analysts.

Guideline 4.2
Contestable, such that decisions are taken with genuine opportunity for consideration of the goals, evidence, alternatives/options and risks.

Guideline 4.3
Proposals for transformational policy reform need to be *timely* so that evidence and options are available when needed and when decision makers are receptive.

Guideline 4.4
Adaptive, such that there is timely/regular review of policy as circumstances change and within the "policy cycle" that includes actions that specify, identify, act, monitor and update (SIAMU) the policy process.

Guideline 4.5
Transparent as to what the policy problem is that needs fixing, the evidence for the policy, and what the policy implementation will (and will not) achieve.

Guideline 4.6
Envisioned, such that there is a compelling narrative which guides implementation, accounts for who loses and who gains, who acts and who is acted upon, and provides a vision of what the policy is intended to achieve.

Four assessments of public policy

National Competition Policy

Purpose and process

The Australian National Competition Policy (NCP) was formulated under the prime ministership of Paul Keating in the early 1990s. It was signed as an intergovernmental agreement between the federal, state and territory governments in April 1995. Broadly speaking, the NCP is an overarching microeconomic reform framework intended to liberalise all sectors of the Australian economy and promote competition.

The foundational development of the NCP occurred throughout the end of the 1980s and the start of the 1990s as a result of growing recognition that Australia's economy functioned as eight separate economies based on state and territory boundaries, tightly bound by respective state and territory regulation. For example, road rules differed, as did trade practice regulations, and there was limited consistency in water and electricity standards.

The NCP provided a common framework for reform, identified reform priorities and allocated transfer payments from beneficiaries of reform to those undertaking the reform. The three key documents for the NCP, developed through the Council of Australian Governments (COAG) in April 1995, were the National Competition Principles, the National Code of Conduct, and the Agreement to Implement National Competition Policy and Related Reforms.

The development of the NCP took over a decade from the early political announcements through to policy implementation (Figure 4.1). It benefited from problem formation and academic analysis in the 1980s and 1990s, especially by the

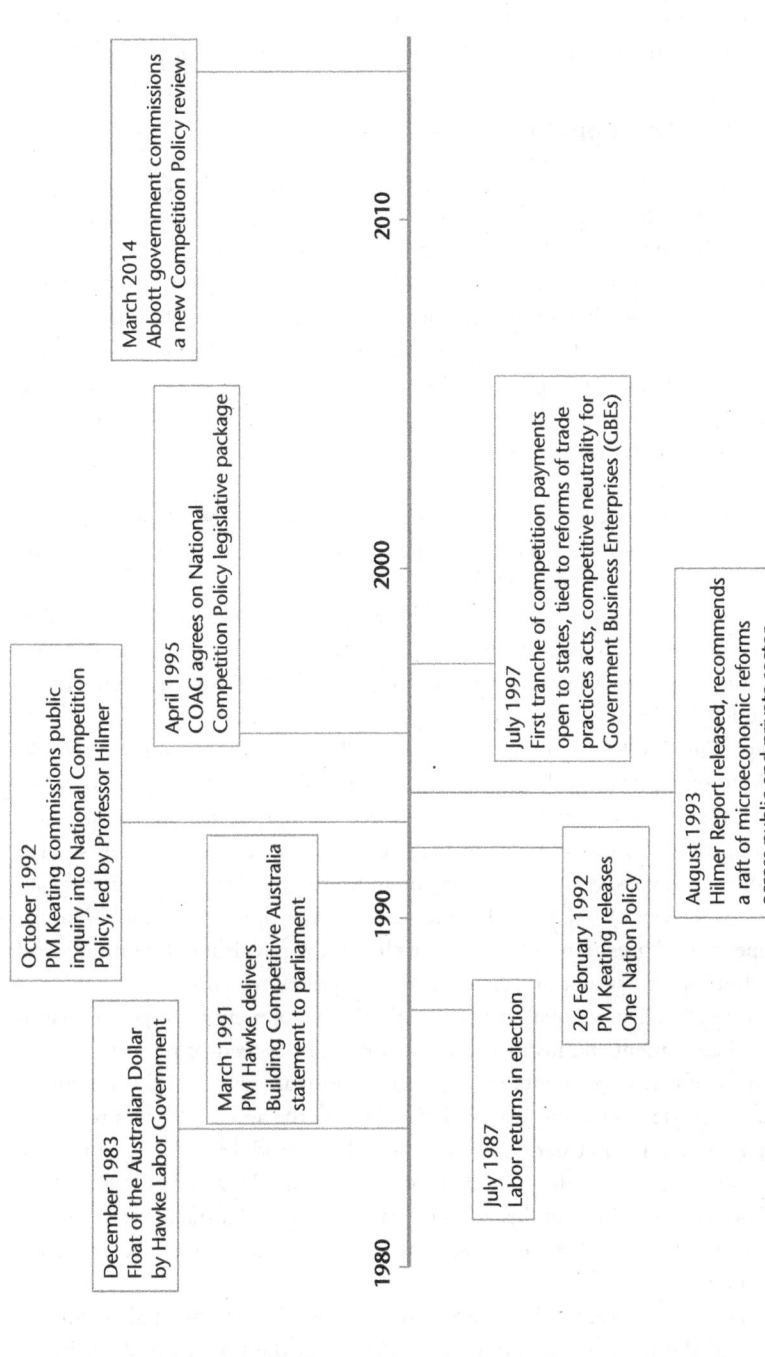

FIGURE 4.1 Timeline for National Competition Policy reform

Industry Commission (IC, 1995b, 1995a) and the Hilmer Review (Hilmer et al., 1993), stages of consultation particularly in the 1992–95 period, and recognition by both major parties of the necessity of reform. The key aspects of the NCP are described below using the six criteria for the assessment of resilient public policy.

Assessment of the six guidelines

- *Evidence-informed.* The formation of the NCP benefited from the build-up of evidence, first from specific sectors and then as an overarching framework provided by the Hilmer Review that laid out the evidence for and steps to undertake reform. In the years preceding the development of the NCP there were premiers' and chief ministers' conferences that sought to align regulations between states. The Hilmer Review, conducted over 12 months, provided substantive analysis (425 pages) of both framework and sectoral gains from microeconomic reform. Further independent analysis was provided by the Industry Commission in 1995, and subsequently by the Productivity Commission (PC, 1999).
- *Contestable.* The NCP itself was contestable, open for public and political comment, and followed a remarkable period of public debate about economic reform. The public debate followed on from a recession in the early 1990s which had raised competition as a key area of reform in early 1992. The Hilmer Review, COAG statements and policy intent were reviewed and contested for three years prior to the signing of the National Competition Principles Agreements with the states in 1995.
- *Timely.* The NCP was timely in that it allowed time for policy contest, development and political agreement on the problem, and the policy solution. As the Hilmer Review stated there was "widespread recognition of the critical role effective competition can play in the transformation of the Australian economy necessary to meet our current and future challenges" (Hilmer et al., 1993, page xxxix). Within 12 months of the signing of the National Competition Agreements there was a change of government at the federal level, but bipartisan support remained for the policy reforms.
- *Adaptive.* The adaptive qualities of the NCP development process are seen in the final agreement and institutional structure. The agreed-to reforms allowed flexibility of state implementation, subject to national review, with competition payments made over a ten-year period following the agreement. A strong and adaptive institutional structure was developed as a product of the NCP process and implementation: the Council of Australian Governments (COAG). COAG has remained an important feature of the Australian institutional landscape, reform focused and testament to the needs for adaptability in policy implementation.
- *Transparent.* Significant "closed-door" negotiations were undertaken for the NCP, but the process was transparent in terms of the policy problem, intent and response. The framework and sectors were clearly specified in COAG

responses to the Hilmer Review and then policy intentions (COAG, 1994, 1995).
- *Envisioned.* As the NCP was developed and negotiated, the accompanying vision became compelling and accessible. Competition reforms were embedded in the key policy statements of the Keating government, but there was advocacy for reform outside of parliament. The Productivity Commission estimated the gains from the NCP and these estimates were used in the budgeted competition payments to the states and territories.

Outcomes

The recognition of the NCP importance, the breadth of the NCP's scope and the value of federal–state financial transfers associated with the NCP endowed COAG meetings with substantial public policy impact. Lasting institutional structures were established through the COAG framework and these structures are continuing to serve ongoing reforms..

In 2005 the Productivity Commission conservatively estimated the gains resulting from implementation of the NCP as an increase in GDP of 2.5 per cent or A$20bn, or about A$1,500 per person (PC, 2005). The observed effects can be seen in real price reductions in electricity, water, rail transport, port charges, telecommunications and milk.

The overall resilient public policy assessment of the NCP, using the assessment scale provided in Table 4.1 is "A". The process and outcomes were delivered in a timely and cost effective manner, and to plan, with decades of serious rigorous analysis and public consultation by the Industry Commission, leading to widespread acceptance from multiple stakeholders and as part of the policy cycle.

TABLE 4.1 Assessment score of resilient public policy

Overall grade	Assessment
A	Process and outcomes delivered to plan in a timely and cost effective manner, with widespread acceptance from multiple stakeholders and as part of the policy cycle.
B	Deficiencies in implementation, but overall design and approach appropriate with generally favourable outcomes.
C	Substantial deficiencies in design and implementation, but has or is expected to generate some beneficial outcomes.
D	Widespread failures in design and implementation, inadequate consideration of risks, and a failure to achieve key goals or creation of other large and unanticipated costs.
E	Complete failure in design, implementation and outcomes.

Murray–Darling Basin Plan

Purpose and process

The Murray–Darling Basin Plan (the Plan) was developed in response to poor environmental outcomes and severe drought throughout Australia's largest river system. Significantly, development of the legislation needed to prepare the Plan achieved bi-partisan support. The process that developed the plan originated in the 2004 National Water Initiative and a 10 point and A$10 billion 2007 National Plan for Water Security in response to a worsening drought in the Murray–Darling Basin (Connell and Grafton, 2008). The National Water Initiative itself had followed from several years of intense drought along the east coast, increasing concerns about the environmental health in Australia's largest river system (the Murray–Darling Basin), and stalled water reforms previously undertaken through the National Competition Policy (NCP).

The Murray–Darling Basin Authority was established as an independent expert agency under the Federal Water Minister and was given the task of developing the Plan under the federal government's Water Act 2007. The Plan included the following three objectives (there were seven in total):

- the establishment and enforcement of environmentally sustainable limits on the quantities of surface water and ground water that may be taken from the Basin water resources (including by interception activities);
- the use and management of the Basin water resources in a way that optimises economic, social and environmental outcomes; and
- improved water security for all users of Basin water resources.

A 2008 assessment of water reform in the Murray–Darling Basin noted that there was:

> insufficient transparency about the measurable environmental goals of water reform, inadequate consideration of interdependencies in terms of future environmental watering plans, insufficient rigour in the processes being developed to assess trade-offs in using public funds, ... and in-built inflexibility in the Basin Plan.
>
> (Connell and Grafton, 2008: 83)

Over the period 2007 to 2010 the *Guide to the Proposed Plan* (the *Guide*), which was in two volumes and four parts, was developed as a precursor to the Plan (see Figure 4.2). With the release of the *Guide* in October 2010 (MDBA 2010a) there was major backlash in the rural areas of the Murray–Darling Basin. In part, this was because the *Guide* had been developed in a process that ignored advice provided to it and never explicitly responded to the inherent conflict between the objectives for the Plan nor effectively engaged with communities. The rural community opposition

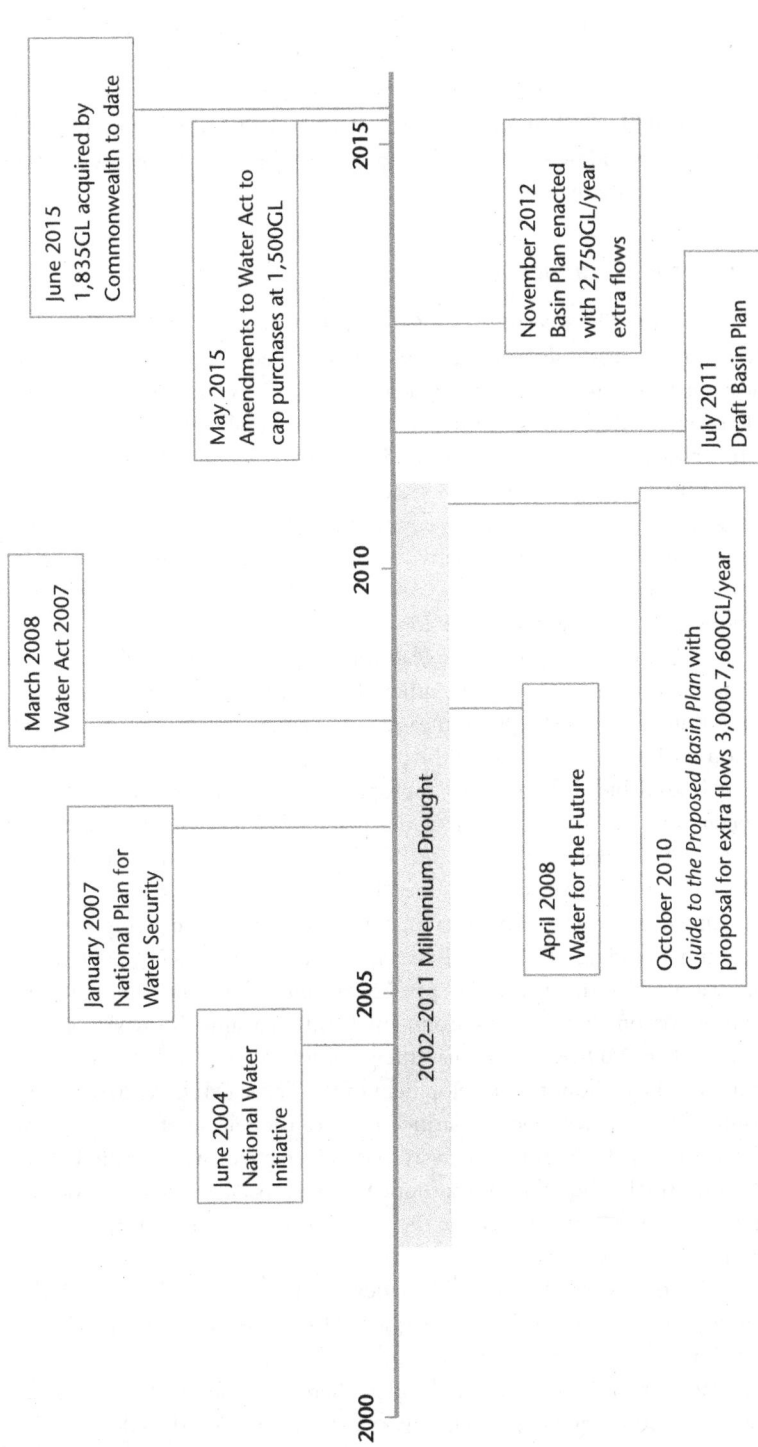

FIGURE 4.2 Water reform in the Murray–Darling Basin (GL = gigalitre = 1 billion litres)

to the *Guide* was substantial and arose from their perception that their interests were secondary in the preparation of the *Guide* (Boully and Maywald, 2011).

The final Basin Plan was signed into law in November 2012 (see Figure 4.2) against a background of acrimony, "closed-door" negotiations, and disputes surrounding the costs and benefits of reallocating water between irrigators and the environment and among regions.

Assessment of the six guidelines

- *Evidence-informed.* The release of the *Guide* in October 2010 led to claims by irrigator groups that the evidence used was inadequate or inaccurate. In response the federal government sought a compromise with rural constituents, and there was much less scientific evidence, and much of it contested, to support the final allocations of water under the Basin Plan. Indeed, the *Guide* in 2010 outlined a minimum of 3,856GL (MDBA, 2010b: 114) reduction in surface water diversions to achieve environmental water requirements while the actual agreed-to reductions relative to baseline diversions under the Basin Plan was 2,750GL, coupled with a 40 per cent *increase* in groundwater extractions relative to baseline diversions (MDBA, 2012).
- *Contestable.* The development of the Plan was highly contested, but debated in public at such a normative level, rather than factual, that there was not a proper consideration of the goals, means and alternatives. A far more helpful discussion of the policy goals should have occurred prior to the release of the *Guide*. It is arguable that the most appropriate timing of the contest should have been prior to the inception of the National Water Initiative and the Water Act 2007. Before the release of the *Guide*, there were conflicting interpretations of the goals such that the National Water Commission (NWC) recommended as a matter of urgency that it was essential to "develop a shared national understanding of sustainable levels of extraction" (NWC, 2008, page 21) and warned that there was still "no agreed approach to understanding and balancing trade-offs between environmental and consumptive uses" (NWC, 2009: vii). The MDBA stated that they consulted with stakeholders and governments throughout the development of the *Guide* (MDBA, 2010a: xvi), but conflicting goals were never clarified prior to the release of the *Guide*. At its release, the evidence for change in existing practices was disputed (Lee, 2010). Surprisingly, the solution was not contested: to spend billions of dollars on irrigators to assist them to reduce their level of extractions so as to increase environmental flows.
- *Timely.* The timing of the Basin Plan development was awkward for the government of the day. The process, legislated for in the Water Act 2007, was distinctly proscriptive in the timing and deliverables. Unfortunately, at the due delivery dates for the *Guide* and then the Plan, there was a minority government, existing only with rural independent support. Two days after the release of the *Guide*, a parliamentary inquiry was commissioned, and chaired by one of the

rural independents. The inquiry report eventually declared that the *Guide* "sent shockwaves through the regional communities of the Basin for no good reason" (Commonwealth of Australia, 2011: ix). The willingness and capability for difficult decisions in policy making was severely weakened.
- *Adaptive*. The challenge of revisiting the Water Act 2007 meant that the Basin Plan specifications and process were tightly fixed, such that the policy-making process was less adaptable than it could have been. With rural independent support, the minority government of the day could only agree to prioritise funding for infrastructure efficiency. This circumstance is an example of what Hollander and Curran (2001) observe as a common trait of policy processes that fail to account for political context.
- *Transparent*. Although the content requirements of the Plan were legislated, and thus transparent, the negotiations for water allocation were opaque. The "surprise" about the contents and recommendations for the *Guide* were mirrored by surprise by scientists about the final allocation of water, including an increase in groundwater diversions (Grafton *et al.*, 2014), under the eventually negotiated Basin Plan. Moreover, the overarching negotiations for water reform through COAG, and separately between the federal government and state governments lack transparency (NWC, 2011: 5).
- *Envisioned*. The vision was ineffectively articulated, or, at least, the mixed vision of both sustaining rural communities and increasing environmental flows was viewed by many as inconsistent or even incompatible. There were clear signs that conflicting interpretations of the goals and means existed (NWC, 2008: 21), yet the political leadership to resolve these differences was largely absent in the lead up to and release of the *Guide*. In twenty months prior its release (October 2010) there had been two prime ministers, three water ministers and a close federal election followed by a month of negotiations before one party could emerge with a minority government. At the release of the *Guide*, the Minister for Water had been in the job for less than a month. Championing major change in water management, particularly provoking emotive rural responses to water, required a compelling narrative about change that the Murray–Darling Basin Authority did not, could not, or would not do.

Outcomes

The enacted Basin Plan is now within the five-year adjustment period before coming into force. The planned reductions in baseline diversion of 2,750GL of surface water beginning in 2019 are currently being sought through water entitlement buybacks from farmers and irrigators (the A$3.2bn Restoring the Balance program) and from irrigation scheme efficiency improvements (the A$5.2bn Sustainable Rural Water Use and Infrastructure Program). The 2013 Intergovernmental Agreement to progress MDB water reform (Commonwealth of Australia, 2013) provided an ongoing work program for adjustment to the sustainable diversion limits (SDLs) that prioritise investment in efficiency infrastructure ahead of the buyback of water entitlements. As of the end of June 2013, direct water entitlement purchases had acquired about 40 per cent of the planned reductions under the Basin Plan (Grafton and Horne, 2014).

The intended environmental outcomes associated with the Basin Plan will not now be realized until the commencement of the implementation of sustainable diversion limits in 2019. Nevertheless, the renewal of dredging in early 2015 at the Murray Mouth (ABC, 2015), despite the fact that the whole of the Basin is not in drought, is a worrying sign that current environmental flows are inadequate. Equally as important are the expenditures on achieving reform, which were accounted to be almost A$13 billion, and which could have achieved the same level of environmental flows for billions less (Grafton, 2010; PC, 2010). This suggests that there were very large missed opportunities to support Basin agriculture, communities and landscapes under the Basin water reform process (Wentworth Group of Concerned Scientists, 2010).

The overall resilient public policy assessment of the Murray–Darling Basin Plan and reform process is a "C" (see Table 4.1), which indicates that the policy process had substantial deficiencies in design and implementation, but is expected to generate some beneficial outcomes, despite being very poor value for the billions of dollars expended (Young, 2014).

The Home Insulation Program

On Tuesday, 3 February 2009, Prime Minister Rudd and Federal Treasurer Wayne Swann announced a A$42bn economic stimulus package for Australia (Nation Building – Economic Stimulus Plan). The stimulus package was a response to a looming global economic recession. A key component of the Plan was the Energy Efficient Homes Package, valued at approximately A$2.5bn. The Energy Efficient Homes Package included the Home Insulation Program (HIP), the Low Emissions Assistance Plan for Renters (LEAPR) and the Solar Hot Water Rebate. The Home Insulation Program was the largest part of the Energy Efficient Homes Package.

The HIP was intended to boost employment opportunities for low-skilled workers in the construction industry with funding provided by the federal government. Monitoring of standards for safe installation of insulation were perceived to be the remit of state and territory governments.

The HIP was implemented in two phases. The first phase (February to 30 June 2009) had Commonwealth rebate payments made directly to households, following the installation of the insulation. The second phase (1 July 2009 until program suspension in 19 February 2010) had rebates paid directly to the installers (see Figure 4.3).

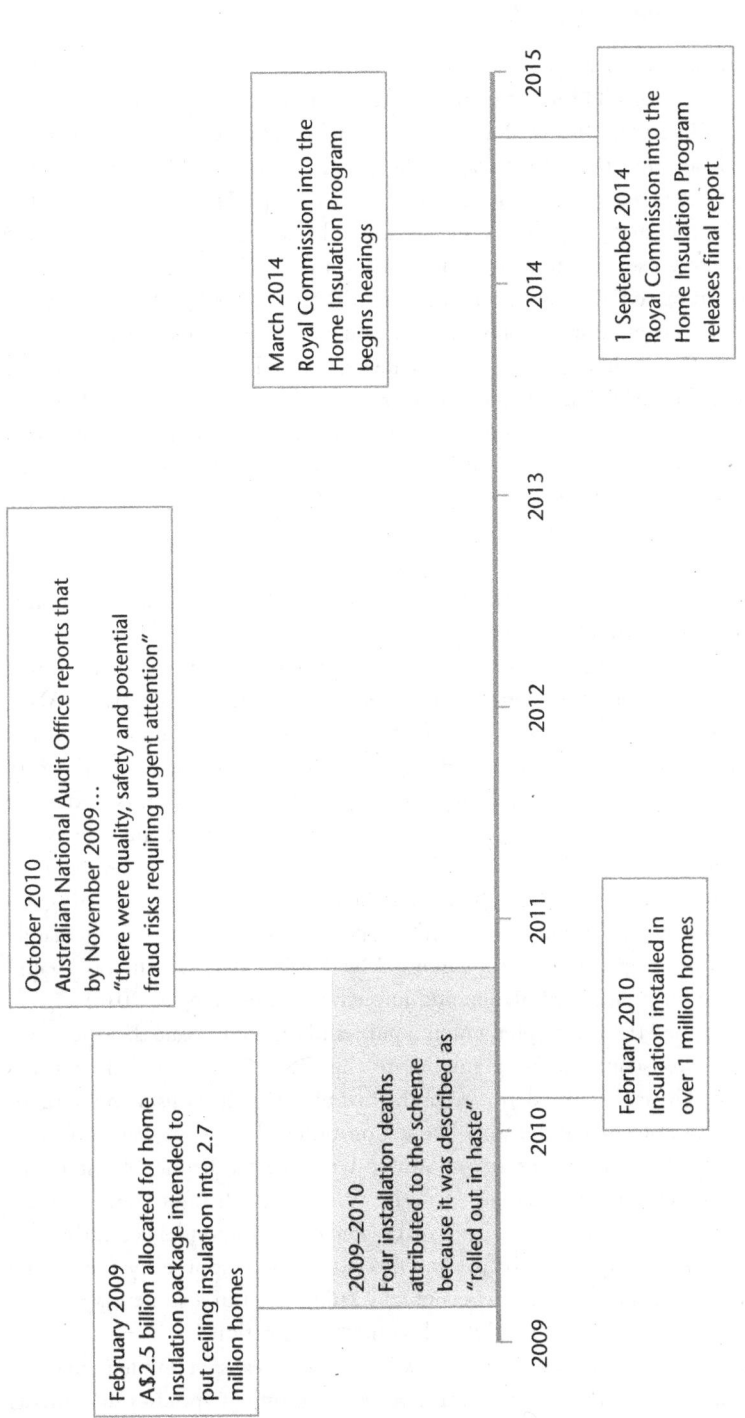

FIGURE 4.3 Home Insulation Program

Assessment of the six guidelines

- *Evidence-informed.* Evidence in favour of economic stimulus was supported by the IMF and OECD for mitigating the real economic impacts of the financial crises (IMF, 2009; OECD, 2009a, 2009b). However, as the subsequent Royal Commission into the HIP declared, the external advice and assistance on risk and project management was "patently inadequate" (Hanger, 2014: 5). For example, the safety experience in proximate locations (New Zealand) found similar safety issues with insulation installation in 2007, but this evidence was not incorporated into program design (O'Rourke, 2007). As the external advice was given confidentially, the inadequacy was never exposed.
- *Contested.* The policy goals, evidence, alternatives and risk were never publicly contested for the HIP despite the fact the program expenditure was over A$2.5bn. If it had been, the conflicting goals of employment for low-skilled construction workers and safe and effective installation of insulation would have been identified (Hanger, 2014: 5), the regulatory frameworks of the states and territories tested, and the feasibility of timely roll out questioned. There was pressure to roll out the program quickly despite a forecast risk to worker safety and the insulation manufacturing industry (Commonwealth of Australia, 2010), because economic stimulus goals of the HIP overrode other goals (ABC, 2010).
- *Timely.* The use of a stimulus package to support the Australian economy during the economic downturn was generally supported domestically (ABC, 2009) and was consistent with Keynesian standard fiscal stimulus. In terms of effective implementation, the HIP depended on effective state and territory regulation. Key regulations, such as the supervision requirements under the HIP were not defined and, thus, where lax state legislation prevailed, the supervision of unskilled and untrained workers was not of the standard assumed by the architects of the HIP (Queensland State Coroner, 2013). The program was announced in February 2009, with the pilot program effective immediately and the full program to be implemented by 1 July 2009, which was a rapid timeframe for policy formulation and implementation (Hanger, 2014).
- *Adaptive.* The HIP was implemented rapidly and on such a scale that there was little time to adapt the program before the first evidence of safety issues appeared. The early risks identified in the first phase by the consultants, Minter Ellison, did not change the implementation timetable, which was unrealistic (Hanger, 2014). The Minister responsible wrote to the Prime Minister four times recommending changes to the program, changes which were implemented several months later (Ministerial Correspondence, 2010). As concerns arose with the HIP the interpretation and response by the federal government was defensive, but eventually culminated in a suspension of the program in February 2010 and its subsequent termination.
- *Transparent.* The HIP was clear in its goals and means of implementation. However, critical appraisal was missing as government, politics and media were concerned with the financial crisis and the macroeconomic impacts.

- *Envisioned.* The vision for the HIP was principally associated with employment benefits, rather than being an efficient and safe program of home insulation. As such the state and territory regulators were unaware of their looming responsibility, or the response of the building industry within their jurisdiction. The actions by those who needed to regulate the home insulation industry was "too little too late".

Outcomes

There were some qualified successes of the HIP in the popularity of uptake and in the innovation of the federal disbursement system. Over the year of operation (February 2009 to February 2010), out of an existing Australian housing stock of more than 8.5 million households, there were 1.1 million insulation instalments (ABS, 2012; Hanger, 2014). In terms of innovation, the existing federal payment systems for Medicare were used for the first time to process and manage payments to government suppliers (installers of insulation).

As multiple subsequent enquiries have found, the HIP was hastily developed, poorly designed and implemented and resulted in poor quality practices and insulation outcomes. As an example of the haste, the state and territory governments were consulted *after* the HIP was announced (Hawke, 2010: 15), even though they had a critical role in the safe and effective implementation (see Table 4.2). A Queensland Coroner's court heard that a A$2.5bn program, such as the HIP, would be expected to take two years to develop and implement, whereas the program was announced on 3 February 2009 for implementation five months later, on 1 July 2009 (Queensland State Coroner, 2013).

The poor administration of the HIP has been directly linked to the deaths of four tradesman and hundreds of house fires as a consequence of a surge of untrained and inexperienced installers joining the insulation industry to take advantage of the business opportunity. A significant safety and remediation program was implemented after the closure of the HIP, estimated to have cost approximately A$425m (ANAO, 2010). A Royal Commission, two independent reviews and two coroner's investigations have been undertaken in relation to the HIP and the associated deaths. The HIP, by encouraging a huge influx of installers into the insulation industry and by bringing forward several years of installation, effectively destroyed the market for incumbents and resulted in multiple bankruptcies of established home insulation companies.

The overall assessment of the Home Insulation Program is a "D" (see Table 4.1), indicating that the policy process had widespread failures in design and implementation, inadequate consideration of risks and had inadvertently led to large, unintended costs and the loss of life of improperly supervised insulation installers. This is notwithstanding the fact that the HIP did involve rapid spending of federal money, as was intended, and a substantial increase of homes with home insulation, as planned.

TABLE 4.2 Stakeholders engaged before and after announcement of the Home Insulation Program (HIP)

Parties engaged prior to announcement of HIP	Parties engaged subsequent to announcement
Commonwealth government: • Prime Minister and Cabinet (in particular the Office of Coordinator-General) • Department of Environment, Water, Heritage and Arts (Renewables and Energy Efficiency Division, REED) • Department of Treasury • Department of Finance and Deregulation **Other parties** • Insulation Council of Australia and New Zealand (ICANZ) • Council of Australian Governments (COAG) (on the National Strategy on Energy Efficiency, a separate policy)	**Industry associations (examples):** • Construction and Property Services Industry Skills Council (CPSISC) • Insulation Manufacturers' Association of Australia • Master Builders Australia • Housing Industry Association • Australian Building Codes Board • National Electrical and Communications Association • Master Electricians Australia • ElectroComms and Energy Utilities Industry Skills Council • Standards Australia **Commonwealth government (examples):** • Department of Education, Employment and Workplace Relations (in particular Federal Safety Commissioner) • Department of Human Services (Medicare and Centrelink) • Australian Taxation Office **State government (examples):** • Queensland Electrical Safety Office • Workplace Health and Safety Queensland • Queensland Building Commission • Queensland Building Services Authority • South Australia Building Authority • Victorian Coordinator-General

The Mineral Resources Rent Tax

Purpose and process

In early May 2008, Prime Minister Kevin Rudd and Treasurer Wayne Swan appointed a committee, chaired by the then Secretary of the Treasury, Ken Henry, to review the Australian tax system for the twenty-first century. The Henry Review took more than a year to complete, held fora with many leading domestic and international economists, and provided multiple public technical and discussion papers. The final report provided a wide range of recommendations, including dealing with inefficient state taxes, a reduction in the company income tax rate, and the introduction of a mineral resources rent tax on non-renewable resources

(Henry et al., 2009). The federal government received the Henry Review in December 2009 (The Treasury, 2010b).

On 2 May 2010 the Henry Review was officially released to the public, but was overshadowed by the federal Budget the following week. The 2010–11 Budget contained a provision for the Resources Super Profits Tax (RSPT), a type of a mineral resources rent tax, to be implemented from 1 July 2012. The May 2010 Budget estimated the RSPT to return A$3bn in 2012–13 and A$9bn in 2013–14 (The Treasury, 2010a). The timeline of the policy development is presented in Figure 4.4.

Immediately after the announcement of the Budget, Australian and international mining companies launched a public advertising campaign against the RSPT. The campaign included full page advertisements in all daily metropolitan newspapers and television advertisements in the evenings. The cost of the political advertising by the mining companies was A$22m, as reported to the Australian Electoral Commission (Davis, 2011).

In part due to the negative response of the mining and resource sector, Prime Minister Rudd lost a leadership contest in June 2010 that saw Julia Gillard elected by the Labor Party Caucus as the new Prime Minister. On 2 July 2010, Prime Minister Gillard and a selected group of mining companies' representatives reached an agreement on an alternative to the RSPT, to be called the Mineral Resources Rent Tax (MRRT). The mining companies' political advertising ceased. On 17 July PM Gillard called an early election for 21 August which returned her to office, but in charge of a minority government and the tax was eventually repealed in 2013.

Assessment of the six guidelines

- *Evidence-informed.* There was sound economic theory and experience supporting a resource rent tax, but the detailed evidence used to develop the MRRT was inadequate in the context of the policy discussion and the subsequent negotiations of the MRRT that occurred in July 2012. Australia had an existing resources rent in the offshore petroleum sector, dating to 1988, and the proposal for a minerals resource rent tax was founded on the thorough and impartial assessment of the tax policy in the Henry Review. When the negotiations between Prime Minister Gillard and the mining companies finally took place, the mining companies provided much of the data that Treasury used to model the tax.
- *Contestable.* With the release of the MRRT in the 2010 Budget, without prior contest of the problem, the context of debate about the merits of policy became polarised as for-or-against the government itself. This did not result in any meaningful consideration of the goals, merits, alternatives and risks associated with the MRRT.
- *Timely.* Tax reform in Australia is a constant refrain, but the timeliness of policy development for the MRRT affected the quality of the policy outcome. The 2010 budget with the RSPT announcement and subsequent leadership

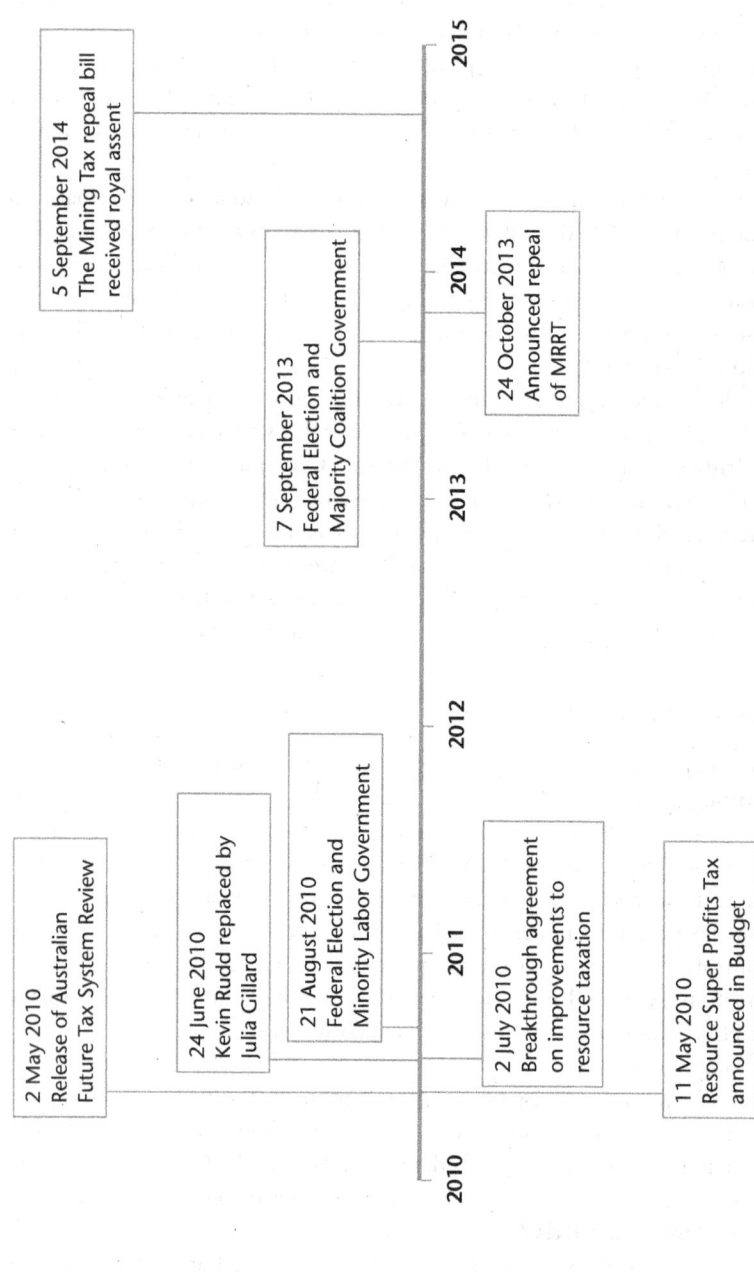

FIGURE 4.4 Timeline of Mineral Resources Rent Tax

change meant that the negotiation of the eventual MRRT (like the HIP) owed more to solving a political problem than developing sound policy. As evidence of the political value with which the Gillard government accorded the MRRT negotiations, an election was called within two weeks of the completion of the deal. The timely evidence in favour of the sound policy was missing, as demonstrated by the consistently overoptimistic forward revenue projections of A$12 billion compared to the revenues actually received by the federal government (see Figure 4.5).

- *Adaptive.* The policy process for the MRRT became adaptive to solving a political problem, rather than making sound policy. The policy process was perhaps too adaptive to the political process – alternative goals, approaches, policy designs could not be assessed in the rush to solve a political problem. As the MRRT was implemented, with receipts far less than expected, the political history prevented renegotiation of the policy. The subsequent government that was elected in September 2013 repealed the MRRT.
- *Transparent.* In the negotiations for the MRRT there was very little transparency around the tax design. There was no public scrutiny of the tax arrangement until after the agreement was signed. As a result, a poorly designed tax was agreed to and implemented before it could be critically appraised and contested.

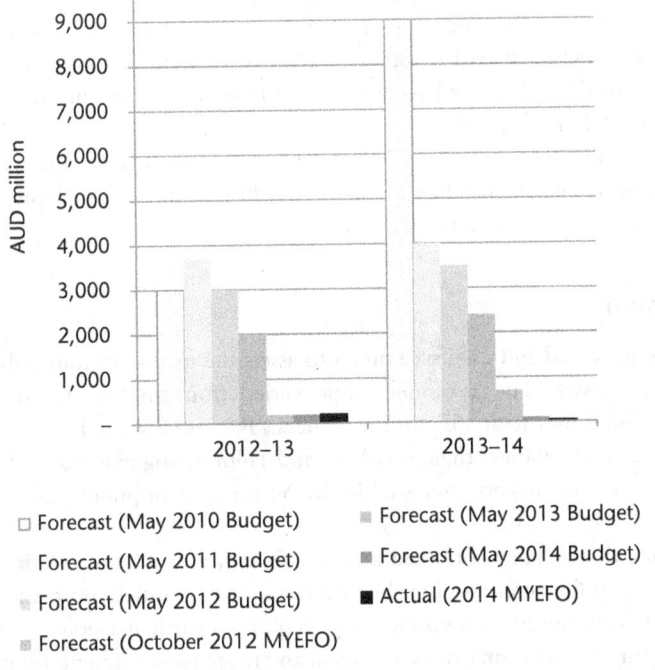

FIGURE 4.5 Estimated and actual revenues of Mineral Resources Rent Tax

- *Envisioned.* The vision for the MRRT was never effectively communicated. The mining companies appeared to win the public relations battle, and contributed to the toppling of a sitting Prime Minister (Davis, 2011).

Outcomes

The Mineral Resources Rent Tax delivered barely a fraction of the revenues proposed. Figure 4.5 provides the revenue estimates and actual receipts over time. This gap between the projected and actual revenues supports the view that it was designed, intentionally or not, in such a way as to capture very little resource rent.

The MRRT, unlike the RSPT, was directed at two commodities only: iron ore and coal. Mining companies established a tax liability for coal or iron ore projects and the tax calculated was a proportion of profits above a certain margin and size. The negotiated agreement with the mining companies did not fix the base value, and, as was later reflected upon by Dr Parkinson, Treasury Secretary, it had "no legal obligation on them [the mining industry] to have settled on the starting base. They had the opportunity to go back and think about what their starting base should be" (APH Hansard, 2013).

A key flaw of the MRRT in terms of the revenue it generated for the federal government was the arrangement that mining companies could deduct from their tax liability the amount of tax paid to state governments. State governments took advantage of this allowance: in the September 2012 budget, the Queensland government increased coal royalties in a move expected to raise A$1.6bn from miners that might otherwise have gone to the federal government's revenues raised by the MRRT (Hurst, 2012).

The overall assessment of the MRRT is an "E" (see Figure 4.1), as the policy process can be characterised by a complete failure in design, implementation and achievement of its intended outcomes.

Discussion

We have provided and used six criteria to assess the quality of four public policy-making processes. The assessment scale varied from an "A" for the National Competition Policy to an "E" for the Minerals Resource Rent Tax. A comparison of the four case studies, their successes and failures, suggests the following key insights for policy makers interested in delivering resilient public policy:

- Policy that is both contested and envisioned, as with the NCP, and which survives public contest of problem and response, is much more likely to result in the recognition of a problem that requires a particular policy response and ongoing cooperation from subsequent and related governments for its delivery. Thorough diagnosis is a prerequisite for sound policy.

- Very short timelines ("haste is waste"), as shown by the HIP and the MRRT, greatly increase the risks of failure in implementation to achieve the defined objectives.
- Policy that is not fully evidence-informed ("proof bears fruit"), as was the case of the development of the Basin Plan, may fail to deliver on key legislated outcomes and risks generating conflict and opposition to the policy.
- Transparency about process and timelines are integral to the success of resilient public policy, as shown by the NCP.
- Public policy processes can never be fully predictable, must "adapt" and quickly adjust to evidence and public responses. Using pilot programs, detailed simulations, and extensive public consultation greatly reduce the potential for adverse "surprises". An inability or unwillingness to adjust or respond in a timely fashion, such as with the HIP, increases the risks of failure.
- Public policy worth doing is worth explaining. Neither the *Guide* to the Basin Plan nor the MRRT were properly explained and, as a consequence, the backlash to the policy change was exacerbated.

Contestability of policy and two-way communications are not the same as "tick the box" consultation. Contestability that supports durable policy, as seen with the NCP, involves a contest of ideas about the policy, its goals and how it is implemented. By comparison, in the Basin Plan consultation processes the policy was "explained" to stakeholders.

Conclusions

Much public policy is not resilient in the sense that it is not durable, even if beneficial, or it is durable when it is not beneficial. This should not be a surprise because it requires successful delivery in multiple dimensions and should be: evidence-informed, contestable, timely (but not rushed), adaptive and transparent, and envisioned with a clear narrative about who wins (and loses), what it is intended to achieve and why. This will, typically, require effective co-ordination among those who decide on policy, elected officials, and those who advise and implement policy. If the policy actors are not "on message", or there are too many priorities, resilient public policy is unlikely to result.

Our assessment framework provides valuable starting and end points for both policy deciders and policy doers. The framework does not guarantee success: there are multiple factors that will encroach on good policy making such as unreasonable deadlines, lack of staff to do the work, inconsistencies with existing policies and even mistrust among policy actors. What the framework does do is to identify likely policy pitfalls that can result in policy failures, provide a benchmark to judge policy performance, and give a guide as to what should be done in the "best of all possible policy worlds".

References

ABC (2009) "Initial praise for Govt stimulus package". Australian Broadcasting Commission, 3 February [Online]. Available at: www.abc.net.au/news/2009-02-03/initial-praise-for-govt-stimulus-package/282008 (accessed 30 April 2016).

ABC (2010) "Jobs more important than safety: insider". Australian Broadcasting Commission, Four Corners, 26 April [Online]. Available at: www.abc.net.au/news/2010-04-26/jobs-more-important-than-safety-insider/410458 (accessed 30 April 2016).

ABC (2015) "First of two Murray Mouth dredging operations begins in South Australia". Australian Broadcasting Commission, 9 January [Online]. Available at: www.abc.net.au/news/2015-01-09/murray-mouth-dredging-operation-begins/6008530 (accessed 30 April 2016).

ABS (2012) "Australian Social Trends 4102.0". Canberra: Australian Bureau of Statistics.

Althaus, C., Bridgman, P. and Davis, G. (2013) *The Australian policy handbook*. Sydney: Allen and Unwin.

ANAO (2010) "Audit Report No. 12 2010–11: Home Insulation Program". Australian National Audit Office, Canberra.

APH Hansard (2013) "House Economics Committee – 14 February (2013)". Australian Parliament House, Canberra.

Bardach, E. (2011) *Practical guide for policy analysis: the eightfold path to more effective problem solving*. Los Angeles: Sage.

Boully, L. and Maywald, K. (2011) "Basin bookends, the community perspective". In: Connell, D. and Grafton, R. Q. (eds.) *Basin Futures: Water Reform in the Murray–Darling Basin*. Canberra: ANU Press.

COAG (1994) "Council of Australian Governments" Communiqué, 19 August 1994'. Council of Australian Governments, Darwin.

COAG (1995) "Council of Australian Governments" Communique, 11 April 1995'. Council of Australian Governments, Canberra.

Colebatch, H. K. (2005) Policy analysis, policy practice and political science. *Australian Journal of Public Administration* 64: 14–23.

Commonwealth of Australia (2010) "Energy Efficient Homes Package (ceiling insulation)". Report of the Senate Environment, Communications and the Arts References Committee, Canberra.

Commonwealth of Australia (2011) "Of drought and flooding rains: Inquiry into the impact of the Guide to the Murray–Darling Basin Plan". House of Representatives Standing Committee on Regional Australia, Canberra.

Commonwealth of Australia (2013) "Intergovernmental Agreement on Implementing Water Reform in the Murray–Darling Basin". The Commonwealth of Australia and the Governments of New South Wales, Victoria, Queensland, South Australia, the Australian Capital Territory and the Northern Territory, Canberra.

Connell, D. and Grafton, R.Q. (2008) "Planning for Water Security in the Murray–Darling Basin". *Public Policy* 3(1): 67–86.

Davis, M. (2011) "A snip at $22m to get rid of PM". *Sydney Morning Herald*, 2 February.

Dovers, S. and Hussey, K. (2013) *Environment and sustainability: A policy handbook*. Sydney: Federation Press.

Grafton, R. Q. (2010) "How to increase the cost-effectiveness of water reform and environmental flows in the Murray–Darling Basin". *Agenda* 17: 17–40.

Grafton, R. Q. and Horne, J. (2014) "Water markets in the Murray–Darling Basin". *Agricultural Water Management* 145: 61–71.

Grafton, R. Q., Pittock, J., Williams, J., Jiang, Q., Possingham, H. and Quiggin, J. (2014) "Water Planning and Hydro-Climatic Change in the Murray–Darling Basin, Australia". *AMBIO* 43: 1082–92.

Hanger, I. (2014) "Report of the Royal Commission into the Home Insulation Program". Australian Government, Canberra.

Hawke, A. (2010) "Review of the Administration of the Home Insulation Program". Australian Government, Canberra.

Henry, K., Harmer, J., Piggott, J., Ridout, H. and Smith, G. (2009) "Report on Australia's Future Tax System". Commonwealth Treasury, Canberra.

Hilmer, F., Taperell, G. and Rayner, M. (1993) "Committee of Inquiry into a National Competition Policy for Australia". AGPS, Canberra.

Hollander, R. and Curran, G. (2001) "The Greening of the Grey: National Competition Policy and the Environment". *Australian Journal of Public Administration* 60: 42–55.

Hurst, D. (2012) "Coal-fired bid to get budget back in black". *Brisbane Times*, 11 September.

IC (1995a) "The Growth and Revenue Implications of Hilmer and Related Reforms: A report by the Industry Commission to the Council of Australian Governments". Industry Commission, Canberra.

IC (1995b) "Implementing the National Competition Policy: Access and Price Regulation". Industry Commission, Canberra.

IMF (2009) "Global Economic Policies and Prospects: Staff note for G20 meeting". International Monetary Fund, London.

Lee, T. (2010) "Murray authority chairman faces uphill battle". ABC Landline, 18 October 2010.

MDBA (2010a) "Guide to the proposed Basin Plan". Murray–Darling Basin Authority, Canberra.

MDBA (2010b) "Guide to the proposed Basin Plan". Murray–Darling Basin Authority, Canberra.

MDBA (2012) "Basin Plan". Murray–Darling Basin Authority, Canberra.

Ministerial Correspondence (2010) "Minister Garrett's Letters of Correspondence on Home Insulation Program". Australian Parliament, Canberra.

NWC (2008) "Update of progress in water reform". National Water Commission, Canberra.

NWC (2009) "Second biennial assessment of progress in implementation of the National Water Initiative". National Water Commission, Canberra.

NWC (2011) "Biennial assessment". National Water Commission, Canberra.

OECD (2009a) "Economic Outlook June (2009)". Organisation for Economic Cooperation and Development, Paris.

OECD (2009b) "Employment Outlook (2009)". Organisation for Economic Cooperation and Development, Paris.

O'Rourke, S. (2007) "Coroner slams Govt over electrocutions". *NZ Herald*, 12 September.

PC (1999) "Impact of Competition Policy Reforms on Rural and Regional Australia". Productivity Commission, Canberra.

PC (2005) "Review of National Competition Policy Reforms". Productivity Commission, Canberra.

PC (2010) "Market Mechanisms for Recovering Water in the Murray–Darling Basin". Productivity Commission, Canberra.

Queensland State Coroner (2013) "Inquest into the deaths of Matthew James FULLER, Rueben Kelly BARNES and Mitchell Scott SWEENEY". Office of the State Coroner, Queensland Courts, Brisbane.

The Treasury (2010a) "Budget Overview 2010–11". Commonwealth of Australia, Canberra.
The Treasury (2010b) "Timeline of Australia's future tax system review" [Online]. Commonwealth of Australia. Available at: http://taxreview.treasury.gov.au/content/Content.aspx?doc=html/timeline.htm (accessed 29 April 2016).
Wentworth Group of Concerned Scientists (2010) "Sustainable Diversions in the Murray–Darling Basin: An Analysis of the Options for Achieving a Sustainable Diversion Limit in the Murray–Darling Basin". Wentworth Group of Concerned Scientists, Sydney.
Young, M. (2014) "Trading Into Trouble? Lessons from Australia's Mistakes in Water Policy Reform Sequencing". Chapter 11 in Easter, W. and Huang, Q. (eds) *Water Markets for the 21st Century: What we have learned?* Dordrecht: Springer.

5
LESSONS FROM REFORMING FOSSIL-FUEL SUBSIDY REGIMES

Georgeta Vidican

Relevance of reforming fossil-fuel subsidies

Climate change concerns and the need to transition to more sustainable energy systems have triggered renewed attention to the ever increasing fossil-fuel subsidies.

Worldwide subsidies to conventional fuels (measured on a pre-tax basis) reached US$548 billion in 2013 (IEA, 2014) and could exceed US$600 billion by 2020 without policy reforms (IEA, 2011).[1] Many of these subsidies are located in emerging and developing countries.[2] For some products, such as coal, post-tax subsidies are substantial because prices do not reflect negative externalities (on environment and health). Energy products are taxed much less than other products.

In developed countries the main reason why governments continue to subsidize fossil fuels is to protect energy industries and employment (UNEP, 2003). This is particularly the case for coalmining subsidies in Germany, Japan and Spain, and for peat in Finland and Ireland (UNEP, 2003). Such protectionist measures are, however, declining in importance in developed countries. For this reason, this chapter focuses mostly on fossil-fuel subsidy reform in emerging and developing countries.

While the justification for sustaining subsidies is made on economic and social equity grounds, there is meagre evidence to support their continued use. By making conventional energy cheaper, subsidies lock in fossil-fuel-based energy generation and distort the market for clean energy. Subsidies also place a high burden on government budgets, especially in developing countries, reducing fiscal space for other spending items (e.g. education, health, infrastructure). Further, there is abundant evidence that subsidies benefit disproportionally the middle- and upper-income groups, while the low-income groups receive only a small fraction of the subsidies.

On average, the richest 20 per cent of households in low- and middle-income countries capture six times more in total fuel subsidies (43 per cent of total subsidies) than the poorest 20 per cent of households (7 per cent of total subsidies) (Arze del Granado *et al.*, 2012). By reducing the price of conventional energy (including electricity), subsidies also encourage overconsumption of such products, contributing to higher air pollution and environmental degradation.[3]

A reduction of fossil-fuel subsidies, therefore, could have profound effects not only on economic and social parameters, but also on pollution and health outcomes (Aldy, 2013). For instance, the IEA (2010) estimates that eliminating all fossil-fuel subsidies could reduce CO_2 emissions by about two gigatons per year by 2020. By removing subsidies global oil consumption could be reduced by 4.7 million barrels per day by 2020, representing a decline of about 5 per cent of current consumption (Aldy, 2013). Furthermore, subsidy elimination could reduce CO_2 emissions by 23 per cent and could raise government revenues through savings and taxation equivalent to 2.6 per cent of GDP (GSI, 2014). These savings from subsidy reform could then be targeted towards low-carbon development and supporting investment in health, education and infrastructure. For example, renewable energy targets until 2020 in the Middle East and North Africa could cost up to US$200 billion, but this amount is less than one year's worth of fossil-fuel subsidies in the region, a total of US$237 billion (GSI, 2014).

To address the challenge of reforming fossil-fuel subsidies, in 2009 G20 leaders agreed to "phase out and rationalise over the medium term, inefficient fossil-fuel subsidies, while providing targeted support for the poorest" (G20, 2009). Although dozens of countries have started reform in the past few years, the track record of reform remains unimpressive, so far, in spite of mounting evidence on the negative effects of fossil-fuel subsidies at different levels. In fact, because of rising oil prices, global consumption subsidies more than doubled from 2009 to 2012 (Lang, 2011). A recent study (IMF, 2013a) synthesizes evidence from selected countries in different regions, showing mixed experiences from several reform episodes. While successful reform outcomes[4] were found in a few cases, in most countries governments were not able to sustain reform for a long period of time, reversing initial actions by increasing subsidies under pressure from different interest groups.

Experiences from different country contexts (mostly developing and emerging economies) point to several challenges with reforming fossil-fuel subsidies, generally related to politics and policy implementation. Firstly, energy pricing is highly politicized and subsidies are rooted in a "political logic that is often difficult to alter" (Victor, 2009), oftentimes being used as a legitimizing mechanism for incumbent regimes. Therefore, finding ways to deal with the complex political economy of reform should be one of the main priorities for decision makers. Secondly, reforming subsidies requires rapid, systematic, and carefully planned actions in order to avoid negative effects on vulnerable population groups and reduce opposition from interest groups.

Key guidelines learned from reforming fossil-fuel subsidies

The reform of fossil-fuel subsidies is not a new item on the agenda of policy makers. Even when subsidies take up a large share of a government budget, attempts at reform tend to have mixed results as energy pricing is a highly politicized process. Typically, the main challenge resides in understanding the political economy of initiating and sustaining a subsidy reform over a long period of time. *Previous experiences illustrate that identifying the right time to reduce a subsidy and thereby increase energy prices, has long-lasting effects on the probability of success.*

Mapping the interests and power of various stakeholders that benefit from subsidies and are affected by their removal is critical in building the transformative coalitions needed to gather the political and social support needed to implement the reform. Throughout this process, extensive communication campaigns that focus on the costs and benefits from reform can prove critical in increasing transparency with regard to the reform process and hence build trust in the state, as initiator of reform. Furthermore, integrating systematic learning and experimentation in the policy cycle can be decisive on the outcome of reform.

Critical junctures

Guideline 5.1
Search for windows of opportunity – critical junctures – to initiate a reform. In the meantime, build knowledge about the nature of and the case for the policy reform and seek opportunities to communicate the need for change.

Critical junctures is a concept that derives from the historical institutionalism literature used to assess institutional change. Windows of opportunity for institutional change – critical junctures – are defined as brief phases of institutional flux in relatively long periods of path-dependent institutional stability. During critical junctures, there is a substantially heightened probability that agents' choices will affect the outcome of interest (Capoccia and Kelemen, 2007).

Critical junctures include major events, such as societal cleavages (Hogan, 2006) or situations of political, financial, or economic crisis, in which "structural (i.e. economic, cultural, ideological, organisational) influences on political action are significantly relaxed for a relatively short period of time." During political junctures, "the range of plausible choices open to a powerful political actor expands substantially". In addition, "the consequences of their decisions for the outcome of interest are potentially much more momentous" (Capoccia and Kelemen, 2007). Such crises "can bring abrupt institutional change, as they present leaders with an opportunity to enact new plans and realize new ideas by embedding them in the institutions they establish" (Hogan, 2006). Hence, junctures are critical because they place institutional arrangements on trajectories that are difficult to alter (Pierson, 2004). Unanticipated events (critical junctures) are not the only source of change, but they can prove to be critical in discrediting and bringing into question existing institutional arrangements and policies (Cortell and Peterson, 1999; Haggard, 1998).

The relevance of critical junctures for the reform of fossil-fuel subsidies relates to the following aspects. Firstly, a reform of fossil-fuel subsidies implies a drastic change of policy that has defined a long-standing social contract between the state and society. Secondly, such a change (i.e. an increase in energy prices) can have dramatic implications on the society at large in terms of loss of welfare, lower competitiveness in the private sector, inflationary effects, etc. For these reasons, the political risk associated with the commencement of a transformational reform tends to be very high. Therefore, those interested in pursuing a transformational reform need to search for ways of increasing the "tensions" that help lead to critical junctures and open up windows of opportunity for reform.

In the case of fossil-fuel subsidy reform, critical junctures can be the result of internal factors (e.g. budgetary pressures, changes in political regimes) or external factors (e.g. increase in oil prices, economic crisis, loan conditionality imposed by donors). The trigger for reform does not necessarily have to be negative (i.e. a situation of crisis). Rather, situations of economic progress could also open up venues for reform, as the population at large could better internalize the negative effects from increasing energy prices. The sudden unexpected drop in fossil-fuel subsidies in late 2014, for example, led several authors and quite a few journalists in the media to argue for the removal of fuel subsidies and/or the introduction of carbon taxes.

Large external and fiscal deficits and rising public debt often create critical opportunities for reform. This was the case in Poland and the Czech Republic, for example. Another example is Egypt, where the budget deficit became increasingly unsustainable in recent years. According to the IEA (2014), Egyptian energy subsidies reached 10.2 per cent of GDP in 2012, one of the highest levels worldwide. This is despite the fact that, since 1977, Egyptian governments have made repeated attempts to reduce them. When it became clear that Egypt was about to face a major fiscal crisis and there was a change in the political regime, the government announced major measures that would result in an increase in energy prices for both businesses and residents (Bridle *et al.*, 2014). While it is still too early to assess how successful this reform has been, existing evidence points to promising results and an unprecedented scale of change. That is, *the emergence of a critical juncture in the form of a major fiscal crisis created a reform opportunity that had not previously been there.*

Jordan is another case where internal and external crises have created a window of opportunity for taking action on reducing fossil-fuel subsidies. Most of Jordan's energy requirements are met by importing natural gas and oil (Electricity Regulatory Commission, 2012). The government began to spread the message that existing subsidies would place significant pressure on Jordan's fiscal sustainability – especially as population increased and economic growth occurred. The opportunity to reduce subsidies, however, suddenly emerged in 2010 when a major disruption to the Arab Gas Pipeline forced a reduction in imports of natural gas and increase in oil imports (Bridle *et al.*, 2014). Increasing fiscal pressure resulted and, in response, the Jordanian government increased electricity tariffs and removed the remaining subsidies on oil prices while stressing the importance of energy security to national development (Bridle *et al.*, 2014).

Critical junctures can also be created by structural reforms or periods of economic prosperity. For example, Turkey started to liberalize its energy pricing system at the time it introduced economy-wide reforms in expectation of entering the European Union in the early 1990s (IMF, 2013a). Improved economic conditions led to little opposition to reforms and limited negative effects on vulnerable consumer groups.

These examples suggest that the timing is an important element to consider when planning to reduce fossil-fuel subsidies. Identifying such circumstances and taking advantage of them is an important step. Reform is possible, however, if and only if the prior empirical and policy research has been completed and well communicated.

Mapping stakeholder interests and power

Guideline 5.2
Map stakeholder interests and power in order to design a reform that is closely aligned with the needs of different stakeholder groups.

Changes to a fossil-fuel subsidy regime, like most other transformational reform agendas, tend to be highly political. As a general rule, interest groups that demand subsidies tend to be well organized and should be expected to concentrate around arrangements that make reform difficult (Victor, 2009). Often this is done intentionally in an attempt to persuade governments to let vested interests prevail and ensure that they are "unwilling, unable and afraid of implementing reforms" (Blatter and Buzzell, 2013).[5]

Knowledge about the constellation of interests and power among different stakeholders, therefore, and the rationale behind their interests and factors, is critical in working out how to present arguments and can prove to be more important than political will and leadership. In particular, it is critical to map out the structures and nature of the considerations that shape the interests of each stakeholder group (Moore, 2011).

Guideline 5.3
Proposals for compensation can be used to build early support for a reform.

Aside from a clear understanding of interests and power relations, development of state capacity and familiarity with each stakeholder group is critical so that those involved in the reform process can begin the process of reorienting stakeholder interests and building trust. One of the most common ways of doing this is to find the means to assure potential losers that compensatory measures will be implemented.

As a general rule, the population at large is an important source of opposition to fuel subsidy reform. In the case of low-income groups, subsidies can be seen as an essential form of welfare support – even though the majority of the benefits from a subsidy may go to middle and upper-income groups. As the experience of various countries shows (e.g. Indonesia, Egypt, Tunisia), removing this financial support can result in mass protests and even the destabilizing of an existing regime or government. Hence, while economically low-income households tend to have limited power, as a collective entity they can exert strong influence on policy actions which can then be supported quietly by middle- and upper-income households.

The business sector can also be an important source of opposition, as increases in energy prices are likely to be seen as a threat to the competitiveness of firms. However, as Blatter and Buzzell (2013) argue, the business sector typically finds it difficult to develop a coherent position as many low-energy industries understand that the removal of fuel subsidies can be used to free up the capital they need for investment. Wise policy reformers can take full advantage of this argument. In Tunisia, for example, the fragmentation of opinions and weakening of business associations led to a political realization that the business sector was not strongly opposed to subsidy reform (Blatter and Buzzell, 2013).

Guideline 5.4
Build transformative alliances among key stakeholder groups to support reform implementation.

Trade unions, which by their nature seek to protect the interests of workers, are generally opposed to the removal of fossil-fuel subsidies due to the negative effects these reforms tend to have on consumers. However, it remains unclear as to whether trade unions are generally powerful enough to impede development of the case for reform. Drawing again on the experience of Tunisia, unions appear to be more willing to support reform if they are included in the debate, and if the government adopts a transparent approach that invites the union movement to focus on implications for low energy users (Blatter and Buzzell, 2013).

Among other actors, obviously, governments are the most relevant stakeholders in the majority of transformational policy reform processes. To enact reform, a government must have the political will needed to tackle complex subsidy reforms. Strong political capital is also necessary to develop the case and minimize political opposition as a reform is implemented. Lack of political will from within the government can be due to ideological reasons, corruption, fear of losing legitimacy, or weak administrative capacity to enact a complex reform. Governments are not monolithic actors. Rather, tensions and conflicting interests prevail within the government structure. For example, a Ministry of Finance might try to push forward reform for reasons of fiscal sustainability, while a Ministry of Interior might try to block it for political stability concerns. In Morocco, this situation resulted in the ultimate abandonment of an attempt to reduce fossil-fuel subsidies (Vidican, 2014).

The constellation of interests and power is highly context specific. Therefore, while the above description of interests can apply more generally, strong variations can be observed from place to place. Each country is faced with specific political, economic and social framework conditions, which will result in more or less unique conditions. Therefore, when planning a reform, thorough political analysis is necessary. Careful mapping of all the factors that support or obstruct reform is worthy of early consideration by researchers as well as those who aspire to implement a proposed reform.

To this end, Mitchell *et al.* (1997) provide a useful classification scheme that can be used to assess likely stakeholder responses to an energy subsidy reform process. According to this scheme there are three key attributes that a stakeholder (in relation to a focal organization) can possess: power, legitimacy, and urgency.

The identification of the focal organization is also relevant. Mitchell and others classify stakeholders into seven categories: definitive stakeholders, dangerous stakeholders, dependable stakeholders, dormant, discretionary, and demanding stakeholders (see Figure 5.1).

While this classification is useful, it does not clarify the specific view that each stakeholder has. Hence, further focus group and consultative analysis is needed to understand the specific position that each actor has (support, opposition, ambivalence), the rationale for their position, and the factors that might contribute to a change in their initial position. Such an in-depth assessment can help in

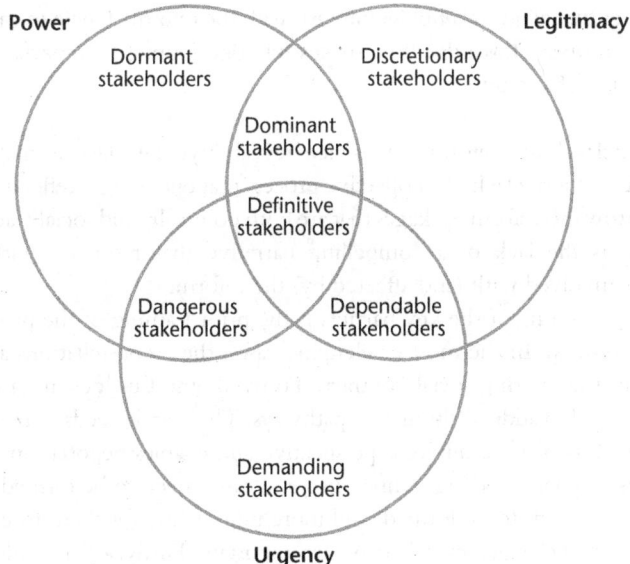

FIGURE 5.1 Stakeholder identification and salience based on three attributes (Mitchell *et al.*, 1997)

identifying how incentives can be reoriented towards supporting certain reform outcomes. In Brazil, for example, a stepped approach to reform was adopted, tailored to the specific interests and power of various stakeholders. Careful attention was then paid to sequence reforms in a politically acceptable manner. Specifically, the first products to lose subsidies were those associated with politically weak stakeholders (asphalt, lubricants and gasoline for aeroplanes), while politically more difficult subsidies for the fuels used in transport and by local industry were removed last (IMF, 2013a).

Guideline 5.5
Sequence reforms to increase prospects for success. Early emphasis on fostering dialogue among different stakeholders is critical to the avoidance of setbacks.

While such assessments of interests and power might take place on a haphazard basis during the preparation of reform, there is limited literature on the need for a systematic approach to map interests and power of different stakeholders. Yet, given the complex politics surrounding the reform of subsidies, such an assessment can help decision makers identify potential alliances for reform and seek alternative strategic interventions to satisfy interest groups.

Building transformative alliances

Guideline 5.6
Investment in the creation of new stakeholder coalitions and the development of new narratives that align stakeholder interests with the reform objectives can be used to speed progress towards the successful development, repackaging and implementation of a reform.

Past fossil-fuel subsidy reform experience reveals two key factors that obstruct reform. The first is the lack of a collective process that encourages reflection on and negotiation towards reform packages that are both politically and socially acceptable. The second is the lack of a compelling narrative that resonates with various stakeholders involved with (and affected by) the reform.

In many cases, one of the key barriers is the prior framing of the problem and governance process. In the most challenging cases, these constellations are deeply embedded in the existing social contract. To overcome this lock-in, a collective process is needed to address alternative pathways. The search needs to be for a new narrative that articulates a different perspective and enables negotiation involving different stakeholder groupings which, in some cases, need to be formed.

For new coalitions to be formed, and more importantly for them to enable and sustain a process of change, several factors are important. Firstly, a clear understanding of interests and power relations (as discussed above) is necessary so that ways around a political bottleneck can be found. Secondly, state capacity needs to be developed so that the processes which draw attention to these new interest groups (coalitions) can be established. Thirdly, these processes should be used to reorient interests towards the reform goal, develop understanding of the case for a reform and build trust.

Extensive information and communication campaigns are necessary not only to justify the need for reform but also to ensure transparency of the reform process. Building transformative alliances depends strongly on all these three factors. Figure 5.2 illustrates strategic interventions necessary to build internal and external support for reform, where these three main factors play an important role.

Peiffer (2012) offers a comprehensive review of the literature on reform coalitions, defined as:

> a (formal and informal) political mechanism and process utilized and formed by state and business actors, initiated by either, which enables them to work cooperatively to address specific state and market collective action problems through institutional and policy reform in pursuit of a specific reform agenda.

Such alliances need to include a broad set of actors (state, business, academia and civil society) with different interests and motivations. This diversity is important as "the chance of effective cooperation increases dramatically if players with different motivations are brought into the picture" (Johnson et al., 2014). Yet, alliances among stakeholders with heterogeneous interests are more difficult to build. To address this challenge, the analysis of stakeholder interests and power needs to focus on ways to build bridges among new interest groups and form new alliances.

Guideline 5.7
Conduct extensive information campaigns to explain the rationale for and progression of reform and proposed measures to mitigate negative effects.

In the process of building transformative alliances the realistic goal should not be to achieve full consensus. Rather, the goal should be to find a narrative that encourages different stakeholder interest groups to converge and work together to negotiate win–win policy interventions.

In the case of fossil-fuel subsidies, the state is the critical driving force for reform, as subsidies place a high burden on government budgets, legitimize incumbent elites, and offer benefits to various societal groups. Thus and with care, bargaining between state and society actors can be used to stimulate collective action, channel demands, identify common interests, build consensus and, ultimately, allow political leaders to be seen to be responding appropriately as they propose and then implement a transformational reform (Moore, 2011: 10).

A recent IMF report (IMF, 2013b) assessing lessons learned from the reform of fossil-fuel subsidies stresses the point that close consultation with stakeholders can be used to build consensus. They can, for example, be invited to participate in the formulation of a reform strategy. Taking this approach, in mid-2007 the Federal Government of Germany worked with states that contained coal mines, the unions and the RAG Deutsche Steinkolhe AG (the company which carries out all

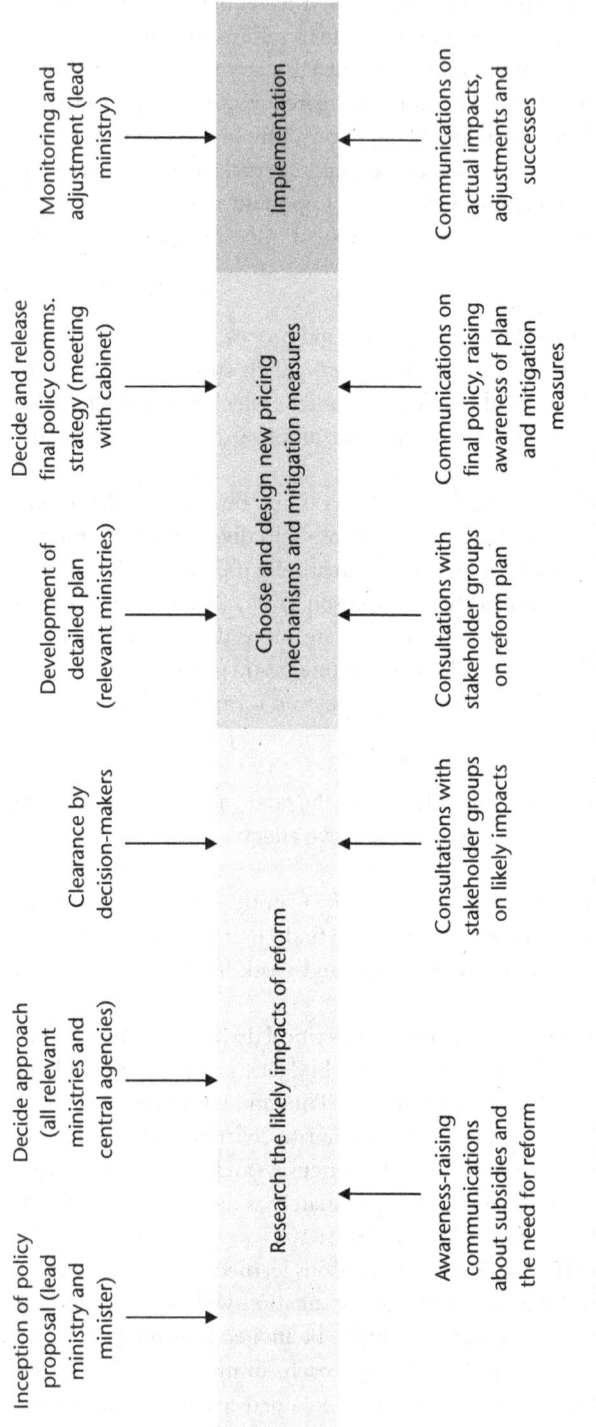

FIGURE 5.2 Model policy cycle showing strategic points for internal and external support building (based on GSI, 2013)

production of black coal) to prepare a detailed roadmap to end all coal subsidies by the end of 2018 (OECD, 2013).

Guideline 5.8
Using extensive information and communication campaigns to explain the rationale for and nature of proposed mitigation measures can play an important role in building support for change.

Continuous dialogue among stakeholders is necessary to ensure that reform can be carried out.[6] In 1996, the Namibian National Energy Council established a National Deregulation Task Force to examine options for fuel price deregulation that required a consultative process involving all stakeholders. This resulted first in a White Paper stressing the importance of keeping subsidies in remote areas, information transparency and gradual deregulation (Namibia's Ministry of Mines and Energy, in IMF, 2013b). In retrospect, it can be seen that this process was critical in securing widespread support for the reform (IMF, 2013b). In Niger, the government opted for a similar approach. They set up the Comité du Différé in 2010 to discuss ways to advance fuel subsidy reform. This committee's role was to ensure that all relevant stakeholders were on board and forge a consensus for the main elements of reform (IMF, 2013b). These experiences and others suggest that gradual development of the case for reform can be critical to success. Sufficient time needs to be set aside to do this. In Niger, it took six months to ensure that all stakeholders were on board and agreed with the main elements of proposed program reform (IMF, 2013a).

Conducting extensive information campaigns

Efforts to diffuse opposition to a reform can be as important as development of the case for it. To reduce opposition to reform, extensive communication campaigns and the development of proposed mitigation measures may be necessary. Communication about the need for reform and proposed mitigation needs to reach a wide audience. Based on experience in various countries, Table 5.1 illustrates various communication messages about fossil-fuel subsidy reform (GSI, 2013). Active communication is needed throughout the entire reform process. In Tanzania, for example, a specialized regulatory agency was established to keep the public informed about the price structure of fuel products (Kojima, 2009). A similar effort to increase energy pricing transparency to ensure continuity of reform has been used in South Africa (Clemens et al., 2014).

The literature abounds with examples of how communication can enable or constrain reform. In 2005, for instance, Ghana performed a poverty and social impact analysis (PSIA) that showed how the rich benefited disproportionately from energy subsidies and quantified the likely impact of reform on the poor (Laan et al., 2010). The results of the PSIA were made public and discussed in a dialogue with various stakeholders, including trade unions (Laan et al., 2010). The government

TABLE 5.1 Negative and positive communication messages about fossil-fuel subsidy reform

	Raise awareness of subsidy problems	Neutralize opposition	Raise awareness of gains from reform	Raise awareness of reform plans
Example focus of messages	Costs, inefficiencies, comparison with other countries, impacts on the poor and the environment.	Identifying smuggling and corruption, countering misconceptions.	Savings, target aid to the poor, more social spending, better standard of living.	Explaining reforms and mitigation, showing relevance to stakeholder needs, noting successes.

Source: GSI (2013).

then engaged in widespread communication campaigns, including public addresses by the President and the Minister of Finance, explaining how resources freed from subsidizing energy products, would, in part, be reallocated to social priorities (IMF, 2013a; Laan et al., 2010).

In India, a public report showing that 40 per cent of subsidized kerosene was diverted to the black market and did not reach the intended recipients contributed to the government taking action on reforming subsidies (Shenoy, 2010). On the other hand, in Nigeria, the absence of good quantitative information about the refining industry and the subsidy mechanism being used precluded a transparent discussion about the merits of the reform in 2011 (Clemens et al., 2014). As a result, the National Assembly voted against the removal of petrol subsidies on the grounds that there was a lack of firm data about the size and incidence of subsidies (Ogbu, 2012).

Another illustrative example comes from Iran, which has one of the highest levels of fossil-fuel subsidies in the world. In the past, it had experienced strong opposition to increasing energy prices. In 2010, after nearly three years of negotiation, Iran implemented an ambitious subsidy reform program. This process began in 2008 when the President announced a plan to search for a way to reduce subsidies. During the development phase, an extensive communication campaign was used to inform the public about the cost of subsidies and their unequal distributive effects. Several months before these subsidies were to be reduced, households were asked to open a bank account and document the number of people living in the house, so that they could receive compensation payments on the day that energy prices increased (Salefi-Isfahani, 2014).

Policy learning and experimentation

Guideline 5.9
Transformational policy reform needs to be seen as an ongoing iterative process that benefits from the development of new understandings and adjusts to the changes induced by the reform. Learning during implementation and from experience elsewhere can be critical to success and durability.

Ensuring the durability of reform is a challenging process. Various countries that seemed on the way to successful reform have reverted to the use of subsidies when international oil prices went up. Recent examples of such reversions can be found in Jordan, Ghana and Indonesia.

Successful policy reform involves systematic learning (Vidican, 2014). The mixed experience with fossil-fuel reforms worldwide and the heavy dependence of reform on the specific political circumstances suggest that learning should be at the centre of the policy-making process. Beaton et al. (2013) stress that governments often use "one another's innovations" to assist with the development of the case for a reform.

To this end, several elements are important (Vidican, 2014). Firstly, the cataloguing of international experience can be used to provide insights about likely impacts and benefits. International experience can be used to show that targeted compensation measures have been effective in some countries, but not effective in others. The reasons for this can then be used to justify exploration of alternative approaches. Secondly, experimenting with alternatives and making choices is important. Iran's experience with the reform of subsidies in 2010 illustrates this point. Initially the government sought to provide compensation only to specific groups. When Iran encountered opposition to this approach, it immediately switched to a proposal for uniform compensation payments (Hassanzadeh, 2012). This rapid policy switch suggests that experimentation and learning occurred and enabled future inefficiencies to be avoided. In the process of making this shift, Iran also reshaped its narrative (Vidican, 2014).

Observations like these suggest that policy learning should be continuous and ongoing rather than a one-off process. In its effort to redistribute income, the Iranian Government set the level of cash transfers well above new revenues from the price increases and printed money to pay the deficit. The resulting inflation eroded public support for the program and caused the parliament to freeze further price adjustments (Salefi-Isfahani, 2014). What initially appeared to be successful reform, therefore, turned out to be ineffective, mainly because the government failed to consider the long-term effects of at least one policy intervention.

A third element needed to support systematic policy learning is willingness to reconsider overall policy objectives. Evaluating the progress of reform is also important here, as are phase-out strategies for compensation schemes and the replacement of cash handouts with in-kind mitigation measures as the negative impact of subsidy removal diminishes. Further, to ensure durability of reform it is highly important that policy makers continue consulting and communicating even when the automatic fuel pricing mechanism is operational.

What these experiences show is that systematic policy learning must occur across two dimensions: learning from others and learning over time. In addition, cycles of learning should be integrated in the policy-making process, where reviews and revisions of goals and achievements are regularly made (Lütkenhorst et al., 2014). The World Bank's "learning spiral" (see Figure 5.3) is one of the most compelling approaches to integrate learning in the policy-making process

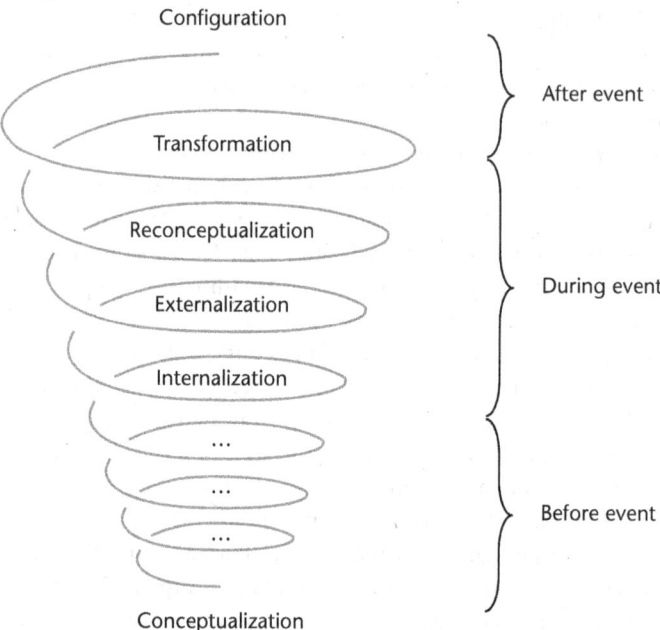

FIGURE 5.3 The learning spiral concept (adapted from Blindenbacher, 2010)

(Blindenbacher, 2010). Such an approach can be highly relevant when a complex policy reform is being considered. At its core, there is a need for an iterative process that searches for feedback loops and allows the integration of new knowledge and ensures adaptation to the responses that the reform induces. Reforms induce change and innovation and, as they occur, they need to be accounted for (Lütkenhorst et al., 2014). To this end, "learning brokers" can be used to moderate the interactive learning process and facilitate dissemination of new knowledge and ongoing reform (Lütkenhorst et al., 2014).

Concluding remarks

Fossil-fuel subsidies have reached unprecedented levels and, without policy reform, are likely to increase further. Their distortionary effects on the economy, society and the environment are undisputed. Yet, while some progress on reducing their incidence has been made in recent decades, extensive and long-lasting reform is lagging behind in most countries. There is wide agreement that the main challenge to reforming fossil-fuel subsidies resides in the complex political dynamics associated with changing a social contract that supports vested interests of various stakeholder groups.

Experience with reform suggests that several factors could contribute to improving the track record. Firstly, in order to implement a successful transformational reform it can be wise to establish the knowledge needed to begin implementation and then wait for a critical juncture that creates the window of opportunity needed to break stakeholder alliances and escape from path dependencies. Critical junctures typically centre around major events, such as political, financial or economic crises. Economic prosperity and/or a price fall can also open up an opportunity. Given the risks of social unrest and strong opposition from powerful interest groups timing is critical. A severe budgetary crisis in Morocco, political change in Egypt and energy security concerns in Jordan are examples of critical junctures that enabled the successful removal of fossil-fuel subsidies without major opposition or protest.

Once a decision to engage in the reform of fossil-fuel subsidies is made, a thorough exploration of the constellation of interests and power among different stakeholders is necessary. This needs to be coupled with attention to the rationale behind interests likely to oppose reforms and the search for measures that might turn opposition into support. Motivations to support or oppose a specific policy are not static, but rather are determined by certain framework conditions and circumstances that can change quickly.

While political will and leadership are imperative for initiating reform at a critical juncture, a focus on the structures and institutions shaping interests of different groups is more important. Given the complex political dynamics around the reform of subsidies, such an assessment can assist decision makers in building potential political alliances for reform and in seeking alternative strategic interventions to satisfy interest groups.

Knowing the sources of opposition and support among various stakeholder groups can assist decision makers to build transformative alliances. Such alliances enable consultations with a diverse group of stakeholders in order to reflect and negotiate different interests towards elaborating solutions that are both politically and socially acceptable. The lack of a compelling narrative that resonates among many stakeholders can often be a major barrier to enabling and sustaining reform of fossil-fuel subsidies. The relevance of such coalitions or transformative alliances for reform has been shown in several countries.

The development of extensive information campaigns that reveal the cost of subsidies to specific groups is an important factor necessary for enabling the formation of transformative coalitions and for increasing their effectiveness during negotiation processes.

Continuous communication and transparency with respect to the reform process is critical for building trust in government, as the initiator of the reform, and also in reducing opposition as each step is taken. Gradual implementation allows time to build transformative alliances across stakeholders and communicate the consequences of the next step effectively.

Identifying the right time to initiate reform (i.e. the critical juncture), mapping the interests and power of different stakeholders, building reform coalitions and ensuring communication and transparency on the reform is not enough of themselves to achieve a long-lasting reform. In addition to these, ongoing systematic learning and experimentation is essential.

The mixed experience with fossil-fuel reforms worldwide and the heavy dependence on the specific political circumstances suggest that learning should be at the centre of the policy-making process. Learning has two dimensions: learning from others and learning over time. To this end, it can be useful to document international experience about reform pathways, experiment with alternatives, be prepared to adapt and show willingness to reconsider proposed policy measures. The experience in many countries shows that failure to take a systematic learning approach can seriously hamper the reform of fossil-fuel subsidies and lead to their undoing.

Another lesson learned from the reform of fossil-fuel subsidies is that state capacity is critical. State capacity can be defined as the ability to "implement official goals, especially over the actual or potential opposition of powerful social groups or in the face of recalcitrant socioeconomic circumstances" (Skocpol, 1985). Strong state capacity is critical for effective implementation of reform. More in depth research at country level is needed to identify ways to strengthen capacity.

Subsidy reform requires rapid, systematic and carefully planned actions in order to avoid negative effects on vulnerable population groups and reduce opposition from interest groups.

Notes

1 At the same time, subsidies for renewable energy account for only one-fourth of the subsidies to fossil-fuels, the same being true for investments in energy efficiency globally (GSI, 2014). When calculated on a post-tax basis, fossil-fuel subsidies are much larger, amounting to US$2 trillion in 2011 (IMF, 2013a). The advanced economies account for about 40 per cent of the global total, topped by United States, China and Russia (IMF, 2013a).
2 Pre-tax fossil-fuel subsidies prevail primarily in the Middle East and North Africa (about 48 per cent of global level) and emerging and developing Asia (over 20 per cent) (IMF, 2013b).
3 The largest share of local air pollution and the carbon dioxide emissions that contribute to global warming are a by-product of fossil-fuel combustion (Aldy, 2013). Harm to the environment can occur many years after the end of a subsidy. For example, the United Kingdom has some 900 abandoned coal mines, from which 400 are leaking methane, which cannot be fully captured, into the atmosphere (IEEP, 2007).
4 As discussed in the IMF report (2013a), successful reform outcomes occur when countries implement reforms that lead to a permanent and sustained reduction of subsidies. Partial success is recorded in countries that achieved a reduction of subsidies for at least a year but where subsidies have re-emerged or remain a policy issue. Reform is considered to have failed where price increases or efforts to improve efficiency in the energy sector have been rolled back soon after the reform began.
5 An increase in energy prices leads to withdrawing rents from powerful groups in the society (e.g. middle and upper classes, energy intensive industries or businesses in general) and increasing the vulnerability of large low-income population groups.
6 Currently, however, in light of continuous pushback from the coal industry, it is not clear whether subsidies will be phased out completely by 2018.

References

Aldy, J. (2013) *Designing Energy and Environmental Fiscal Instruments to Improve Public Health*. Global Health Working Papers. Available at: http://globalhealth2035.org/sites/default/files/working-papers/designing-energy-environmental-fiscal-instruments.pdf (accessed 1 May 2016).

Arze del Granado, J., Coady, D. and Gillingham, R. (2012) "The Unequal Benefits of Fuel Subsidies: A Review of Evidence for Developing Countries". *World Development* 40: 2234–48.

Beaton, C., Gerasimchuk, I., Laan, T., Lang, K., Vis-Dunbar, D. and Wooders, P. (2013) "A guidebook to fossil-fuel subsidy reform for policy-makers in Southeast Asia". Global Subsidies Initiative (GSI) of the International Institute for Sustainable Development, Geneva.

Blatter, D. and Buzzell, Z. (2013) "The Subsidy Trap: Why Tunisia's Leaders are Unwilling, Unable, or Afraid to Abandon Fuel Subsidies". IMES Capstone Paper Series. The Institute for Middle East Studies (IMES), The Elliot School of International Affairs, The George Washington University.

Blindenbacher, R. (2010) *The Black Box of Governmental Learning: The Learning Spiral: A Concept to Organize Learning in Government*. Washington, DC: The World Bank.

Bridle, R., Kiston, L. and Wooders, P. (2014) "Fossil-Fuel Subsidies: A Barrier to Renewable Energy in Five Middle East and North African Countries". GSI Report, September. Global Subsidies Initiative (GSI), International Institute for Sustainable Development, Geneva.

Capoccia, G. and Kelemen, R. D. (2007) "The Study of Critical Junctures: Theory, Narrative, and Counterfactuals in Historical Institutionalism". *World Politics* 59: 341–69.

Clemens, B., Coady, D., Fabrizio, S., Gupta, S., Alleyne, T. and Sdralevich, C. (eds) (2014) *Energy Subsidy Reform: Lessons and Implications*. . Washington, DC: International Monetary Fund.

Cortell, A. P. and Peterson, S. (1999) "Altered States: Explaining Domestic Institutional Change". *British Journal of Political Science* 29: 177–203.

Electricity Regulatory Commission (2012) "Jordan Tariff Structure and the Energy Efficiency". Available at: pubs.naruc.org/pub/53889B58-2354-D714-51E5-98A610B0EDD1 (accessed 9 May 2016).

GSI (2013) "A Guidebook to Fossil-Fuel Subsidy Reform for Policy-Makers in Southeast Asia: Executive Summary". Global Subsidies Initiative (GSI), International Institute for Sustainable Development, Geneva.

GSI (2014) "Paying the Polluter: How Fossil Fuel Subsidies Hold Us Back from a Low-Carbon Future". Available at: www.iisd.org/gsi/sites/default/files/FFSR_and_climate_infographic_snd10-12_0.jpg (accessed 1 May 2016).

G20 (2009) *Leaders' Statement: The Pittsburgh Summit, September 24–25 2009*. Available at www.treasury.gov/resource-center/international/g7-g20/Documents/pittsburgh_summit_leaders_statement_250909.pdf (accessed 1 May 2016).

Haggard, S. (1998) "The Institutional Foundations of Hegemony: Explaining the Reciprocal Trade Agreements Act of 1943". *International Organization*, 42(1): 91–119.

Hassanzadeh, E. (2012) "Recent developments in Iran's energy subsidy reforms". *Policy Brief*, October 2012. Global Subsidies Initiative (GSI), International Institute for Sustainable Development, Geneva.

Hogan, J. W. (2006) "Remoulding the Critical Junctures Approach". *Canadian Journal of Political Science* 39(3): 657–79.

IEA (2010) *World Energy Outlook 2010*. International Energy Agency, Paris. Available at www.worldenergyoutlook.org/media/weo2010.pdf (accessed 9 May 2016).

IEA (2011) *World Energy Outlook 2011*. International Energy Agency, Paris. Available at www.worldenergyoutlook.org/weo2011/ (accessed 9 May 2016).

IEA (2014) "Fossil-fuel Consumption Subsidy Rates as a Proportion of the Full Cost of Supply". International Energy Agency. Available at: www.worldenergyoutlook.org/weo2014/ (accessed 9 May 2016).

Institute for European Environmental Policy (IEEP) (2007) *Reforming environmentally harmful subsidies*. Final report to the European Commissions's DG Environment, March 2007.

IMF (2013a) *Case Studies on Energy Subsidy Reform: Lessons and Implications*. Washington, DC: International Monetary Fund, 28 January.

IMF (2013b) *Morocco: Selected Issues*. IMF Country Report No. 13/110. International Monetary Fund, Washington, DC. Available at: www.imf.org/external/pubs/ft/scr/2013/cr13110.pdf (accessed 1 May 2016).

Johnson, O., Altenburg, T. and Schmitz, H. (2014) "Rent Management Capabilities for the Green Tranformation". Chapter 2 in A. Pegels (ed.), *Green Industrial Policy in Emerging Countries*. Abingdon: Routledge.

Kojima, M. (2009) *Government Response to Oil Price Volatility: Experience of 49 Developing Countries*. Extractive Industries for Development Series No. 10. Washington, DC: The World Bank.

Laan, T., Beaton, C. and Presta, B. (2010) "Untold Billions: Strategies for Reforming Fossil-Fuel Subsidies: Practical Lessons from Ghana, France and Senegal". The Global Subsidies Initiative. International Institute for Sustainable Development, Geneva.

Lang, K. (2011) *The First Year of the G-20 Commitment on Fossil-Fuel Subsidies: A commentary on lessons learned and the path forward*. The Global Subsidies Initiative (GSI), International Institute for Sustainable Development (IISD), Geneva. Available at www.iisd.org/gsi/sites/default/files/ffs_g20_firstyear.pdf (accessed 1 May 2016).

Lütkenhorst, W., Altenburg, T., Pegels, A. and Vidican, G. (2014) "Green Industrial Policy: Managing Transformation under Uncertainty". DIE Discussion Paper 28/2014. German Development Institute / Deutsches Institut für Entwicklungspolitik, Bonn.

Mitchell, R. K., Agle, B. R, and Wood, D. J. (1997) "Toward a Theory of Stakeholder Identification and Salience: Defining the Principle of Who and What Really Counts". *Academy of Management Review*, 22(4): 853–86.

Moore, M. (2011) "The Governance Agenda in Long Term Perspective: Globalization, Revenues and the Differentiation of States". Working Paper Series 378. Institute of Development Studies, Sussex.

OECD (2013) 'Inventory of Estimated Budgetary Support and Tax Expenditures for Fossil Fuels 2013'. Organisation for Economic Development and Cooperation. OECD Publishing, Paris.

Ogbu, O. (2012) "The Removal of Oil Price Subsidy in Nigeria: Lessons in Leadership and Policymaking in a Trust-Deficit Environment". Brookings Institute. *Opinion*, January 26.

Peiffer, C. (2012) "Reform Coalitions: Patterns and Hypotheses from a Survey of Literature". Concept Paper 03, May, Developmental Leadership Program, Policy and Practice for Developmental Leaders, Elites and Coalitions. Available at: www.dlprog.org/publications/reform-coalitions-patterns-and-hypotheses-from-a-survey-of-the-literature-.php (accessed 9 May 2016).

Pierson, P. (2004) *Politics in Time: History, Institutions, and Social Analysis*. Princeton, NJ: Princeton University Press.

Salefi-Isfahani, D. (2014) "Iran's Subsidy Reform: From Promise to Disappointment". Policy Perspective No. 13. Economic Research Forum, Cairo.

Shenoy, B. (2010) "Lessons Learned from Attempts to Reform India's Kerosene Subsidy". The Global Subsidy Initiative (GSI), International Institute for Sustainable Development, Geneva.

Skocpol, T. (1985) "Bringing the State Back in: Strategies of Analysis in Current Research". In Evans, P.B, Rueschemayer, D, and Skocpol, T. (eds.), *Bringing the State Back in*. Cambridge: Cambridge University Press.

UNEP (2003) "Energy Subsidies: Lessons Learned in Assessing their Impact and Designing Policy Reforms". United Nations Energy Program, Geneva.

Victor, D. (2009) "The Politics of Fossil-Fuel Subsidies". Global Subsidies Initiative (GSI), International Institute for Sustainable Development, Geneva.

Vidican, G. (2014) "Reforming Fossil-fuel Subsidy Regimes in the Middle East and North African Countries". Chapter 7 in A. Pegels (ed.), *Green Industrial Policy in Emerging Countries*. Abingdon: Routledge.

6

TWO STEPS FORWARD, ONE STEP BACK

The ongoing failure to capture synergies in natural resource management (Australia)

Andrew Campbell

The Australian political narrative – exemplified by Megalogenis (2012) and Keane and Razer (2014) – commonly holds that transformational policy reform has become too difficult, that vested interests have become too powerful, and that governments are less bold and less able in the 24-hour media cycle to make and sustain a compelling case for a fundamental reform.

This contention holds true up to a point but transformational reform is not impossible, just more difficult. This is arguably especially the case for policy reforms that favour long-term conservation over short-term resource exploitation and development.

The beneficiaries of environmental protection measures are usually the general public, the environment (other species) and future generations. The last two of these beneficiaries don't vote and can't donate to political parties. For individual members of the public, the environment may not be a top-order issue, or the benefits of an individual reform may be modest or difficult to detect. Ministers and their offices may perceive that they are doing something brave or controversial, notwithstanding that reform may be grounded in the best available science and there may be an overwhelming (albeit silent) majority in favour of it. Opposition to reform may be loud, fierce, well-organised and increasingly well-funded, even if only from a vocal minority with a vested interest. It will have its own narrative, crafted to suit its own agenda, and using evidence selectively if at all.

Moreover, few politicians suffer a backlash for sacking public servants, and public sector cuts can frequently be dressed up as efficiency measures, savings, reducing 'green and red tape', rather than being seen as reducing services or undermining the public interest. As a consequence, while many environmental challenges are inherently public good issues, cost-cutting measures are often incorrectly seen as virtuous within the dominant political narrative with adverse consequences for environmental projects.

In addition, the impact of environmental cuts and lax development approval processes is usually felt well after the perpetrators have moved on. A pollutant spill, aquifer contamination or responsibility for the over-allocation of fishery resources is rarely sheeted home to the minister or government that first weakened the regulation, allocated too many permits or licences, cut research budgets or reduced compliance staffing levels.

Moreover, the conservation movement and environmental Non-Government Organisations (NGOs) in the main have not been well prepared for, nor have they responded well to, the changing political landscape to which they are being exposed. They have relied on essentially the same advocacy tools they were using twenty years ago, and on the whole they have not inspired Generation Y and the Millennials. Digital-savvy organisations such as Get Up have been more nimble and occasionally more effective in mobilising community concerns and focusing political pressure on single issues. Nevertheless, they remain essentially reactive and don't have a coherent forward-looking agenda. Individual events such as 'March in March' can mobilise more than 100,000 people and yet be so disparate and unfocused as to have negligible political impact.

So how can we engender long-term public-good environmental policy reform in the era of wicked problems, big data, sophisticated well-funded campaigns by vested interests against reform, declining scientific literacy within mainstream media and politicians, and a 24/7 news cycle with a myopic and ephemeral attention span?

This chapter attempts to explore the question of how to bring about a successful transformational policy reform through the lens of the Australian Landcare movement, within the broader policy context of land, water, vegetation and biodiversity management in Australia, which is usually shortened to natural resource management (NRM). Along the way, a set of fifteen transformational policy reform guidelines are identified.

Over the past twenty years of environmental and NRM programs in Australia, there have been three key investments in processes that sought to transform the way Australian landscapes are managed and used. The three major reforms, with a short running title, were:

- *Localism*: an attempt to catalyse a large voluntary, community-based Landcare movement;
- *Regionalism*: the evolution of a regional-scale NRM delivery model based on catchment management organisations; and
- *Centralism*: a more recent push for more evidence-based, targeted national environmental investment and reporting coupled with increasing use of market-based mechanisms for allocating resources.

These approaches are described in turn below as three distinct phases, but in reality it is more accurate to think of the past twenty years as an environmental policy reform journey. At the time of their inception each was lauded as a ground-breaking reform. Each reform was expected to make a fundamental difference to the future of Australian agriculture and the lands associated with it.

Landcare in Australia: nourishing grass roots environmental cooperation (localism)

The introduction of a joint proposal for a Decade of Landcare was presented to the then Prime Minister, Bob Hawke, in 1989. They were heady days, infused with optimism underpinned by the solid foundations of community enthusiasm, bipartisan support, the NFF–ACF partnership and a decade-long funding commitment.

Landcare means different things to different people. At its core, Landcare is about promoting sustainable environmental and natural resource management through voluntary collective action at a neighbourhood or district level. Landcare groups build social capital, change social norms, develop a shared community understanding of environmental problems and their solutions, and promote those solutions, often through on-ground local demonstration projects (Campbell, 1994).

By the mid-1990s, more than one-third of all Australian farm families were actively involved in one of more than 6,000 local Landcare groups, and in many regions well over half of all landholders were engaged. They often employed their own staff, and were supported by the National Landcare Program and a range of associated state- and commonwealth-funding programs and government agencies. There were programs in schools and urban areas, corporate support was strong, and there were high profile and very popular awards at state and national levels. Brand recognition for the Landcare "caring hands" logo among the general public was comparable to that for Coca-Cola and the golden arches of McDonald's.

Conceptually, the primary role of voluntary Landcare groups and the professionals assisting them is not directly about managing soil, vegetation, water or even farms. Those tasks are carried out by farmers and other landholders operating their individual enterprises. Of course those landholders may be members of a Landcare group, but they are managing natural resources in the course of their own business, not as a Landcare activity per se. Rather, the role of Landcare, and the measure by which its success or otherwise should be judged, was to change social norms within rural communities (e.g. the definition of what it means to be seen as a "good farmer") and to promote more sustainable land management practices. This is a subtle but important distinction. It means that within a given catchment or district, Landcare could be doing a good job, yet landscapes could still be degrading, because of factors outside the control of Landcare groups (e.g. climate, markets, demography – or the fact that a sustainable farming system may not yet have been developed in a particular region).

The problem for Landcare – in particular for the Australian federal government-funded Decade of Landcare – was that the formal objectives of the program were expressed in biophysical terms as the reversal of land and water degradation in

Australia. So when the Australian National Audit Office (ANAO) evaluated Landcare as a government program, it invariably found that land degradation was still occurring, if not accelerating, as various State of Environment Reports and the National Land and Water Resources Audit documented in great detail without due regard to other factors. Therefore, measured against its own objectives by the ANAO, Landcare was not considered to be an effective commonwealth government program (ANAO, 2008).

Guideline 6.1
When setting formal policy objectives, expect these same objectives to be used as the basis for subsequent reviews. Beware of aspirational objectives.

Most informed observers would agree that, in terms of mobilising community engagement, building partnerships within rural communities and between urban and rural communities, changing norms about what it means to be a 'good farmer' and providing a framework for community involvement in and ownership of NRM programs, Landcare has been one of the most successful extension programs in Australian history (Marshall, 2008, Curtis et al., 2014).

During the Decade of Landcare, the program was recognised globally as one of the most successful exemplars in critical aspects of sustainable development and was lauded as an amazing achievement for any country. At the time more than one-third of all farm families in Australia were involved in voluntary environment groups undertaking cooperative conservation activities at a community level. Politicians and senior officials in the United Kingdom and the European Union found it hard to believe that this level of community engagement could be delivered across a whole continent at a cost of less than A$30 million per year.

Scaling up: Australia's regional natural resource management (NRM) framework (regionalism)

Landcare evolved along slightly different pathways across the six Australian states and territories from the early 1980s, but in all regions a key driver was an understanding that land and water degradation issues which crossed farm boundaries needed to be tackled at a scale of planning and action greater than the individual farm. Landcare groups predominantly are neighbourhood groups, comprising up to a few dozen families in traditional agricultural districts, and more in peri-urban settings with a predominance of lifestyle farms or rural residential blocks. Typically, they were organised around already-established social groupings such as a school, a fire brigade or a sporting team. The advantage of this approach is that the core group of people, including group leaders, are well known to each other and already identify with that community.

For some issues such as fixing soil erosion hotspots, establishing wildlife corridors through revegetation, controlling pests such as rabbits or a particular weed problem, the scale of activity of a Landcare group working across 20–30 farms is quite appropriate. For many other NRM issues, however – for example dryland salinity or water quality in southern Australia or fire regimes in northern Australia – degradation processes operate at larger spatial scales. For such issues, restoration measures and the information base to support them need to be organised at a larger watershed or landscape scale outside the focus of a typical Landcare group. Moreover, many early Landcare groups were focused on one or two issues (often pests and weeds), but tackling the full suite of NRM issues requires a more integrated approach that necessarily needs to be organised at a scale commensurate with the ecological and hydrological drivers of those processes.

The need for a more regional or catchment-based approach to NRM was recognised in the 1980s under the banner of integrated catchment management (ICM), and some jurisdictions formed catchment-based organisations at that time. Regionalisation was the obvious next step to take in the process of making Landcare more effective.

The Australian Government established the Natural Heritage Trust (NHT) in 1997, funded through the part sale of its telecommunications company, with the expressed aims of funding "on-ground works" to tackle land degradation problems and fund environmental restoration activities. The Natural Heritage Trust explicitly funded local Landcare groups, but also funded catchment and regional NRM bodies to undertake planning activities and to perform an integrative function at a scale larger than community groups (Marshall, 2008). No long-term funding arrangement was put in place.

By the late 1990s, Australia had evolved what became known as the Regional NRM Model, based on 56 regional or catchment organisations. These 56 organisations, called Catchment Management Authorities in some jurisdictions and Regional NRM bodies in others, were configured and governed in different ways in different jurisdictions. They ranged from statutory Catchment Management Authorities in Victoria (with their own rating powers initially) and later in South Australia and New South Wales, through incorporated committees initiated and supported by state and territory governments in Tasmania, the ACT and Northern Territory, to unincorporated community groups in Western Australia and Queensland. By 2005, commonwealth and state/territory governments had invested almost A$400m in the 56 regional bodies to prepare and implement regional NRM plans and investment strategies (Robins and Dovers, 2007).

They identified a range of factors outside the control of regional bodies (demographic, economic, biophysical and political) that substantially influenced their ability to achieve their objectives. They proposed a typology of ten regional types, which they likened to aircraft, from "Jumbo" to "Ultralight", noting that some regions close to major population centres containing universities and other research capacity, and with high levels of human capital, are much better able to access the decision makers and the resources they need to develop and implement their plans.

However, the process of establishing and supporting the regional model was essentially a "top down" exercise, of governments attempting to rationalise resource delivery. An increase in commonwealth investment in NRM was accompanied by a parallel process of state governments reducing their own investment in agricultural research and extension, closing down and selling off research farms and district offices, withdrawing staff positions back to regional centres, and often shifting funding for their own staff to commonwealth programs including the National Landcare Program. In some jurisdictions (notably New South Wales) regional bodies under the commonwealth's regional model were established through the wholesale transfer of staff from state government agencies, in a blatant case of cost-shifting from state to commonwealth level.

The establishment of the regional model was ostensibly about "scaling up" and operating at a more effective scale for the problems being tackled, and helping to establish a better framework within which the activities of individual farmers and Landcare groups could combine for greater aggregate impact. But it was also about rationalising resource allocation and service delivery, and these two policy drivers were not always working in the same direction. In contexts where the former driver held sway, regional bodies saw themselves as facilitators of grassroots community action, and essentially tried to deliver resources to and make life easier for voluntary community Landcare groups. In fact one CEO of a Catchment Management Authority described himself as the "servant" of local Landcare groups, and he meant it. But many other regional bodies saw themselves as the "professionals" in NRM taking a more strategic view as opposed to local Landcare groups as the "amateurs" with necessarily local priorities. In one case the regional body evicted from its offices a highly successful Landcare group that had won national awards, employed several professional staff and managed multi-million dollar projects.

In the early stages of the development of "the regional model", regionalisation and Landcare were seen as complementary and reinforcing. Those involved in the day-to-day operation of each process, however, rarely appreciated this. With hindsight, those responsible for implementing the regional framework should have seen improving the effectiveness of voluntary Landcare as one of their core objectives.

On paper, Australia in establishing the regional NRM model to complement community Landcare created an exemplary model of what Graham Marshall (2008) calls "nested multi-level systems of community-based governance". But Marshall goes on to emphasise the importance of vertical trust between the different layers of governance if such systems are to realise their potential. He analysed several regions and found that where local groups and farmers trusted the sub-regional and regional organisations they were more likely to implement practices consistent with the regional strategy, but in other regions there was significant distrust and suspicion between the levels of organisation.

Landcare is now struggling in many, if not most, districts, having lacked strategic attention for more than a decade. Some of Landcare's problems and loss of momentum are symptomatic of policy neglect. The regional model for NRM program delivery has undermined voluntary community Landcare in many regions (Curtis et al., 2014). In retrospect, those responsible for developing regionalism failed to articulate how the regional framework should relate to voluntarism and, as a result, undermined it (Marshall, 2008). As regionalism was implemented, the network of Landcare facilitators suffered from cumbersome, stop–start funding arrangements and insufficient strategic support or direction. Those who could do so, left.

From my perspective, as someone who was involved both in the establishment of Landcare at a national level and later in the administration of the NHT, the complementarity of voluntary local action within regional/catchment planning and resource delivery seemed logical and obvious. In retrospect, I think we assumed that regional bodies would support Landcare, and that Landcare groups would want to contribute to a "catchment plan" and, hence, would support the regional bodies. Looking back, we did not pay sufficient attention to the social dynamics at the interface between local and regional scales, and we did not design funding rules and reporting requirements with sufficient emphasis on nourishing and sustaining grassroots action. In too many regions, local groups and regional bodies saw themselves as being in competition for human talent and for funding, rather than as paddlers in a tandem canoe.

Guideline 6.2
As far as possible, lock in long-term funding arrangements and secure bipartisan support that will endure a change in government.

The tendency for the regional NRM policy reform to displace and undermine rather than augment community Landcare was a grave error. The job of catalysing community engagement in environmental management at a grassroots level is essential and perpetual. There is much to be gained from taking the best elements of the Landcare approaches of the 1990s and rejuvenating them for the next decade and beyond. A comprehensive re-think of the relationship between agriculture, the environment and natural resource use in Australia is needed (Campbell, 2009; Marshall, 2008).

National Investment in NRM through a top-down approach (centralism)

Guideline 6.3
Over a long timeframe, consider carefully what a new program is likely to do to existing programs.

By about 2007, the regional NRM model had been in place for around a decade, and federal funding for Landcare for fifteen years. More than A$1 billion had been invested through the NHT and related commonwealth programs. Questions were being asked about the effectiveness of this investment in reducing or reversing land and water degradation and improving the health of the Australian environment. Several sobering assessments are summarised in this quote from Curtis and Lefroy (2010):

Limited understanding of ecological processes plus the challenges of governance faced by small local groups and new regional organisations operating within a federal framework (Stratford *et al.*, 2007) commonly resulted in untargeted investment, poor accountability and a focus on symptoms rather than cause. The expectation that learning and action at local-scale would eventually lead to landscape-scale change has not been realised, as evidenced by four national audits of NRM programs which concluded that there had been focus on outputs rather than environmental outcomes which were often poorly specified, based on untested assumptions, and either not measured or unmeasurable.

The incoming Labor Government in 2007, as part of its election platform, promised a more strategic, assets-based approach to NRM investment. Citing the Australian National Audit Office reports, the new government contended that the prevailing model was spreading resources too thinly and not investing sufficiently in the "jewels in the crown", outstanding natural assets under threat from degradation, habitat destruction and development pressures. It also promised that a greater proportion of funding (including for regional delivery) would be contestable, and that non-government organisations including private nature conservation groups and philanthropic bodies should be able to compete with regional NRM bodies for resources to develop and implement strategies at a landscape scale. Perhaps counter-intuitively, given its initiation by an incoming Labor Government, the "Caring for our Country" program announced in 2008 was characterised by the language of business, investment and the market.

Criticising the past government, the new Labor Government was guided by a national Business Plan that stressed the greater benefits achievable if investment was targeted to priority national assets and access to funds made contestable. With Labor in power, resources for on-ground activities, where appropriate, were to be allocated through market-based instruments such as tenders and auctions.

The Labor Government cut 40 percent of the core funding for regional NRM bodies in order to establish its Caring for our Country program. These cuts quickly served to undermine relationships between regional bodies and local groups. In particular, many of the regional NRM bodies that had provided supporting infrastructure for local groups were no longer able to do so. Most found themselves scrabbling for resources, often against their own local groups. For example, 1,300 proposals were submitted in response to the 2009–10 Caring for our Country Business Plan competitive grants call, of which only 59 were successful. Only 12 of these successful proposals came from a regional NRM organisation (Robins and Kanowski, 2011). In a hard-hitting paper called "Crying for our Country", Lisa Robins and Peter Kanowski (2011) identified eight ways in which the framing and delivery of Caring for our Country undermined the achievements of Landcare and regional NRM:

- Caring for our Country narrowed the agenda for natural resource management.
- Central control was increased at the expense of regionally determined goals and priorities.
- A simple outputs focus ignored real-world complexity.
- Buy-in by state and territory governments was compromised.
- Core funding was reduced and constrained.
- Increased transaction costs meant unproductive "busyness" reached new heights.
- The gap widened between regional bodies and local groups.
- Federal research and development (R&D) funding for regional NRM was diminished.

At the same time as Caring for our Country was further centralising NRM program delivery and investment, Australia was experiencing what became known as the Millennium Drought. Water scarcity affected all of southern and eastern Australia with a severity not experienced over the 200 years of European settlement. As a direct result, an intense focus on national water policy reform emerged and the Commonwealth Government established the National Water Initiative and followed this with unprecedented commonwealth investment in the National Plan for Water Security. Eventually, more than A$12 billion was committed to modernising irrigation and water management infrastructure; standardising water accounting and measurement systems; harmonising water entitlement and allocation regimes across jurisdictions; establishing a functioning water market; buying back water entitlements from over-allocated systems; and managing the purchased "environmental water".

Thinking about policy reform in parallel, rather than in sequence

The three phases of NRM investment described above are highly complementary – at best synergistic – approaches to more sustainable management of the environment and land and water resources, and to public investment. Each is essential, but insufficient on its own to bring about more sustainable management of Australia's natural resources and more resilient rural and regional communities.

Community commitment is an important condition, but not a sufficient condition, to progress sustainable agriculture and resource management at a landscape scale or a continental scale. In the absence of technically and economically viable and adoptable land use and farming systems, no amount of community goodwill will deliver sustainable land, water and biodiversity management. Similarly, in the absence of sensible, integrative regional planning frameworks, there is an increased risk of wasting public and private investment. Many of the big issues in NRM – such as the need for water reform underlined by the Millennium Drought – cannot be tackled effectively at local or even regional levels, but demand a national approach across multiple jurisdictions.

Each of the three approaches outlined above – crudely summarised as localism, regionalism and centralism – is a valid, internally coherent response to an environmental challenge. Each was underpinned by a solid evidence base. Each was also in effect a reasonable response to perceived weaknesses in preceding approaches, and a "natural evolution" of the NRM policy framework. Each development was justified by serious policy documents making the case for reform.

Guideline 6.4
Genuine crises often create the possibility for transformational reform and for "creative destruction" of prior constraints. However, it is crucial that such destruction does not extend to the foundations on which long-term gains rely.

Ideally, and with the benefit of hindsight, Australia should have implemented these three approaches in parallel, each reinforcing the other. But they were seen, unfortunately, as sequential, evolutionary developments. This might have worked out well had Australia paid more attention to ensuring that these approaches built on each other and invested strategically to buttress that the platform that was being built. But Australian administrators did not do this. Instead, exacerbated by the tendency in modern politics for incoming governments to disparage the achievements of their predecessor, each phase of NRM policy reform tended to displace its predecessor and undermine the very platform it was built upon.

An interesting point of contention at the Gough Whitlam and Malcolm Frazer Chair of Australian Studies Transformational Dynamic Change workshop at Harvard University in 2013, which gave rise to this book, was the extent to which policy development needs to be contestable, informed by open, public and possibly intense debate.

Good policy process within a Westminster system, like Australia's, necessarily ensures a contest of ideas. If Cabinet is used appropriately, then all new policy proposals should undergo a Cabinet coordination process run by the Department of the Prime Minister and Cabinet (PM&C). In particular, policy proposals from a given department must be circulated for comment to other relevant departments. Central agencies such as the Prime Minister's Department, Cabinet, Finance and Treasury can exercise significant influence and impose considerable rigour in this process, even if it seems tedious and at times painful for the proposing agency. For difficult, complex or contentious issues, additional mechanisms such as parliamentary inquiries or referrals to an independent agency, such as Australia's Productivity Commission, can be used to explore and test policy reform proposals, seek public input and start new policy discussions.

In Australia, unfortunately, over the past decade or so, irrespective of the party in power, there has been a strong centralising tendency in policy development processes, with seemingly ever greater power concentrated in the Prime Minister's Office (Keane and Razer, 2014). This has tended to lessen the rigour and breadth of scrutiny of new policy proposals, whether or not they are buttressed by a political mandate hardened through the harsh glare of an election campaign. In particular, it is desirable that there is focused scrutiny on proposed implementation measures as well as the policy objectives. Even the best policy can be sadly discredited through misconceived or incompetent delivery.

While contestability is important, it does not necessarily have to be realised through sustained public debate over a long period. If proper policy development processes are followed within a government and its administration, there should be sufficient checks and balances to ensure that policy objectives and program delivery are properly thought through, with ample opportunity for potential risks to be identified and mitigated.

Guidelines for "sticky" policy reform

Reflecting on the Landcare experience and subsequent developments in NRM policy in Australia, ten more general guidelines for the development and implementation of a transformational policy reform that sticks are set out below.

Guideline 6.5
Create a "burning platform" that establishes a compelling rationale for change, then pay careful attention to timing. Impact is likely to be maximised when political planets are aligned and when people are looking for new ideas/initiatives.

Guideline 6.6
Marshall the evidence and facts to support your case for reform, but never assume that the facts will speak for themselves, or be sufficient. If the policy reform is perceived to threaten powerful interests, then assume that opposition will be well organised, well resourced and politically ruthless.

Guideline 6.7
Ensure that the "three lenses of knowledge and influence" (Head, 2008) are all considered, mutually reinforcing and well-aligned with the reform agenda. The three lenses are:

- *political judgement* (the Minister, their office and party, and preferably the Minister's informal advisers);
- *professional practice* (the relevant agencies, including central agencies and also think tanks and NGOs); and
- *scientific research* (policy briefs, refereed literature, professional societies, conferences, learned academies and peak groups).

Guideline 6.8
Build a broad coalition of interests in support of the reform, and try to get engagement from as many different kinds of beneficiary as possible so that the reform has as many parents/champions/sponsors as possible. Don't assume that people have a sophisticated understanding of their own best interests. Try to ensure that at least

one influential group is prepared to "die in a ditch" to protect the reform. Think about polycentric governance and leadership models, and invest heavily in identifying and resourcing leaders and champions at all levels.

Guideline 6.9
Analyse where opposition is likely to come from and work hard to understand its drivers. What values or vested interests (real or perceived) feel threatened? What messages/strategies could be effective in defusing or countering opposition? Could the reform package be recast to capture the interests of potential losers without compromising its intent?

Guideline 6.10
Plan implementation very carefully. There is often a wide gap between policy intent and program practice. Think hard about allocating responsibility and resources at the right level to motivate successful implementation. Build capacity quickly. Ensure that the right people and agencies have the necessary training, resources and instruments to do the job well, and follow through. Implementation is about relationships at multiple levels. It is critical that the operational system is both technically competent and socially rewarding for all involved in policy delivery.

Guideline 6.11
Measure impact systematically from the outset (including impacts on "losers"), and adjust policy and program settings as required. Make sure you have more and better empirical data than anyone else, especially likely opponents of reform. Understand how implementation works and how success is interpreted in terms of the dominant political mores and theories of the day. Communicate benefits as early as possible, without over-reaching or making false claims, and keep communicating and refining the narrative. Never assume that the communication task to mobilise and sustain political support is complete. Reinterpret the burning platform as necessary. Assume that all wins are temporary and the case always needs to be made to claim them.

Guideline 6.12
Celebrate success (even modest wins) and reward champions at all levels.

Guideline 6.13
Be clear about the fundamental policy objectives and guidelines and stay true to them, while being flexible and adaptable in implementation to respond to changing circumstances, improvising practice and tweaking the narrative so that it resonates and legitimises progress as the "current" political context changes. For slow-moving issues such as many environmental problems, driven by ecological or hydrological processes that may operate over multi-decadal timeframes or even longer, it is crucial to remember that much policy reform is necessarily incremental, building on previous developments. Continued investment is often required to ensure that those '"old" measures (such as community Landcare) remain effective. Stay vigilant in

implementing reform to ensure that new measures don't undermine the foundations on which long-term progress ultimately depends.

Guideline 6.14

Continually recruit new political champions and identify new beneficiaries (while honouring the old ones) and help them to see the importance of sustaining the policy reform, so that the policy itself is reinvented if necessary (while remaining true to its principles) and is never taken for granted. Ensure that decision makers (and wider beneficiaries) are always aware that the costs and risks of unravelling or undermining the policy are much greater than any potential benefit from doing so. BUT, if the evidence is clear that the policy is not working, and it is clearly not a problem of poor implementation, then analyse why and start working on the next major reform. Be prepared to "disrupt yourself" rather than waiting for someone else to demolish your program.

Another way of conceptualising a transformational policy reform is to imagine three threads of parallel activity and focus: the policy content (what are we going to do and why); the political process (who will be affected, how, where and when); and the program implementation (what mix of policy instruments will be used, and how they will be delivered). If any one of these is underdone, the policy outcome is unlikely to be "sticky" or durable. It will not withstand the test of time.

Reviewing the Landcare and regional NRM policy reform journey against the ten general guidelines above, the scorecard is mixed (see Table 6.1).

TABLE 6.1 Landcare and regional NRM policy in Australia assessed against 10 guidelines for durable environmental policy reform

6.5	Burning platform	✔✔
6.6	Evidence base	±
6.7	Three lenses	±
6.8	Broad coalition	✔✔✔
6.9	Understand opposition	✗
6.10	Competent implementation	±
6.11	Measure impact systematically	✗
6.12	Celebrate success	✔✔
6.13	Policy clarity	✗✗✗
6.14	Sustaining reform	✗✗

From this analysis the most generous interpretation of Landcare policy reform against the guidelines elucidated above would be 6 out of 10, and a tougher marker wmight give 3 out of 10.

The original lack of policy clarity – that Landcare was essentially a social intervention, not a biophysical intervention, and hence its achievements need to be assessed in primarily social terms – feeds into all the other low scores in this table. This in turn meant that Australian administrators paid insufficient attention to social capital issues such as "vertical trust" between the respective layers of NRM governance. Recognition of this reveals the importance of specifying objectives in a manner that makes it more feasible that a subsequent review will judge the reform to be successful. Failure to do this meant that the wrong things were measured and tracked. Key metrics that underpinned the effectiveness of the whole policy direction were ignored.

Guideline 6.15
Interactions among policy elements are as important as the individual components. Never lose sight of the whole package, and think carefully about how diverse elements work together and how to ensure that they don't undermine previous gains, or each other.

Conclusion

In retrospect, it can be seen that prospects for successful implementation were undermined because there was competition among different elements of the system that should have come together in a collaborative, synergistic fashion. Failures in implementation and in building an evidence base of achievement inevitably corroded the foundations of the policy reform agenda and compromised its ultimate durability. As a result, to a considerable extent all three initiatives have been less successful than they could or should have been. In aggregate they failed to capture the potential synergies inherent in what could have been one of the world's best examples of nested, multilevel systems of community-based governance of natural resources.

Having observed Landcare in Australia for thirty years, as an active participant and leader in the early days and from a greater distance over the past decade, two messages emerge. First, the achievements of Landcare in mobilising such a large proportion of Australian rural and peri-urban landholders in voluntary neighbourhood groups to take responsibility for landscape restoration, changing what it means to be seen to be "a good farmer" in the process, have been remarkable. However, these achievements built a platform for what could have produced a profound transformation in the management of natural resources in Australia, had more attention been paid to the guidelines elucidated here in policy development and program implementation.

References

ANAO (2008) "Regional Delivery Model for the Natural Heritage Trust and the National Action Plan for Salinity and Water Quality", Audit Report No. 21 2007–08, The Australian National Audit Office, Canberra.

Campbell, A. (1994) *Landcare: Communities Shaping the Land and the Future*. Sydney: Allen and Unwin.

Campbell, A. (2009) "It's time to renew Landcare". *Agricultural Science* 2(09): 30–33.

Curtis, A. and Lefroy, T. (2010) "Beyond threat- and asset-based approaches to natural resource management in Australia!" *Australasian Journal of Environmental Management* 17(3): 134–41.

Curtis, A., Ross, H., Marshall, G., Baldwin, C., Cavaye, J., Freeman, C., Carr, A. and Syme, G. (2014) "The great experiment with devolved NRM governance: lessons from community engagement in Australia and New Zealand since the 1980s". *Australasian Journal of Environmental Management* 21(2): 175–99.

Head, B. (2008) "Three lenses of evidence-based policy". *Australian Journal of Public Administration* 67(1): 1–11.

Keane, B. and Razer, H. (2014) *A Short History of Stupid: The Decline of Reason and Why Public Debate Makes us Want to Scream*. Sydney: Allen and Unwin.

Marshall, G. (2008) *Community-based, Regional Delivery of Natural Resource Management: Building System-Wide Capacities to Motivate Voluntary Farmer Adoption of Conservation Practices*. RIRDC Publication No 08/175. Canberra: Rural Industries Research and Development Corporation.

Megalogenis, G. (2012) *The Australian Moment: How We Were Made for These Times*. Sydney: Penguin.

Robins, L. and Dovers, S. (2007) "NRM Regions in Australia: the 'Haves' and the 'Have Nots'". *Geographical Research* 45(3): 273–90.

Robins, L. and Kanowski, P. (2011) "Crying for our Country: eight ways in which Caring for our Country has undermined Australia's regional model for natural resource management". *Australasian Journal of Environmental Management*, 18(2): 88–108.

7

NEVER WASTE A CRISIS

Drought as an opportunity to bring robust water-policy reform to California

Dustin Garrick

Background

California has experienced sustained drought since 2011 with 94 percent of the state experiencing *severe drought* conditions or worse as of July 2015 according to the US drought monitor (Cody et al., 2015); the drought conditions from 2012 to 2014 may be the most severe in 1200 years (Griffin and Anchukaitis, 2014). It is often argued that severe drought creates opportunities for robust water reform provided there is adequate preparation before the window of opportunity opens (Grafton et al., 2013). This chapter uses the ongoing Californian drought since 2011 as a backdrop to search for guidelines that can be used by those interested in shaping policy to reduce systemic risk. The notion of robustness – the proposition that it is possible to design and implement constellations of institutional arrangements that are less prone to cascading failures – is introduced.

On February 14, 2014 President Obama toured California by plane, met with farmers and politicians and committed US$2 billion to relieve California and western US states from one of the most severe droughts on record. Water deliveries from the (California) State Water Project had been reduced to zero (0 percent of full allocations), leaving a vast territory fallowed. The drought, observed by Obama, has since intensified pressure on the state's already stressed ecosystems and infrastructure, leading to the first state-wide mandatory water restrictions in April 2015, followed by curtailment orders for some of the highest priority water rights in the state. In the context of over-allocated water resources and depleted aquifers, it is reasonable to wonder if thresholds and tipping points are nearing for the state's inter-connected food, energy and water supply systems.

Guideline 7.1
Systemic failures are most likely to occur when sustained droughts combine with governance deficits to cause shortage risks that cascade across connected physical, social and economic systems.

The ongoing California drought exposes the systemic risks associated with connected food, energy and water systems in California – a region facing both chronic resource competition and the effects of climate variability and change. The stakes are not trivial. Agriculture was a US$54 billion industry in California in 2014. Although a tiny fraction of the state's economic production, the sector is important in absolute terms and through its role in the global commodity markets. Overall, California produces one-third of the vegetables and two-thirds of the fruits and nuts in the US. Exports to Canada, the EU, China, Japan and Mexico among others comprise US$21 billion per year, linking California with global markets. California therefore brings the drivers, consequences and policy dimensions of food, energy and water into sharp relief and frames a set of important risks and trade-offs both today and in the future.

Systemic risks, systemic response? Striving for policy coherence and multi-level governance capacity

A range of legal, regulatory and incentive-based tools have been developed to reduce systemic risk by empowering users to manage shortage risk before impacts cascade through connected environmental and economic systems. Robustness starts with enhancing information and incentives faced by water users. Dry-year agreements are one prominent option for building robustness and resilience to systemic risks in California. Alfalfa, livestock and relatively low-value agriculture provide a buffer during drought through a market-based mechanism that allows California's large cities to enter into dry-year agreements with large irrigation districts. In dry years, the low-value agricultural land is fallowed and the resultant water savings transferred to urban-water use. Such tools require policy coherence and governance capacity across multiple levels.

Guideline 7.2
Crises create significant opportunities for the introduction of policies that reduce deeply embedded systemic risks.

Systemic risks can lead to "breakdowns in an entire system, as opposed to breakdowns in individual parts or components, and are evidenced by co-movements amongst most or all of the parts" (Kaufman and Scott, 2003, cited in Goldin and Vogel, 2010). In a globalizing and interdependent world, systemic risk is important because of complexity and invisible relationships that contribute to ripple effects and spill-overs that are hard to predict and even harder to control.

Often applied to the financial system, systemic risk provides a compelling lens with which to explore the reasons why so many food, energy and water management systems are failing. The 2013 World Economic Forum (WEF) annual survey of global risks, for example, identified water supply shocks as a "centre of gravity" connecting food, energy and climate threats. The 2014 version of the survey identified water crises and food shocks among the 10 concerns for society and noted their strong interdependencies. By 2015, water crises had been identified as the highest impact risk.

Systemic risk requires systemic policy responses that enable adaptation, strengthen and/or create a suite of institutional arrangements that shift and coordinate responsibilities and expectations (Goldin and Vogel, 2010). In this chapter, the onset of sustained years of "drought" in California is used as a means of identifying how systemic risks emerge and can be resolved. This includes examination of complex policy and governance arrangements, including fledgling efforts to coordinate across sectors.

The overall insight is that crises are powerful because systemic risks present openings for transformational change. However, systemic risks can lead to a robust solution only when transformational policy reforms have already been proposed, tested and accepted by influential policy entrepreneurs prior to the crisis. When knowledge about the nature of a transformational change required to reduce systemic risk is missing, governments still have to be seen to respond. In such cases, typically, they respond by putting in place arrangements that discourage change and tend to have the unfortunate tendency of increasing the probability that the depth of the next crisis will be worse (as argued by Christian-Smith *et al.*, 2014, in their review of adaptations to drought in California from 2007 to 2009). The approach is short-term. Resolution of the long-term underlying problem is left to another day – especially if it is not expected to reoccur for a few years. In the case of a severe drought, for example, and as shown in Chapter 9 in this book, governments routinely ration access and subsidize actions that alleviate short-term impacts.

Guideline 7.3
Clarify roles and responsibilities to ensure accountability and provide incentives for local innovation coupled with trans-boundary coordination.

In the US, authority for water allocation is vested with the state government; therefore systemic risks have required "polycentric", but coordinated, responses to facilitate local action and cooperation by state governments in basin-wide and regional planning. Given the lack of federal authority over water allocation, as noted above, President Obama was able to offer cash – an important pathway to federal influence over water allocation. The White House has since established new initiatives to spur technological innovations in water and enhance the role of private investment and incentives to share access to scarce water resources, promote the development of a culture of preparedness and use the drought as an opening for enhanced federal leadership in water, which has been rare historically. In this context, California has exhibited its willingness to seize the ongoing drought (as of 2016) as an opportunity to identify and respond to systemic risks with two important, if partial, measures: a US$7.5 billion Water Bond and the Sustainable Groundwater Management Act.[1]

California is also part of interstate institutions governing the Colorado River, which has witnessed a transformation in historically antagonistic relations among the seven US and two Mexican states, and cities, tribes, farmers, energy utilities, and ecosystem uses depending on the river. This transformation in relations has been highlighted by the 2007 Record of Decision for coordinated management of Lake Mead and Lake Powell under surplus and shortage conditions, as well as Minute 319, the much celebrated update to the 1944 US–Mexico Water Treaty enacting binational shortage sharing, infrastructure financing and ecosystem restoration. The California groundwater and bond legislation in 2014, and the interstate progress in the Colorado River, show the need to define roles and develop capacity at multiple levels, while establishing platforms to coordinate and resolve conflicts.

California water, drought and resource interdependencies

Droughts highlight the interdependencies and connections across food, energy, environmental and water systems and the economic and political systems they underpin. California's long history of water and economic development sets the context for the challenges and opportunities for transformation today (Hundley, 2001).[2]

Water

Writing in the *New York Times*, Peter Passel noted that "California's water system might have been invented by a Soviet Bureaucrat on an LSD trip" (cited in Hanak et al., 2011). From Hollywood's treatment of the Owens Valley Transfer in *Chinatown* to contemporary images of depleted reservoirs, California's water system has achieved mythic status for its engineering feats (reservoirs, canals) that have harnessed and distributed its variable water supplies and, up until now, limited the need to plan for a severe water shortage.

Guideline 7.4
Define the boundaries of the system and its range of historic and potential future variability.

A distinctive feature of California's development history is that it has largely decoupled from its rivers and aquifers to create an interconnected "system" with "plumbing" that transports water great distances from regions of relative water abundance to relative scarcity. Inter-basin transfers are common. The water supplies of the Colorado River, the Central Valley and the Owens Valley are linked together (Figure 7.1).

FIGURE 7.1 California's surface water system (Hanak *et al.*, 2011)

California's water system emerged in response to its hydro-climatic variability – both spatial and temporal. Some 75 percent of the state's precipitation falls north of Sacramento, while 75 percent of state demand is south of this point. Reconciling this mismatch has led to a system of more than 1400 dams, a byzantine network of canals, and the development of hundreds of groundwater basins (Hanak *et al.*, 2011).

Major sources of water supply include surface water (including imported supplies from the Colorado River), groundwater, and reuse. The water system is a major consumer of energy to move water where it's needed. The environmental cost has been high, and unacceptably so by contemporary standards. For example, the area of wetlands in the Central Valley has declined to 5 percent of historic levels (Department of Water Resources, 2013). This has led to multi-billion dollar restoration and recovery programs, highlighted by the Bay Delta at the confluence of the San Joaquin and Sacramento Rivers of central California.

Superimposed on the spatial mismatches in water supply and demand are seasonal and inter-annual variability buffered by an extensive groundwater source. The majority of annual runoff is derived from snowmelt in late spring and early summer each year; and the region is prone to sustained droughts. Streamflows vary annually from 200 percent to less than 25 percent of average annual levels (Hanak *et al.*, 2011). Sequences of dry years contribute to sustained droughts exemplified by the ongoing drought in California and the unprecedented 14-year period of below-average flows in the Colorado River. The potential for synchronous droughts across California's multiple surface water sources is a systemic risk due to severe shortages on multiple surface water sources, intensifying pressure on groundwater (MacDonald, 2010).

Groundwater forms a critical component of California's water system (Famiglietti, 2014; see also Figure 7.2). Access to groundwater was limited by pumping technology and energy supplies until the early twentieth century, when pumps could reach 300 feet in depth and deeper. Groundwater now comprises up to 40 percent of water use, with the dependence varying by location and access to surface water (from almost 90 percent in the Central Coast to about 10 percent in the Colorado River region) with a tendency to increase as much as two-fold during drought (Hanak *et al.*, 2011; DWR, 2013). Groundwater use provides an important buffer, but temporary relief comes with long-term consequences as water levels decline.

As shown in Figure 7.2, in recent years there has been a dramatic decline in groundwater levels. From 2003 to 2010, central California lost 30 km^3 in groundwater storage. This is the equivalent to the storage contained in Lake Mead on the Colorado River (Famiglietti *et al.*, 2011) – a decrease of over 3 km^3 per year. The current drought accelerated these declines to almost 10 km^3 per year in 2012 and 2013 (Famiglietti, 2014).

Water rights: from prior appropriation to allocation flexibility?

Guideline 7.5
Good measurement and information underpin robust entitlement and allocation regimes.

Water rights have developed in parallel with the state's extensive water infrastructure. The roots of contemporary water institutions and governance arrangements trace back to the Spanish and Mexican customs and laws of the earliest settlers, which gave way to the common law guidelines of nineteenth-century miners. Hanak *et al.* (2011)

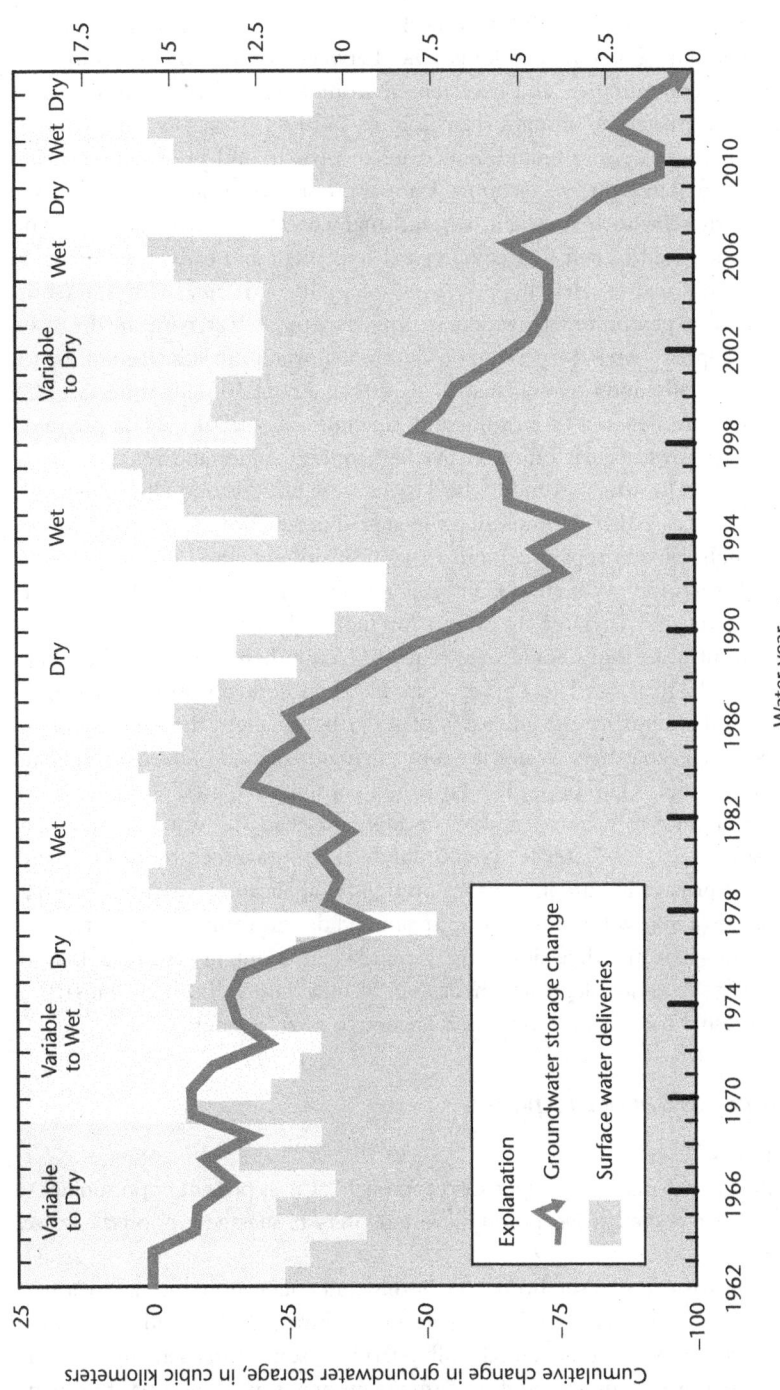

FIGURE 7.2 Cumulative groundwater losses and surface water deliveries in California's Central Valley since 1962 (C. Faunt, USGS, pers. comm., 2016)

identify four eras of this evolution: laissez faire, irrigation development and municipal water supply by local organizations, the hydraulic dam-building era, and the contemporary era of conflict among different users, stakeholders and so on. The contemporary era is marked by conflict between consumptive users in cities and irrigation communities, and between environmental and consumptive users, which are exacerbated by drought (Hanak et al., 2014).

California relies upon a complex mixture of riparian and prior appropriation (first in time, first in right) water rights. Prior appropriation assigns priority during shortage to those who first established and maintained a "beneficial use". This system was designed in part to facilitate rural settlement and early investments in irrigation infrastructure, first by private associations and later with substantial federal capital expenditures. Irrigation is now the largest water use in the state, comprising approximately 80 percent of (developed) water use after accounting for farms and associated industries (Hanak et al., 2011). About 10 million hectares (25 million acres) are devoted to farming and ranching (Ross, 2014). The premium associated with irrigation is captured by the property values and rental rates. In 2011, rental rates for irrigated and dryland farms were US$340 and US$40 per acre, respectively (Ross, 2014). Drought has threatened production, particularly for the perennial high valued crops (Radonic, 2014). Surprisingly, and unlike Australia, agricultural water use in much of California remains unmetered and, hence, there is little incentive for irrigators to search for more efficient ways to save water. Similarly, most water right holders are required to use their water for a beneficial use. As a result, they need to be very careful when contemplating investing in technologies that improve the efficiency of water use financed through the sale of the "saved" water to others. Water use for growing urban and industrial water and energy security needs comprise the next largest consumptive uses.

Allocation patterns have been slow to adjust to changing water supplies and values (Garrick, 2015). Water leases and purchases are governed by a "no harm" standard that places the burden of proof on transfer applicants to demonstrate that proposed transaction will not impair upstream and downstream water rights. Poor measurement of water diversions and groundwater pumping create a lack of accountability, pervasive legal and hydrological uncertainty and high transaction costs. As a result, there is little economic incentive to save water.

Policy and governance responses

Guideline 7.6
Policy coherence depends on a "portfolio approach". Crises present opportunities to identify and overcome barriers posed by vested interests affected proposed reforms.

The drought has exposed the brittleness of this water allocation system, creating a "focusing event" and a catalyst for long-needed reforms. In 2014 and 2015, water deliveries were reduced for Central Valley farmers, some rural settlements were forced to truck water supplies and investments in new supply infrastructure were prioritised. In the past, it had been assumed that more water infrastructure could always be built and/or that groundwater pumping could be used to bridge the gap. The idea that California might have to live with and plan for absolute water scarcity was foreign – at least at the state level – until recent planning initiatives and the 2014 Sustainable Groundwater Management Act required new efforts to plan and monitor groundwater use. The policy mechanisms necessary to enable rapid autonomous responses to absolute water scarcity were and still are largely missing from the dialogue that is underway. Despite similar (or even higher) levels of competition for water in California, the state's water market is limited to approximately 5 percent of annual water use, in contrast with the Southern Connected Murray of Australia, which approaches 40 percent of annual water use.

A "systemic" response to these problems requires a portfolio approach with multiple, complementary safeguards:

- cumulative limits on ground and surface water abstractions;
- proportional shares of available water (as occurs within some irrigation districts and federal projects within California);
- monitoring and compliance with the limits; and
- sustained investment in arrangements that enable the autonomous resolution of supply imbalances.

To date, however, the response has been to leave surface water arrangements largely unchanged. The 2014 Sustainable Groundwater Management Act now requires groundwater users to enact resource management plans prior to 2040. The historic users and infrastructure create dependencies and vested interests that stand to lose from these changes, even if the region and system as a whole is better off. Strategies to build a winning coalition for the reforms require the identification and engagement of those who stand to lose and the recruitment of new champions (stakeholder groups, individuals) for change, such as chambers of commerce.

There have been increasing calls to transform the water-right regime used in California into, for example, one that allows speedy adjustment to changing supply and demand conditions, as enacted in the water planning and water rights reforms in the Southern Connected Murray of Australia. According to Young (2014, 2015), this requires:

- preparation of statutory management plans of such prescriptive detail that allocation decisions, transfers, etc., would rarely end up in the courts;
- conversion of existing water rights into shares of high, medium or low security entitlement pools;
- unbundling of water rights so that:
    - allocations are made in proportion to the number of shares held, recorded in water accounts of guaranteed integrity and made tradeable according to pre-specified rules; and

- beneficial use requirements are transferred to separate site-specific land-use controls;
• creation of independent expertise-based boards empowered, after appropriate consultation, to finalise management plans, make allocations, etc., in a timely manner.

Food

Guideline 7.7
Policy coherence requires accounting for food and energy systems, and the drivers and interactions affecting water supply, demand and allocation during droughts.

With nearly 80 percent of the state's developed water supply being used by the agricultural sector, it is no surprise that farmers and agriculture organizations have had a huge stake, and influence, in the development of water infrastructure and conservation efforts.

California's irrigation systems depend heavily upon water from Lower Colorado Basin and produce more than one-third of the US's vegetables and nearly two-thirds of its fruits and nuts (Ross, 2014). The health of the state's agriculture, especially the amount of irrigated acreage, is largely determined by several factors, including water availability, impacts of drought, the increasing impact of agriculture-to-urban water transfers and land conversion (Cohen et al., 2013). The amount of irrigated acreage within the Colorado River basin in California has declined by about 8.6 percent, or 54,000 acres, between 2000 and 2009 (Cohen et al., 2013).

An important consideration within the agricultural sector in California and throughout the US is the large number of insurance payouts being made to farmers, which has the potential to mask the seriousness of the drought crisis (McColl and Young, 2007). In 2012, a record number of US farmers received payouts, to a grand total of US$15 billion. These kinds of payouts may eliminate risk for larger commodity growers but not independent farmers (Oxfam, 2014). The most recent US Farm Bill, which passed in 2014, shows the stakes are high: the government has allocated, over the next 10 years, US$90 billion for crop insurance (nationwide), an increase of US$7 billion from the last bill, and US$57.6 billion for conservation programs, including the promotion of healthy soil, more ecologically friendly irrigation methods and the reduction of land use (Plumer, 2014) – all key strategies in the effort to mitigate the impacts of the current drought now and in the future.

Energy

The energy sector is second to agriculture in overall water consumption in the US. The water sector is also energy dependent, requiring vast quantities of electricity to move water where it is needed and to treat it. However, over the past several decades, there has been a perceived disconnect between water, food and energy.

Rising energy costs and the need for diversified and renewable energy sources due to climate change have triggered concerns that the energy sector may use (and pollute) an increasing amount of the state's freshwater resources (Newsha and Truelove, 2014).

California's energy crisis in the late 1990s resulted in the development of some of the country's most innovative energy programs, including a 2003 energy action plan that evaluated the potential to save electricity and natural gas by reducing the energy needed to transport, treat and convey water. Against this backdrop, California also implemented in 2006 the Global Warming Solutions Act, with the goal of lowering the water sector's energy needs (Newsha and Truelove, 2014). Six measures were promoted including enhanced recycled water programs, increasing storm water capture, promoting water conservation and increasing renewable energy generation in the water and wastewater sector, such as biomass, solar, wind and in-conduit hydro.

As the state helps lead the development of alternative forms of energy, however, careful attention should be paid to the trade-offs within the water sector. Natural gas, for instance, boasts a low carbon footprint, but research is lacking on the impact of degraded return flows which is discharged into municipal water systems (Newsha and Truelove, 2014; West Wit, 2013). Thermo-electric power generation has even more direct impact on water, with its high-press steam process requiring significant water withdrawals (WITW, 2013). Overall, going forward, climate change will impact the direction of infrastructure within both the energy and water sectors, but communication and coordination between the two will be the key to success.

Hidden trade-offs: connecting knowledge and action

Sustained drought in California has focused attention on the systemic risks confronting California today and in the future. The overview and policy gaps summarized above point to a set of broad guidelines that can be adapted to other contexts.

Despite the growing recognition of systemic risk and resource interdependencies, planning and policy have failed to stimulate systemic responses. The recent commitments to the commencement of long-term water planning in California and the Colorado River have started to address these deficiencies. New plans will, in particular, be expected to account for climate change risks and consider water-energy and water-food interactions. But a commitment to consider issues does not necessarily generate a solution. The efforts are far from what is required to address the underlying systemic failure to establish mechanisms that force businesses and governments to plan and for investors to make trade-offs.

Unless much more robust arrangements are put in place, triage-based approaches will remain the norm with high costs to the environment and to communities. From these observations we can identify several further guidelines.

Guideline 7.8
To reduce the risks of systemic failures, it is necessary to reform the policy arrangements that shape decision making.

Guideline 7.9
The resolution of complex trade-offs requires new optics, new indicators and new means of communication. These need to include arrangements that make the costs and benefits of inaction transparent. Benefits for those that win and costs to those that lose need to be more visible.

Guideline 7.10
Policy coherence involves high transaction costs, and planning can identify where the most urgent gaps and trade-offs merit the expense.

Guideline 7.11
Crises provide the window for change but, when the solution to the crisis is not well understood, also the potential for maladaptation and triage-based approaches that exacerbate systemic risks.

MacDonald et al. (2010) observe that sustainability is at once a simple matter of two variables – supply and demand – but systemic risk brings with it complexity and competition. Writing in the context of projected climate change impacts on California's already stressed water systems, Tanaka et al. (2006) note that:

> adaptation will be costly in absolute terms and include transaction, institutional, and fixed costs not quantified ... but, if properly managed, should not threaten the fundamental prosperity of California's economy or society, although it can have major effects on the agricultural and environmental sectors.
>
> (cited in MacDonald et al., 2010)

In short, systemic risk management requires a system-wide response. In California, a suite of new institutional arrangements and a culture that faces up to and deals with absolute water scarcity is needed. The most fundamental observation that can be made is that the current water rights and water management system has systemic risks. Significant respecification of these rights is needed.

Notes

1. The 2014 Sustainable Groundwater Management Act represents a milestone in groundwater regulation, albeit still partial and with 25 years until full implementation.
2. This section draws heavily from Hanak et al. (2011).

References

Christian-Smith, J., Levy, M.C. and Gleick, P.H. (2014) "Maladaptation to drought: a case report from California, USA". *Sustainability Science* 1–11. doi: 10.1007/s11625-014-0269-1.
Cody, B.A., Folger, P. and Brown, C. (2015) "California Drought: Hydrological and Regulatory Water Supply Issues". 7-5700 (R40979). Washington, DC: Congressional Research Service.
Cohen, M.J., Christian-Smith, J. and Berggren, J. (2013) "Water To Supply The Land: Irrigated Agriculture in the Colorado River Basin". Pacific Institute, Oakland, California.
Department of Water Resources (2013) "California Water Plan". California Department of Water Resources.
Famiglietti, J. (2014) "Epic California Drought and Groundwater: Where Do We Go From Here?". National Geographic Society. Available at: http://newswatch.nationalgeographic.com/2014/02/04/epic-california-drought-and-groundwater-where-do-we-go-from-here/ (accessed 9 May 2016).
Famiglietti, J.S., Lo, M., Ho, S.L., Bethune, J., Anderson, K.J. and others (2011) "Satellites measure recent rates of groundwater depletion in California's Central Valley". *Geophysical Research Letters* 38(3): L03403, doi:10.1029/2010GL046442.
Garrick, D. E. (2015) *Water Allocation in Rivers under Pressure: Water Trading, Transaction Costs and Transboundary Governance in the Western US and Australia*. Cheltenham: Edward Elgar Publishing.
Goldin, I. and Vogel, T. (2010) "Global governance and systemic risk in the 21st century: Lessons from the financial crisis". *Global Policy* 1: 4–15.
Grafton, R.Q, Pittock, J., Davis, R., Williams, J., Fu, G., Warburton, M., Udall, B., McKenzie, R., Yu, X. and Che, N. (2013) "Global insights into water resources, climate change and governance". *Nature Climate Change* 3 (4): 315–21.
Griffin, J. and Anchukaitis, K.J. (2014) "How unusual is the 2012–2014 California drought". *Geophysical Research Letters* 41(24): 9017–23.
Hanak, E. L., Lund, J., Dinar, A., Grey, B., Howitt, R., Mount, J., Moyle, P. and Thompson, B. (2011) "Managing California's water: From conflict to reconciliation". Public Policy Institute of California, San Francisco.
Hanak, E., Mount, J., Chappelle, C. (2014) "California's Latest Drought". Public Policy Institute of California, San Francisco.
Hundley, N. (2001) *The Great Thirst: Californians and Water – A History*, rev. edn. Oakland, CA: University of California Press.
McColl, J.C. and Young, M.D. (2007) "Managing Change: Australian structural adjustment lessons for water". CSIRO Land and Water Report No. 16/05.
MacDonald, G.M. (2010) "Climate Change and water in Southwestern North America special feature: water, climate change, and sustainability in the southwest". *Proceedings of the National Academy of Sciences of the USA* 107: 21256–62.
Newsha, K.A. and Truelove, C. (2014) "A Water-Energy Research Agenda: Building California's Policy Foundation for the 21st Century Water in the West". Stanford Woods Institute for the Environment and The Bill Lane Center for the American West.
Oxfam (2014) "Hot and hungry: how to stop climate change derailing the fight against hunger". Oxfam.
Plumer, B. (2014) "The US$956 billion farm bill, in one graph". *The Washington Post*, 28 January. Available at: www.washingtonpost.com/blogs/wonkblog/wp/2014/01/28/the-950-billion-farm-bill-in-one-chart/ (accessed 9 May 2016).

Radonic, L. (2014) "Drought in the Golden State Challenges Agriculture". The University of Arizona, College of Agriculture and Life Sciences, Spring 2014 Newsletter. Available at: https://wrrc.arizona.edu/drought-california-agriculture (accessed 9 May 2016).

Ross, K. (2014) "California Agricultural Statistics Review". California Department of Food and Agriculture.

Tanaka, S.K., Zhu, T., Lund, J.R., Howitt, R.E., Jenkins, M.W. and others (2006) "Climate warming and water management adaptation for California". *Climatic Change* 76: 361–87.

Water in the West (WITW) (2013) "Water and Energy Nexus: A Literature Review". Stanford Woods Institute for the Environment and Bill Lane Center for the American West.

Young, M. (2014) "Designing water abstraction regimes for an ever-changing and ever-varying future". *Agricultural Water Management* 145: 32–8.

Young, M. (2015) "Unbundling Water Rights: A Blueprint for development of robust water allocation systems in the western United States". NI R 15–01 Durham, NC: Duke University. Available at: http://nicholasinstitute.duke.edu/publications (accessed 9 May 2016).

8

DEVELOPMENT OF WATER MARKETS IN CHINA[1]

Scott M. Moore

China is facing an acute water scarcity challenge. Driven by population growth, demographic change and rapid economic development, a dramatic increase in urban and industrial water use is occurring (Yong, 2009). Given this situation, it is easy to recommend that China should include water rights trading in the suite of mechanisms it uses to manage water scarcity. China, however, is a socialist economy with little history of formal property rights and market-based approaches to environmental policy problems. Given this background, the proposition that China might consider using water rights trading to help resolve its increasingly acute water scarcity challenges seems impossible. Yet, this is what this country is trying to do.

China has made it clear that it wants to and, increasingly, will use water rights trading as one of the foundations for the development of a "water-saving society" (Xia and Pahl-Wostl, 2012). The overall approach being taken emphasises the need to build the water right permitting systems necessary to keep use within limits and trial ways to use water rights trading to allow adjustment within these limits as conditions change. Pilot tests and trials are being used to improve administrative understanding and test the feasibility of this approach. If implemented on a national scale, this proposed reform would transform Chinese water management and investment in water using technoologies (see Figure 8.1).

Anatomy of water rights trading in China

In order to properly evaluate the role that water rights trading has and might play in helping to resolve China's water scarcity challenges, it is necessary first to detail some peculiarities in the development and implementation of water markets in China.

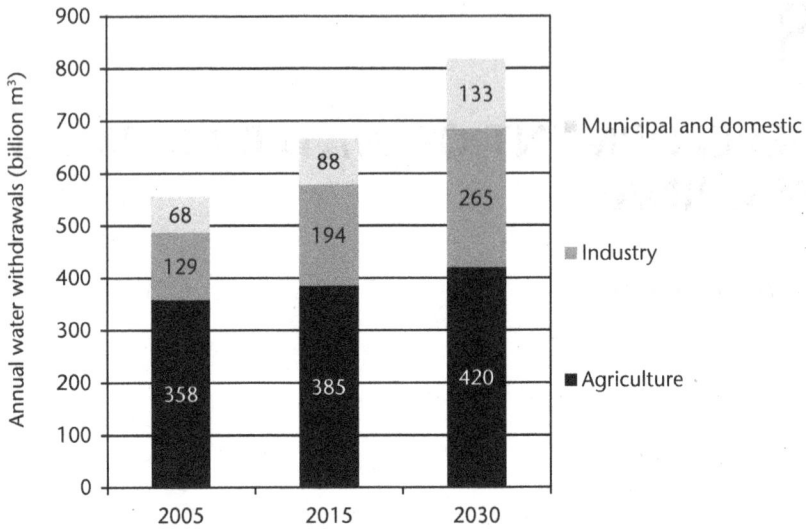

FIGURE 8.1 Predicted changes in demand for water in China (2030 Water Resources Group)

Historically water resource allocation and management has been conducted through administrative usage permissions (Webber *et al.*, 2008). The historical administrative and legal model used is one that first makes it clear that all water rights are owned by the state and that provinces are responsible for the issuing of permits (Gao, 2007; Zhang and Jia, 2012). This abstraction-permit (*qushui kexu*) system for water resource allocation, formalized in China's 1988 Water Law, however, does provide for the "compensated" transfer of abstraction permits (Wang, 2013). The legal opportunity to trade water permits was established many years ago.

Guideline 8.1
Before implementing a policy transformational reform, bed down the institutional arrangements necessary to facilitate the change.

Recognising the extent of the transformation required to enable the wider use of trading, in recent years the Ministry of Water Resources has pursued a policy of "promoting water rights and moving toward the market". To this end, they have been establishing water quantity controls, strengthening the legal foundations of water rights and promoting water conservation (Wang, 2013). Trials and pilot tests are being encouraged.

More forcefully in 2001, the Ministry of Water Resources began to require irrigation districts, cities and other large water users to hold a right, in the form of a permit, to consume a specific quantity of water. These arrangements were formally incorporated into Chinese law through revisions to the Water Law promulgated in

2002. Subsequent regulations have strengthened opportunities to trade water rights between regions. Further emphasising the Ministry of Water Resources commitment to the development of water trading, in 2005, administrators at provincial and local levels were instructed to "take water rights seriously and establish appropriate water rights systems" (Zhang and Jia, 2012). Viewed as crucial for establishing a well-functioning water market, however, the initial allocation of water rights has been left to provincial and local administrators (Shen, 2012).

According to 2006 guidelines issued by the State Council, each province must develop a framework to manage water abstractions, including establishing provisions for reviewing abstraction permit applications. When issuing permits, provinces are supposed to consider sustainability, water scarcity, and other factors in making their decisions, but otherwise are free to formulate their own policies (Gao, 2007).

Three case studies

Further understanding of the Chinese experience can be gained from case studies involving the transfer of water between:

- jurisdictions;
- sectors; and
- individuals.

Each of the case studies is characterised by the fact that the use of water trading had obvious benefits to the entities involved and was neither politically nor administratively challenging.

Transferring water between two cities

Guideline 8.2
When trialling a new policy, begin, if possible, by working with jurisdictions that have a history of collaborating with one another.

The negotiation of an agreement to transfer water between two cities, Yiwu and Dongyang, in Zhejiang Province breaks the top-down regulatory model for water resource allocation in China. In this case, two cities in the same province agreed to work together to find a more efficient way to meet their collective needs.

The level of water conservation investment in Zhejiang was already relatively high, as was the general level of economic development and the resources available to both Yiwu and Dongyang cities. The two cities also enjoyed a history of unusually close cooperation, manifested in a "special partnership" status. City officials communicated frequently and business relationships between the two cities were already extensive at the time of the deal. As several Dongyang leaders put it, "The two cities see themselves as a single integrated market ... and view cooperation from a strategic perspective' (Wang, 2013). Dongyang, for its part, had entered into water supply contracts before, and so was well-disposed to a proposal from Yiwu that they should agree to trade some of their rights in return for money that would enable them to increase the amount of water that they could store.

Billed as a water rights trade, the cities of Yiwu and Dongyang agreed to work cooperatively to improve access to water. The final arrangement required Dongyang to upgrade its reservoir and transfer some of its water entitlement to Yiwu. In return Yiwu would pay Dongyang 200 million RMB plus an annual 0.1 RMB/m^3 reservoir management fee. The long-term nature of the agreement and investment was designed to provide water security for Yiwu. As a city official put it, "spending money buys certainty" (Wang, 2013).

Beginning in 1998, the downstream city Yiwu contributed 3.1 million RMB towards the upgrade of a reservoir upstream of Dongyang. This enhanced Dongyang's ability to store water by 10,000 m^3. A further 35.7 million RMB was also invested in water conservation projects that saved an additional 13,000 m^3. The result made more water available to both cities at a cost of 0.73 RMB/m^3 and, because of the associated transfer of water rights, saved Yiwu 100 million RMB (Yi, 2010; Wang, 2013).

Inter-sectoral transfers: Ningxia and Inner Mongolia autonomous regions

Guideline 8.3
Use pilot tests to demonstrate the extent of the benefits attainable from a transformational reform.

As China develops, it is clear that water will need to be transferred from the agricultural to the industrial and urban sectors. The need for this is particularly apparent in the autonomous regions of Ningxia and Inner Mongolia. In these regions, increasing industrial water demands coupled with physical water scarcity has created a pressing need for the re-allocation of water. To this end, in 2003, Ningxia submitted a proposal for the investment of some 47 million RMB in irrigation conservation projects that would produce 144 million m^3 of water savings that could then be transferred to industry without adversely affecting agricultural production. Along with a further two pilot projects initiated shortly afterwards, some 19.22 km of canals were lined to reduce losses and transfer the 539 million m^3 saved from agriculture to industry. The cost of facilitating this transfer was 2.68–3.1 RMB/m^3 (Zhang, 2012).

Building upon this initial experience, in 2008, the Yellow River Conservancy Commission approved the transfer of a further 26 water rights transfer projects involving the reallocation of a total of 23 million m^3 of water at a cost of 123 million RMB (Wang, 2013). This investment in water conservation reportedly halved the quantity of water required for irrigation and reduced the cost of supplying water to farmers by a third. Investment in these projects, rather incredibly, represented ten times the total investment in irrigation water conservation over the preceding 50 years (Zhang, 2012).

However, much like the case of inter-jurisdictional transfers between Yiwu and Dongyang, inter-sectoral water rights transfer projects in Ningxia and Inner Mongolia do not represent a pure water rights trade. The trade also involves investments that increased the total amount of water available. As several Chinese water resource scholars point out, pilot projects in Ningxia and Inner Mongolia represent transfers of water usage rights under government leadership, rather than true water rights trading between economic actors (Zhang, 2012).

In an attempt to encourage others to search for ways to make similar savings, the Ministry of Water Resources is actively promoting the benefits of coupling water trading with investments in conservation. There remains, however, a long way to go before provinces accept the need for permit holders to keep use within defined limits.

Individual short-term trading: Shiyang River Basin, Gansu Province

Guideline 8.4
Use pilot tests to find ways to help resolve administrative tensions and build capacity.

The third pilot test involves irrigators in the Shiyang River Basin in Gansu Province. The decision to trial water rights trading in the Shiyang Basin was driven primarily by a combination of physical water scarcity and long-standing tensions between upstream and downstream water users. In the early 2000s, groundwater abstraction was estimated at 135 percent of the natural rate of recharge, and irrigation accounted for 86 percent of basin water use (Zhang, 2012). In 2005, the Gansu provincial government approved a plan to reduce basin water consumption by 60 million m^3 annually, largely through agricultural water conservation and strict limits on groundwater use, while also providing for environmental water requirements (Gao, 2007).

The plan involved the initial allocation of water rights to individual water users coupled with an emphasis on the engagement of individual water users and investment in water metering technologies (Zhang, 2012). With these arrangements in place, individual irrigators where encouraged to trade their rights with one another. Distinctive features that differentiate this trial from other water management arrangements include the use of water user associations rather than irrigation districts to hold water rights on behalf of users, the installation of smart meters on individual wells, the monitoring of abstractions and the setting of trading rules (Gao, 2007). In response, the basin has recently developed an online platform in an attempt to increase peasant participation and monitoring capability (see Table 8.1). The Shiyang Basin project thus follows the Western model of individual water rights allocation found in some parts of Australia and Chile (Young, 2014).

TABLE 8.1 Recent water trades in the Shiyang River Basin

Record number	Trade date	Buyer type	Seller type	Market water price (RMB/m³)	Quantity of water traded (10,000 m³)
1	Dec-13	Water User Association	Water User Association	0.03	0.6
2	Dec-13	Village	Village	0.2	8
3	Dec-13	Village	Village	0.2	8
4	Nov-13	Group	Group	0.05	0.26
5	Nov-13	Group	Group	0.05	0.2
	Nov-13	Village	Village	0.2	5
7	Nov-13	Water User Association	Water User Association	0.04	5
8	Nov-13	Village	Village	0.17	0.17

Source: Gansu Shiyanghe Liuyu Jiaoyi Zhongxin (Gansu Shiyang River Basin Trading Center) (2013).

The Shiyang Basin example stands out for the degree to which the central government has encouraged the establishment of water rights trading. The Basin has played host to a number of acute tensions between water users, attracting the attention of the Communist Party Central Committee and the State Council. The degree of high-level interest is indicated by the fact that former Premier Wen Jiabao had, by 2007, visited the Shiyang Basin no fewer than eight times (Gao, 2007). Yet even this high-level attention did not prevent the Shiyang Basin pilot project from experiencing a number of challenges.

Foremost, the initial allocation of water rights in the Shiyang Basin conflicted with the allocation plans of individual localities within the Basin, in the words of one commentator, "undermining the government's credibility and [water users'] respect for the law". Furthermore, the pilot project failed to establish sanctions for abstracting water without possessing the necessary usage rights (Gao, 2007). Finally, as Table 8.1 indicates, both trading prices and the volume traded are quite low, reflecting an immature market for water rights (Gansu Shiyanghe Liuyu Jiaoyi Zhongxin [Gansu Shiyang River Basin Trading Center], 2013). These basic problems may yet be rectified: as one interviewee stated, "the Ministry of Water Resources has plenty of power to implement water rights trading".

Challenges to the development of water markets in China

Documentary sources and interview research conducted for this chapter sheds light on how the distinctive aspects of water rights trading translates into challenges for the future development of water markets both in China and elsewhere.

Definition, enforcement, and participation

Guideline 8.5
Begin by clarifying and formalising existing arrangements. Focus on building the legal institutions and administrative capacity necessary to ensure success.

The first set of challenges concerns definition of rights, knowledge and communication. Chinese water resource experts have long emphasized the unclear legal foundations of water rights trading in China. These deficiencies include a failure in many areas to clearly define rights and make annual allocations. In many cases, the duration of granted water rights is uncertain and, in particular, it is not clear if the rights will remain after the trial has been completed (Gao, 2007). In Ningxia and Inner Mongolia, for example, there is a low percentage of verified water rights trades, large differences between estimated and actual water savings, and uncertainty as to whether water rights refer to abstraction or to actual consumption (Zhang, 2012).

The lack of clarity surrounding water rights entitlements has created two challenges. Firstly, agricultural water use in China is dominated by irrigation districts, which constitute the primary unit of agricultural production (Wang, 2013). Within irrigation districts, water rights are effectively communal, making it very difficult to assign rights to individual users (Moore, 2014: 15-BJ).[2] The lack of clarity surrounding water entitlements within irrigation districts reduces incentives to invest in water conservation technologies, since it is unclear who should benefit from trading the resulting savings (Gao, 2007). One option, being tested in the Gansu Province trial, is to empower water user associations rather than irrigation districts to make and manage allocations. Secondly, the unclear legal foundations for water rights in China undermines the goal of protecting environmental water requirements. Despite being mandated by regulation, it is unclear who is supposed to designate and protect environmental interests and ensure that enough water is set aside for environmental purposes (Moore, 2014: 19-BJ).

Another major impediment to the implementation of water rights trading systems concerns the monitoring and enforcement of water rights. Throughout much of China, individual water user compliance with the permitting system is weak and, consequently, over-consumption of water is rife (Moore, 2014: 21-BJ). Officially, every well is required to have a water abstraction permit but, according to Chinese water resource specialists, permits are rarely obtained and, due to the sheer number of such wells, enforcement is almost non-existent (Gao, 2007). This phenomenon is especially significant in areas such as the Shiyang River Basin, where groundwater abstraction constitutes a high percentage of total water withdrawals.

Integrated coordination and management

Guideline 8.6
When pilot testing a reform, make it clear to all those involved in the pilot test that they should expect to benefit from it and not be made worse off – even if attempts to expand the reform are abandoned.

The lack of institutional coordination among bureaucratic units and administrative jurisdictions is another impediment to progress. In some regions, for example, it is unclear who should be responsible for the facilitation of trans-provincial water trading (Gao, 2007). Indeed, despite the fact that water scarcity is viewed as a strategic issue by the government, interviewees note that water rights trading is seen as an issue only of concern to particular rural areas. Because of this, policies and regulations concerning water permitting are rarely coordinated with efforts to address water scarcity in urban areas, such as water price reform (Moore, 2014: 18-BJ; Moore, 2014: 13-BJ).

The bureaucratic stove-piping described in these interviews is matched by competition between different administrative jurisdictions. Interview accounts indicate that some local governments fear that trading arrangements may offend either agricultural or industrial economic interests. In Ningxia and Inner Mongolia, for example, rapid development has produced dramatic conflicts between agricultural water users and coal companies (Moore, 2014: 24-BJ). An interviewee who works directly with local governments in Ningxia suggested that, under these circumstances, officials prefer to encourage coal companies to finance water conservation measures and then trade the savings, and are very reluctant to approve direct agriculture–industry transfers (Moore, 2014: 28-BJ). In another case, cited by an interviewee in Shaanxi Province, a local government cut off the municipal water supply in order to provide water to a favoured energy production company for a test of hydraulic fracturing techniques (Moore, 2014: 28-BJ). These accounts suggest that, while water rights trading is often seen as a way to resolve multiple contradictions in China's water resource policy (Gao, 2007), without great care, it may exacerbate these problems.

When one looks back over the nature of the trials that have been made, it is clear that Chinese administrators are trying to ensure that future policy changes will build upon commitments already made and will not undo them.

Strategic policy integration

Guideline 8.7
When searching for ways to implement a transformational reform, begin by sending and repeating messages about the nature of the reform.

In 2011, the No. 1 Policy Document issued by the Communist Party Central Committee, stated a goal of enhancing and expanding water rights trading throughout China. This was also the first occasion that the water resource issue had been "raised to the level of a strategic and security issue" (Jia and Yan, 2012). In 2012, the State Council added to the momentum created by the No. 1 Policy Document by issuing a policy intended to cap total national water use by the year 2030.

This cap on total national water use, part of a set of policies known as the "Three Red Lines" (*santiao hongxian*), relies on the formulation of individual caps at the provincial and local government level. Once regulatory caps are in place and enforced then some form of water rights trading becomes essential unless, of course, the government is prepared to remove water rights from some users.

Although the details of the Three Red Lines policy are still being formulated by the Ministry of Water Resources, preliminary indications are that it will rely on the establishment of nested inter-municipal and inter-provincial trading mechanisms (Jia and Yan, 2012). Interviews indicate that province-level jurisdictions such as Ningxia, which have already implemented forms of water rights trading, face significant policy uncertainty as a result of the Three Red Lines regulations (Moore, 2014: 28-BJ). In particular, it is feared that much of the progress already made may have to be undone.

Lessons for transformational environmental policy reform

The development of water markets in China generally, and the development of water rights trading in particular, has made substantial progress in recent years. China has focused first on strengthening the institutional arrangements for associated water allocation, the implementation of pilot projects and communicating the benefits of this approach.

Importantly, the Ministry of Water Resources appears committed to a significant expansion of water rights trading in seven provinces across China, though at this stage it is confined to relatively small areas. Deficiencies in inter-governmental coordination coupled with the allocation and enforcement of permits remain. Some of these challenges pertain mostly to operational issues, and appear to be relatively easy to overcome. Others, however, are likely to require significant reform not only in China's approach to the development of market-based responses to water scarcity, but in its overall water resource management policy.

There is a chance, however, that the emergence of newer technologies, including networked streamflow and well-level monitors, may help. Some of these technologies have been applied in the Shiyang River Basin, but ways to ensure that water rights holders do not exceed their allotted allocations still have to be found. The experience in the Shiyang Basin also suggests that a search for alternative governance structures might help to secure water users willingness to transition to a new regime.

The biggest challenge to the expansion and future development of water rights trading in China, however, concerns its place in China's overall water resource policy framework. At this stage, it is unclear how China plans to align supply-augmentation processes with those designed to keep use with sustainable limits.

When examining the experience from the perspective of other countries, the importance of making a long-term commitment to the broad policy direction is critical. Senior Chinese administrators have made it clear they need to set limits and ensure that all users respect these limits. The search for the most appropriate way to do this, however, is still open to experimentation and learning. The hallmark of the development of water markets in China has been gradual implementation. In retrospect, this gradual approach has proven to be wise in light of the significant administrative changes that have to be made. A high-level commitment of senior Chinese leaders has proven to be crucial in overcoming these challenges.

Finally, and of greatest relevance to other countries, is the willingness of Chinese political leaders and elites to study and adopt policy ideas from other countries. Water rights trading is easily characterized as a Western policy idea ill-suited to developing-country contexts. It is clear, however, that this is not China's view. China's leaders have adopted an open and wide-ranging perspective that begins by building understanding of the need for change and putting in place the institutional arrangements that will ultimately allow that much wider use of water trading as a policy option. Whether or not water trading becomes widespread or not will depend upon China's ability to enforce permits and bring users within the permitting system they are trying to establish.

Acknowledgements

Support for this research from the Sustainability Science Program, Harvard University, and the Italian Ministry of the Environment, Land, and Sea is gratefully acknowledged.

Notes

1. Readers interested in the unquoted sources of the information presented in this chapter should read Moore (2014). This chapter condenses the information in that paper.
2. In order to protect interviewee confidentiality, I employ a coding system that assigns each interviewee a unique number and designation for each interview site. For example Moore, 2014: 15-BJ indicates the fifteenth person interviewed in Beijing.

References

2030 Water Resources Group (2009) *Charting Our Water Future: Economic frameworks to inform decisionmaking*. McKinsey and Company.

Gansu Shiyanghe Liuyu Jiaoyi Zhongxin (Gansu Shiyang River Basin Trading Center) (2013). "Jiaoyi xiangqing (Details of transactions)". Gansu Shuiliting Shiyanghe Guanlibu (Gansu Water Affairs Bureau Shiyang River Basin Management Bureau). Available at:

www.syh-watertrading.com/800/nwt/sys/login_index.action (accessed 21 February 2014).
Gao, E. (2007) *Zhongguo Shuiquan Zhidu Jianshe (Development of China's Water Rights System)*. Beijing: Zhongguo Shuili Shuidian Chubanshe (China Water Conservancy and Hydropower Press).
Jia, S. and Yan, H. (2012) "Weilai shuiquan zhidu jianshe zhanwang (Prospects for the future development of water rights systems)". In S. Jia (ed.), *Zhongguo Shuiquan Jinxingshi: Ge'ermu Anlie Yanjiu (Progress on Water Rights in China: Research on the Case of Ge'ermu)*. Beijing: Zhongguo Shuili Shuidian Chubanshe (China Water Conservancy and Hydropower Press), pp. 140–49.
Li, B. (2013) "Baiyin Shi 'Xiaobu kuaizou' tuijin shuiquan zhidu gaige (Baiyin City takes steps toward advancing water rights system reform)". *Gansu Ribao (Gansu Daily)*. Available at: http://gansu.gscn.com.cn/system/2013/10/03/010466190.shtml (accessed 22 November 2013).
Moore, S. (2014) "Water Markets in China: Challenges, Opportunities, and Constraints in the Development of Market-Based Mechanisms for Water Resource Allocation in the People's Republic of China". Discussion Paper 2014–09, Belfer Center for Science and International Affairs and Sustainability Science Program, Cambridge, Mass.
Moore, S. (2014) 13-BJ, interview with lecturer, Tsinghua University (7 January).
Moore, S. (2014) 18-BJ, interview with professor, Chinese National Academy of Administration (8 January).
Moore, S. (2014) 19-BJ, interview with professor, Tsinghua University (9 January).
Moore, S. (2014) 21-BJ, interview with professor, Renmin University (12 January).
Moore, S. (2014) 24-BJ, interview with campaigner, Greenpeace China (14 January).
Moore, S. (2014) 28-BJ, interview with senior energy associate, World Resources Institute (17 January).
Shen, D. (2012) "Planned water use system in China". *Water Policy*, 14: 581–93.
Wang, Y. (2013) *Zhongguo Shuizhidao Biange (Transformation of China's Water Governance Pathway)*. Beijing: Qinghua Daxue Chubanshe (Tsinghua University Press).
Webber, M., Barnett, J., Finlayson, B. and Wang, M. (2008) "Pricing China's irrigation water". *Global Environmental Change*, 18: 617–25.
Xia, C. and Pahl-Wostl, C. (2012) "The process of innovation during transition to a water-saving society in China". *Water Policy*, 14: 447–69.
Yi, M. (2010) "Dongyang: Yiwu Shuiquan Jiaoyi An (The Case of Water Rights Trading between Dongyang and Yiwu)". Zhongguo Xibu Huanjing Ziyuan Fawang (West China Environmental Resource Law Net). Available at: www.westel.net.cn/Item/Show.asp?m=1andd=1256 (accessed 22 November 2013).
Yong, J. (2009) "China's water scarcity". *Journal of Environmental Management*, 90: 3185–96.
Young, M. (2014) "Designing water abstraction regimes for an ever-changing and ever-varying future". *Agricultural Water Management* 145: 32–8.
Zhang, J. (2007) "Barriers to water markets in the Heihe River basin in northwest China". *Agricultural Water Management*, 87: 32–40.
Zhang, L. (2012) "Zhongguo Beifang Diqu de Shuiquan Gaige Jinxing (Advancing Water Rights Reform in North China)". In S. Jia (ed.), *Zhongguo shuiquan jinxingshi: Ge'ermu anlie yanjiu (Record of Chinese Water Rights Underway: a case study of Ge'ermu)*. Beijing: Zhongguo Shuili Shuidian Chubanshe (China Water Conservancy and Hydropower Press), pp. 43–62.

9
DROUGHT POLICY
Lessons and strategies to change the transformational game

Deborah C. Peterson

Introduction

Transformational policy reform by its very definition involves significant change. It is reform that "changes the game" – it not only leads to substantial and sustained net benefits for the community as a whole, but also changes the way of thinking about problems and how they are addressed.

While transformational reforms have substantial net benefits, they are often long in gestation, have a difficult birth and a not insignificant mortality rate.

This chapter identifies lessons for achieving transformation reform and thus for increasing chances of success, reducing transaction costs and perhaps shortening the time to achieve reform benefits. It focuses on drought policy in Australia and draws on academic literature as well as government reports and media coverage. It also draws on observations from the author's personal involvement in developing, implementing and evaluating reform, and on interviews with a number of participants engaged in drought policy design, and implementation.

What is successful transformational reform?

"Reform" is a word now much overused (Banks 2011) and at risk of being misunderstood. As Paul 't Hart (2011) observes:

> The risk is that even the most timid, technical and trivial policy changes are talked up as "reforms". This gives reform a bad name … . Marginal adjustment of existing practices – however defensible – is not reform; it is public policy as usual.

So what is meant by transformational reform? Here, transformational reforms are defined as those meeting three conditions:

- First, they are reforms that deliver changes intended to make the community as a whole better off in the sense of improved overall wellbeing.
- Second, to qualify as transformational the reforms must be sustained. To satisfy this condition, Banks (2011) suggests the reform must be either broadly accepted from the outset, or become so over time. To be sustained, the reform must also be designed in a way that allows adaptation to changes that inevitably occur over time without compromising the integrity of the reform.
- Third, transformational reforms are significant in their impact, frequently large in scale and/or scope, but they can also begin initially with a small change that provides a catalyst and momentum for further significant beneficial change. This may include redefinition of a problem as well as adoption of concepts and management strategies that might have been used elsewhere, in other countries, perhaps, or in other contexts. An approach used in fisheries, for example, might be applied in water policy.

Assessment as to the height of the bar to qualify as transformational is necessarily arbitrary, but marginal or incremental changes, while they may be laudable, are not considered to be transformational.

Drought in Australia

Australia's climate is highly variable across the continent as well as across seasons, years and decades. Drought is a frequently recurring feature of the Australian environment. The characteristics of individual droughts in Australia are also highly variable. Droughts differ considerably in their length and intensity, and the time between occurrences, as well as in rainfall, temperature and other climatic factors between events. They also vary in their geographic spread and it is not uncommon for some regions to have good rainfall while others are in drought.

There is no universal definition of drought, which complicates policy response to the problems it causes. Drought, in general terms, is a prolonged period when there is not enough water for users' normal needs. Drought is not simply low rainfall. What constitutes drought depends on departure of water availability from perceived "normal" conditions and needs.[1]

One of the features of drought is that its condition develops gradually, making its onset difficult to determine. Likewise the end of a drought is hard to define because the effects may continue for some time after precipitation increases. There may be false ends to dry periods, with rain for a short period followed by a return to dryness.

Water availability depends on a range of factors. Rainfall patterns affect the availability of surface water and groundwater, and high temperatures and high rates of evaporation can exacerbate low rainfall. Water availability is also affected by factors such as afforestation, bushfires, irrigation management practices and return flows (see Productivity Commission, 2006). Due to the rainfall variability, many Australian agricultural producers supplement rainfall with irrigation so water allocation and dam management policies are critical.

The impacts of drought can be significant, especially for droughts that are intense, widespread and/or long such as those of 1982–3, 2002–3 and the Millennium Drought of 2001–11. The effects on different types of agricultural system, and the extent to which these effects can be ameliorated, are varied. Dairy farmers, for example, may buy in feed during droughts or use agistment or non-irrigated grazing for non-milking cows. Buying, transporting and feeding out purchased fodder is expensive, and, to be agisted elsewhere, milking cows need to be dried off and consequently do not produce income (Productivity Commission, 2009). Irrigators, on the other hand, experience relatively little disruption during shorter droughts if there is plenty of water in storage. As a drought lengthens, irrigators may seek to maintain production through buying water allocations on the temporary market, but prices may rise sharply as water allocations decrease. Some irrigators may be able to substitute purchasing surface water with pumping of ground water. Others may temporarily switch to dryland farming (Productivity Commission, 2009; Appels et al., 2004).

While drought without doubt imposes large costs, there are some who benefit.[2] There are opportunities for farmers interested in expanding, for example by purchasing land from farmers wishing to sell. There is also an increase in employment for business and property planning advisers (O'Meagher, 2003).

Effects at state and territory level, as well as on the nation as a whole, can be significant. The impact of the 2002 drought on the farm sector, for example, is estimated to have reduced GDP growth by 1 percentage point and taken around ¾ of a percentage point from employment growth (Lu and Hedley, 2004). The Productivity Commission provides a comprehensive discussion of the wider impacts of drought, including economic, social, environmental and political impacts (Productivity Commission, 2009).

Drought policies affect other policy areas such as urban water quality and availability, as well as the environment. Some drought preparedness measures, such as laser grading and installing more efficient irrigation infrastructure, can reduce the volume of water running off the farm to flow back to rivers and groundwater, but this has been the perverse effect of reducing the amount of water available for other farmers and for environmental flows. Fodder subsidies, a common form of assistance in times of drought, encourage overstocking of land and aggravate land degradation issues. Such policies need to be well aligned to be as effective and efficient as possible as well as to avoid unintended consequences.

The converse is also important: policies outside the agricultural portfolio interact with drought-related policies. These include broad policies such as trade, health, education and training, industrial relations and taxation which affect farm business performance and the wellbeing of people in rural and regional communities. Other policies, such as those related to climate change, water, land-based natural resource management, are also relevant considerations (Productivity Commission, 2009). Such policies influence how farmers respond to drought conditions. Positive effects from other policies create opportunities for beneficial change. For example, the ability to trade water can help mitigate the effects of drought, which contributes to farmers being able to manage their own risks in line with national reform directions.

Lessons for reform success

Attempts to reform drought policy in Australia have been ongoing for many decades (see DAFF, 2014; Productivity Commission, 2009) and have consistently fallen short of the transformational reform sought. Various efforts have been partially successful or unsuccessful, or have even taken steps backwards.

Persistence is a virtue

Guideline 9.1
Persistence and patience improves the prospects of reform and chances of implementation.

The first lesson for would-be reformers is the need for persistence and patience. While some significant reforms in Australia, such as the 1973 across-the-board tariff cut of 25 percent, have been introduced overnight, it is more common for major reforms to be many years in the making (Banks 2005). To achieve a sustainable reform, extensive groundwork often needs to be laid and adjustments made for unexpected events that can delay desired change.

Drought assistance by Australian governments is a good example of the need for patience and persistence. Drought policy reform has a long history, dating back to the mid 1800s. The early focus was on attempts to drought-proof agriculture by expanding irrigation. Australian government policy shifted in 1971 when droughts came to be treated as natural disasters. This enabled support to be provided under the Natural Disaster Relief and Recovery Arrangements which provided assistance for disasters such as floods, bushfires and cyclones. State and territory governments also implemented their own drought policies. These included concessional interest rate loans (for example, for harvesting crops and buying fodder), as well as subsidies and rebates (for example, for transporting stock, fodder and water), to allow farms to continue in business.

It was not until almost 20 years later that drought was acknowledged to be different from other natural disasters, being slow moving and without an easily identifiable start or end. So, in 1989, drought was removed from the disaster relief arrangements, marking a fundamental shift in policy direction, and the foundations of potentially transformational reform.

Amid rising concerns that drought support distorted farm input prices, acted as a disincentive for farmers to prepare for drought and was poorly targeted, an independent Drought Policy Review Taskforce concluded in 1990 that it is not possible to develop an objective, scientific and universally accepted definition of drought, and rejected the option of being able to identify the severity of a drought. The Taskforce went on to affirm that drought should be considered a recurring, natural feature of Australia's environment.

If assistance were to be provided, the Taskforce considered that it should be through concessional loans and not transactions-based and other specific subsidies. Such subsidies can discourage drought preparedness actions such as early destocking or diversification of income sources, and can distort production decisions by leading farms to use the subsidised input in excess of what would otherwise be the case (Productivity Commission, 2009). Where subsidies were provided, the Taskforce suggested they should be based on the circumstances of the individual farmer and that they should contain performance criteria.

However, when the Senate Standing Committee on Rural and Regional Affairs considered the Taskforce's recommendations in late 1991, they continued to draw a distinction between severe droughts and lesser droughts. Although the Committee accepted the idea of a drought policy based on self-reliance and risk management, there were considered to be limits to self-reliance, and the Committee in fact proposed additional assistance during extreme drought events.

A multitude of reviews and reports followed over subsequent decades. In each case, while the conclusions were similar, changes actually made fell short of fulfilling the promise of transformational reform. For example, when the 1992 National Drought Policy was introduced, the view that responsibility for managing drought lies with farmers was reiterated, with the role for government to be limited to creating an environment conducive to risk management. Nevertheless, there remained provision for assistance in "exceptional downturns" for otherwise viable farms facing temporary financial difficulty. These "exceptional circumstance" (EC) provisions were added to the existing Rural Adjustment Scheme. They allowed for interest rate subsidies on new and existing loans when received alongside the interest rate subsidy paid for productivity improvements (Productivity Commission, 2009).

It was not until 2011, on the back of the Millennium Drought, that another significant step forward was made when primary industries ministers agreed to a new framework to support farmers and their families without the need for EC declarations (sometimes known as "lines on maps" because of the need to determine the geographic boundary of the exceptional circumstance). Drought was once again acknowledged to be just one of a number of hardships that can adversely affect farmers. The role of farmers in natural resource management and their role in maintaining vibrant rural communities were acknowledged, and the need to maintain and support the natural resource base during drought and climate change was agreed by the Standing Council on Primary Industries in 2011. Importantly, the new package did not include the national EC Interest Rate Subsidy. This was in recognition that the interest rate subsidy neither helped the farming community to prepare for drought, nor did it improve risk management (Ludwig, 2012).

Be prepared

Guideline 9.2
Be prepared: opportunities to implement a transformational reform tend to emerge quickly and, when the groundwork needed to enable speedy implementation is missing, opportunities to adjust are just as quickly lost.

Kerr (2010) observes that "the longer the reform takes, the more chance that pressures will assemble to overturn reforms". The former Deputy Director General at the Queensland Department of Natural Resources and Mines also observed that the longer the period, the greater the likelihood that those affected may believe the government is not serious about actually implementing reforms. In practice, she notes, when participants are confident that reforms are occurring, faster adjustment is facilitated (Gentle, pers. com.).

Crises capture attention and create a sense of urgency to act. Moreover, they can help demonstrate the unsustainability of the status quo, interest disrupting coalitions that may have previously resisted reform, and may suddenly may reveal increase willingness to accept risks of change (OECD, 2010).[3] The sense of urgency can lift the issue at hand to the top of an already full political agenda and provide a trigger and mandate for reform (Althaus *et al.*, 2007). However, launching unprepared into rapid change on the back of a crisis, especially with inadequate stakeholder engagement, can result in poor or even negative outcomes and unintended effects, leading to a reversal of the change – sometimes not long after the reform is introduced.

To maximise chances of success, groundwork for reform needs to have been laid early, with evidence gathered to support the desired reform, stakeholder engagement undertaken to ensure the benefits of reform are well understood and accepted, and a potential transition plan mapped out.

A clear example of reform that drew on groundwork laid well in advance is when Australia's then Prime Minister John Howard used the crisis of the 1996 Port Arthur Massacre[4] to transform gun control in Australia. The reforms included a ban on all semi-automatic rifles and all semi-automatic and pump-action shotguns, a nationwide gun buy-back program that was coupled with the introduction of restrictive conditions on ownership and storage. As the Australian Constitution prevents the taking of property without just compensation, the federal government raised the money needed to recover the predicted cost of gun buy-backs through a once-off increase in the Medicare levy.

The buy-back scheme purchased and destroyed more than 630,000 firearms. Almost 20 years on, Leigh and Neill (2012) report there have been no gun massacres since 1996, compared with 13 during the previous 18 years. Total gun deaths have been significantly reduced in the early 1990s, about 600 Australians died each year by gunfire; that statistic is now fewer than 250 annually. The reforms also reduced overall homicide and suicide rates (Leigh and Neill, 2012).

Six years earlier, in 1990, the National Committee on Violence had developed a detailed case for a suite of recommendations. Consistent with Guideline 9.2, "be prepared", this work enabled the Prime Minister, immediately after the Port Arthur Massacre, to act quickly. If Prime Minister Howard had acted less swiftly, for example by holding an inquiry or review, momentum for reform may well have been lost. Opponents of reform would have had time to mobilise once media attention moved on and public outrage about the massacre had lessened. Sound policy had already been developed and was ready for adoption – the opportunity was seized.

Crises such as drought evolve more slowly. The Millennium Drought, considered to be the most severe and widespread drought on record for southeast Australia, began in 2001 (some say even earlier) with the final areas not declared drought free until 2012. The period from 2001 to 2009 was the longest uninterrupted series of years below median rainfall in southeast Australia since 1900 (van Djik et al., 2013). Particularly severely affected were river ecosystems and irrigated and dryland agriculture in the Murray–Darling Basin, Australia's most important agriculture region. This drought was so intense and widespread that severe water restrictions were introduced in most mainland cities. Electricity prices increased and there were many large-scale bushfires.

As with previous droughts, the aftermath of the Millennium Drought triggered a major review of drought policy and by 2011 the circumstances were conducive to change. The drought conditions over much of the country had eased considerably, providing an opportunity for reform away from media pressure and some farming groups lobbying for more support. The public, as a whole, however, were still aware of the adverse impacts of drought and the importance of drought policy. Further, budget pressures on Australian federal, state and territory governments had mounted to critical levels, making interest rate subsidies no longer palatable from a fiscal perspective. But the groundwork that had been laid by repeated public inquiries and studies was critical to the adoption of significant policy changes.

Build wide acceptance of the case for change

Guideline 9.3
Use compelling narratives to build broad acceptance of the case for reform and have strategies to deal with stories likely to impede acceptance.

Complacency is the enemy of reform: traction on reform cannot be expected when most people feel the status quo is not so bad ('t Hart, 2011). Building awareness and understanding about why change is needed and developing a broad acceptance of a mandate for reform substantially increases the likelihood of success.

Governments that win elections by a large margin are often considered to have an electoral mandate to implement policies that formed a major part of their election platform. Research by the OECD suggests an electoral mandate is particularly important in respect of wide-ranging reforms such as those related to labour markets, pensions and the environment (OECD, 2010).

Paul 't Hart (2011) emphasises the need for a compelling narrative – "killing arguments" – to sell the reform:

> This is not about spin; it is about building a public case designed to make people face the need for major change … In the absence of a compelling narrative, a reform effort misses the chance of making a significant discursive impact; it will not change the language in which we think and talk about ourselves and the challenges we face. That is a missed opportunity, as discursive interventions cost little yet can have great effects.

In the case of drought reform in Australia, the compelling narrative for change has been missing. The media invariably communicated the depth of suffering caused by drought and developed narratives that resulted in enormous political pressure to provide assistance to drought-affected farmers. Every time there is a drought, newspapers, radio and television have consistently run dramatic headlines and pictures of cracked earth, dying animals and stressed farm families. Such reports have done little to support a view that drought can be planned for and is not a national disaster.

The 1992 National Drought Policy illustrates a timing challenge. The "new" policy was announced just as Queensland and New South Wales were beginning to feel the effects of a severe drought and, arguably, could not have been introduced at a worse time: "the National Drought Policy, which demanded farmers prepare for drought, came into effect in the worst financial period for farmers in 40 years, when few had the ability to put any resources aside" (Walquist, 2003).

At the time, a highly successful and large-scale fund raising appeal also significantly contributed to the public narrative. The Farmhand Appeal highlights included a live concert and Telethon event. Farmhand reportedly collected around A$19 million (Walquist, 2003) and told a story which contributed to a view that the new drought policy was a failure. Walquist observes how, at the time, Prime Minister Paul Keating:

> was seen to be most unsympathetic, after making the statement that drought was just a normal part of the Australian landscape. To be fair to Keating, this was simply restating National Drought Policy. But the drought of 1994–95 was looking exceptional.

There were farmers and others critical of drought support, which they felt primarily went to farmers who had done little to prepare for a drought. But these stories were by and large not being heard. Walquist cites Neil Inall, a rural news reporter, who received calls from farmers angry that their neighbours were receiving government aid. When Inall asked if he could write that story, however, invariably the answer was no because they did not wish to be seen as critical of their neighbours. Inall was:

> frustrated about the lack of communication of the 1992 decision to reduce assistance, and that farmers should look after their own risk management. "It hasn't got out at all, hardly at all". It is vital, Inall says, to get good information about drought, and drought policy, across to the general audience (Walquist, 2003).

As the drought continued to deepen, Prime Minister Paul Keating in September 1994 personally toured drought-affected Queensland, with considerable media attention focusing on the plight of affected farmers and rural communities. The Australian Government then announced an additional income support payment, known as the Drought Relief Payment, as a financial supplement available to farmers living under exceptional circumstances in drought areas without regard to the long-term viability of their farm. Clearly, no compelling case for change to a program that encouraged farmers to plan for drought had been made.

Engage with stakeholders

Guideline 9.4
Engage early with stakeholders. Use this process to improve and gain acceptance of the proposed reform.

Early engagement with those likely to be affected by change can increase the probability of success. Despite the costs of doing so, there can be gains from better design and from buy-in by those likely to benefit. These people can then be used to help speed adoption and sustain implementation. These benefits should not be underestimated.

Robert Kerr, a former Head of Office of the Australian Productivity Commission and Financial Counsellor at the Australian Embassy in Japan (1978–82) has drawn attention to the Japanese practice 'Nemawashi (根回し)' – the process of laying the foundation for new proposals by talking to the people concerned in order to seek feedback and gather support (Kerr, personal communication, 30 January 2014). In Japan this has long been regarded as an essential element in any major change, carried out before any formal steps are taken. Kerr observed that, while this makes the development and discussion phase of reforms seem long, the implementation phase is often much faster and the likelihood of sustainable reform is significantly enhanced.

Inclusive consultative processes are no guarantee of lack of conflict when sensitive reforms are introduced. However, as the OECD notes:

> such approaches seem to pay dividends, not the least by creating greater trust among the parties involved, which may make the expected losers from

reform more willing to rely on commitments to steps that will mitigate the cost of reform for them (OECD, 2010).

The circumstances leading up to the 2012 drought policy contrasted with those of the 1992 reform attempts described earlier. First, the reforms were not introduced until the drought conditions had eased, providing a window of opportunity for reform outside the pressure of a crisis. But another key difference related to extensive stakeholders engagement.

The blueprint for drought policy reform in 2012 was built on a national review of drought policy commissioned in 2008, which comprised three separate assessments:

- an economic analysis by the Productivity Commission (2009);
- an assessment by the Bureau of Meteorology and CSIRO of likely future climate patterns and the exceptional circumstance standard of a 1-in-20-to-25 year event (Hennessy et al., 2008); and
- an assessment by an expert panel on the social impacts of drought (Drought Policy Review Expert Social Panel, 2008).

Importantly, there was extensive engagement with stakeholders during the conduct of these studies. The Productivity Commission, for example, received 188 submissions, held many informal discussions, visited many rural areas and a range of agriculture operations in all states, ran 29 round tables and held open regional forums as well as seven public hearings. Likewise the Expert Social Panel consulted extensively: regional consultation forums and meetings were held across rural Australia, in capital cities and major regional centres and over 250 written submissions were received.

Using pilot tests to inform and learn

Guideline 9.5
Use pilot tests to demonstrate benefits, build administrative capacity and build confidence about the likelihood of success.

In response to the national review, the Australian Federal government and the Western Australian government initiated a pilot of drought reform measures in 2010 (see Keogh et al., 2011). This tested a range of program elements and was designed to inform the development of a new national approach to drought policy. The results were reviewed in 2011 by an independent and widely respected advisory panel. The pilot was observed by all jurisdictions and the results were reported to a ministerial council comprising state, territory and Australian ministers for agriculture. The pilot not only benefited from experimentation, learning and adaptation; it gave ministers confidence that the program design was sound, and that there was unlikely to be unexpected unpleasant surprises. It also provided ministers with direct evidence about benefits of drought-preparedness and the narrative needed to counter arguments for drought assistance.

Transformational reform of drought assistance came into effect late in 2012 when ministers for primary industries agreed to a new framework to better support farmers and their families without the need for Exceptional Circumstance declarations or "lines on maps". The role of farmers in natural resource management and their role in maintaining vibrant rural communities were acknowledged, and the need to maintain and support the natural resource base during drought and climate change was agreed (SCoPI, 2011).

Understand and manage distributional impacts

Guideline 9.6
Focus early on the development of mechanisms to minimise adverse distributional impacts.

Significant change often involves distributional consequences, with both winners and losers from reform. Governments as well as those affected want to know more than whether a reform is expected to deliver a net benefit: they want to know where the expected gains and losses fall, their scale, and when they will happen.

In assessing potential costs and adjustment implications of reform, a number of factors need to be considered, such as:

- the capacity for autonomous adjustment. McColl and Young (2005) note, for example, that relatively rapid autonomous structural adjustment has been a feature of Australian agriculture and rural communities for years. Nevertheless, the effects of significant policy changes can be large and there can be lags in adjustment that may have negative economic, environmental and social impacts;
- whether the existing distribution is preferred. It may reflect outcomes of past government policies bestowing special privileges on certain groups and use of the existing distribution as a benchmark implies an inbuilt bias in favour of the status quo (Productivity Commission, 2001); and
- the costs associated with "doing nothing". For example, while tariff reform has impacts on employment, over time without tariff reductions there would also be lower growth and reduced employment opportunities.

Addressing adjustment challenges is an important aspect to the success of transformational reform. Anticipation of adverse consequences leads people facing losses to defend their interests. Typically concerns about such losses are expressed more strongly than support for gains from reform.

While it might be argued that the social security and tax systems and generally available adjustment measures can be the most appropriate ways of assisting adjustment and reduce adverse distributional impacts of change, they are not well suited to all circumstances. In some situations there is a case for additional measures to ensure both efficient and equitable outcomes (Productivity Commission, 2001). Such measures, individually or in combination, may include:

- packaging complementary reforms together, which can lessen the adjustment issues arising from a series of separate reforms, potentially providing some mitigating benefits to those adversely affected by individual reforms (Productivity Commission 2001; Banks 2005);
- reducing the scope of the proposed reform, for example by modifying elements imposing large adjustment costs or unpalatable distributional consequences;[5]
- applying a "no disadvantage" test as part of the reforms to the industrial relations framework as an example of this strategy (Productivity Commission, 2001); and
- managing the pace and order of reform. Phasing in changes is one approach, and, where possible, staging changes to get early, easier wins on board – "nothing succeeds like success".

Consideration can also be given to adjustment assistance. For individuals this may involve training or relocation assistance to help improve prospects of employment. For businesses, support for research and development or market development may be warranted. For businesses and regions, capacity-building support can be provided. Removing impediments to adjustment can also facilitate change. In the context of drought, removing barriers to trade in water is one such example (Productivity Commission, 2006; McColl and Young, 2005).

Another important consideration is the question of compensation. The distinction between compensation and adjustment assistance is sometimes blurred. McColl and Young (2005) consider that:

> compensation is something paid for the loss of a right or an opportunity that is owned via a legal arrangement ... The distinction between adjustment assistance and compensation depends on the answer to the question as to whether or not as a result of the change made, a court of law would require a payment to be made to an entity affected by the change. In principle, if a court of law would not require payment then it should be regarded as assistance not compensation.

However, as McColl and Young (2005) go on to observe, often a pragmatic choice is made between compensation and adjustment assistance as there are situations where "the wider community, generally expressed through the political process, supports the provision of adjustment assistance even though there is no legal case for compensation".

Regardless, consideration needs to be given to expectations raised about assistance or compensation on other occasions or to other industries. As the OECD (2010) notes, in "repeated games", perceived weakness in government encourages agents to push for maximum compensation. In the case of drought assistance, governments have been at pains to distinguish the situation of farmers from that of other businesses that have not been provided assistance to give a sense of fairness around decision-making.

Watch for backsliding

Guideline 9.7
Keep the impetus going. Include in the reform package arrangements that lock in the new regime and make backsliding difficult.

While benefits of major reforms are substantial, they are often diffused over a large group of people, while losses are concentrated on particular industries, regions or communities. Further, the losses may be felt either immediately or soon after the reform is introduced, while gains can be slower to emerge. Consequently, attention is needed to sustaining support after the reform has been introduced, particularly in a period where transitional costs are being incurred.

By 2013, drought conditions had returned to large areas of inland eastern Australia. January 2014 saw temperatures soar and drought conditions intensify and, as lock-in arrangements were missing, it was not long until there were once again calls for financial support including calls for interest rate subsidies. Following a national government change, a new drought assistance package was announced late in February 2014. Backsliding occurred with A$320 million to support farm businesses, farm families and rural communities facing hardship. Significantly, the package saw a return to subsidised loans.

In announcing the new package, both the Prime Minister Tony Abbott and Treasurer Joe Hockey referred to drought once again as a natural disaster – a flash back to the 1970s and 1980s. A nationally agreed narrative was missing and, hence, it was relatively easy for the Prime Minister to rejected suggestions that the additional measures were inconsistent with the tough position generally taken on industry assistance. By invoking the rhetoric of natural disaster, the government attempted to distinguish assistance to farmers in drought from assistance recently refused to other industries, including the car manufacturer Holden and fruit canner SPC Ardmona, whose closure threatened thousands of jobs.

The 2015 Agricultural Competitiveness White Paper was subsequently delivered with the promise that "the Government will always stand by farmers in drought" (Commonwealth of Australia, 2015). The White Paper committed almost A$3 billion in assistance, including concessional loans for farms with "sound prospects for a return to commercial viability", of A$250 million annually over ten years, which had been provided for in the 2015–16 Budget Papers.

Conclusion

Successful reforms that deliver significant, sustained benefits to the community as a whole often take time to achieve and repeated attempts are commonplace. This chapter looks at the history of Australian drought policies to identify lessons and guidelines which, if followed, are likely to improve the odds of success. Several guidelines emerged:

- Resilience and persistence in the face of repeated setbacks are essential characteristics of eventual success.
- While crises open up narrow opportunities to act, the groundwork for reform needs to have been laid early to reduce the risk of poor policies and implementation. When the groundwork is missing or weak, crises can result in the subsequent reversal of the intended reform.
- Early engagement with stakeholders increases the likelihood of successful reform. This enhances the speed of the roll-out phase and increases the likelihood that reform will be sustainable.
- Broad awareness and understanding of the case for change and support for the reform needs to be developed. This includes developing a "compelling narrative" to win hearts and minds of the community and lock in recognition of the cost of undoing a reform.
- Pilot tests can be used effectively to demonstrate benefits, build support and refine detail.
- For reform to succeed, it is essential to try to understand the size, distribution and timing of costs and benefits of reform.
- Prepare strategies to manage the negative consequences of a reform.

Finally, attention is needed to sustain support for the reform after it has been introduced, particularly during the early phases when adjustment costs are most likely to be significant.

Notes

1 See Wilhite and Glantz (1985) for an informative discussion of the role of definitions of drought.
2 The Productivity Commission (2009) provides a comprehensive discussion of the wider impacts of drought, including economic, social, environmental and political impacts. See also Lu and Hedley (2004).
3 The OECD suggests, "In normal circumstances, when immediate losses do not threaten, the combination of risk aversion and endowment effects tend to lead individuals to overestimate the risks and underestimate the benefits of reform. Yet these same factors mean that agents will often take greater risks to check possible loses than they would to realize potential gains of equal size. Faced with a crisis that threatens their existing endowments, therefore, they may become less risk averse" (OECD, 2010).

4 In the Port Arthur Massacre, 35 people were killed and 23 wounded when a man opened fire at a popular tourist venue in Tasmania using semi-automatic weapons. The event shocked and horrified the Australian public and received extensive media coverage.
5 If such a strategy is followed, notes the Productivity Commission, it is helpful to have a plan for under what circumstances and how the reform can eventually be broadened (Productivity Commission, 2001).

References

Appels, D., Douglas, R. and Dwyer, G. (2004) *Responsiveness of demand for irrigation water: A focus on the southern Murray–Darling Basin*. Productivity Commission Staff Working Paper, Melbourne. Available at: www.pc.gov.au (accessed 2 May 2016).

Althaus, C., Bridgman, P. and Davis, G. (2007) *The Australian Policy Handbook*, 4th edn. Crows Nest, NSW: Allen and Unwin.

Banks, G. (2005) "Structural reform Australian-style: Lessons for others?". Presentation to the International Monetary Fund, World Bank, Washington DC 26–27 May and OECD (Paris, 31 May). Productivity Commission, Melbourne. Available at: www.pc.gov.au (accessed 2 May 2016).

Banks, G. (2011) "Successful reform: Past lessons, future challenges". Annual Forecasting Conference of the Australian Business Economists, Sydney, 8 December 2010, Productivity Commission, Canberra.

Commonwealth of Australia (2015) "Agricultural Competitiveness White Paper". Available at: http://agwhitepaper.agriculture.gov.au/ (accessed 9 May 2016).

DAFF (2014) "History of drought assistance and reviews". Department of Agriculture, Fisheries and Forestry. Available at: www.agriculture.gov.au/ag-farm-food/drought/drought-policy/history (accessed 9 May 2016).

Drought Policy Review Expert Social Panel (2008) "It's about people: Changing perspective". A report to Government by an Expert Social Panel on Dryness prepared for the Minister for Agriculture, Drought Policy Review Expert Social Panel. Department of Agriculture, Fisheries and Forestry, Canberra.

Hennessy, K., Fawcett, R., Kirono, D., Mpelasoka, F., Jones, D., Bathols, J., Whetton, P., Stafford Smith, M., Howden, M. Mitchell, C. and Plummer, N. (2008) "An assessment of the impact of climate change on the nature and frequency of exceptional climatic events". Bureau of Meteorology, Canberra.

Keogh, M., Granger, R. and Middleton, S. (2011) "Drought Pilot Review Panel: A review of the pilot of drought reform measures in Western Australia", Canberra, September.

Kerr, R. (2010) "Structural reform: Easy to say, hard to do". Background paper for APEC Study Group presentation, February.

Leigh, A. and Neill, C. (2012) "Do gun buy backs save Lives: Evidence from panel data". Available at: http://andrewleigh.org/pdf/GunBuyback_Panel.pdf (accessed 2 May 2016).

Lu, L. and Hedley, D. (2004) "The impact of the 2002–3 drought on the economy and agricultural employment", *Economic Roundup*. The Australian Government Treasury, Canberra, Autumn.

Ludwig, J. (2012), "Australia to be drought free". Media release, Minister for Agriculture, Fisheries and Forestry, Canberra, 27 April. Available at: www.selbywatson.com.au/news/australia-to-be-drought-free.aspx (accessed 9 May 2016).

McColl, J.C. and Young, M. D. (2005) "Managing Change: Australian Structural Adjustment Lessons for Water". CSIRO Land and Water Technical Report No 16/05, September. Available at: www.clw.csiro.au/publications/technical2005/tr16-05.pdf (accessed 9 May 2016).

OECD (2010) *Making Reform Happen: Lessons from OECD Countries*. Paris: OECD Publishing.

O'Meagher, Bruce (2003) "Economic aspects of drought and drought policy". In Botterill, L. and Fisher, M. (eds) *Beyond drought: People, policy and perspectives*. Collingwood, Vic: CSIRO Publishing.

Productivity Commission (2001) "Structural adjustment: Key policy issues". Commission Research Paper, AusInfo, Canberra.

Productivity Commission (2006) *Rural Water Use and the Environment: The Role of Market Mechanisms*. Productivity Commission Research Report, Melbourne. Available at: www.pc.gov.au/inquiries/completed/water-study/report/waterstudy.pdf (accessed 9 May 2016).

Productivity Commission (2009) "Government drought support". Report No. 46, Final Inquiry Report. Productivity Commission, Melbourne.

Standing Council on Primary Industries (SCoPI) (2011) Attachment A: Standing Council on Primary Industries' principles for reform. Available at www.agriculture.gov.au (accessed 19 August 2016).

't Hart, Paul (2011) "Epilogue: Rules for reformers". In Lindquist, E. A., Vincent, S. and Wanna, J. (eds) (2011) *Delivering Policy Reform: Anchoring Significant Reforms in Turbulent Times*. Canberra: Australian National University E Press.

van Dijk, A.I.J.M., Beck, H.E., Crosbie, R.S., de Jeu, R.A.M., Liu, Y.Y., Podger, G.M., Timbal, B. and Viney, N.R. (2013) "The Millennium drought in southeast Australia (2001–9): Natural and human causes and implications for water resources, ecosystems, economy, and society". *Water Resources Research* 49 (2): 1040–57.

Walquist, A. (2003) "Media representations and public perceptions of drought". In Botterill, L. and Fisher, M. (eds) *Beyond Drought: People, Policy and Perspectives*. Collingwood, Vic.: CSIRO Publishing.

Wilhite, Donald A. and Glantz, Michael H. (1985) "Understanding the Drought Phenomenon: The Role of Definitions". Drought Mitigation Center Faculty Publications, Paper 20. Available at: http://digitalcommons.unl.edu/droughtfacpub/20 (accessed 9 May 2016).

10

THE COLLISION OF ASPIRATION AND REALITY IN PAYMENTS FOR ECOSYSTEM SERVICES

James Salzman

Largely taken for granted, our landscapes provide a variety of critical goods and services. Created by the interactions of living organisms with their environment, the suite of "ecosystem services" – purifying air and water, detoxifying and decomposing waste, renewing soil fertility, regulating climate, mitigating droughts and floods, controlling pests, and pollinating vegetation – quite literally provides necessary conditions for human society. One cannot begin to understand flood control, for example, without realizing the impact that widespread wetland destruction has had on the ecosystem service of water retention; nor can one understand water quality without recognizing how development in wetlands or forested watersheds has degraded the service of water purification.

Since the late 1990s, there has been an explosion of interest in ecosystem services from scientists, economists, government officials, entrepreneurs, and the media. Virtually anywhere one looks, interest in ecosystem services is on the rise around the globe and still rising. Much of the attention has focused on the possibility of payments for ecosystem services (PES). Some champion the concept as allowing nature to pay its own way, others as a win–win for conservation and development. A recent overview of the ecosystem services field concluded that "Across the world, then, supranational entities, governments, NGOs, regional administrations, scientists, policymakers, and resource managers are learning to govern nature in the form of services, often priced and occasionally commodified" (Dempsey and Robertson, 2013). Each group has seen the potential of an ecosystem services approach to further its own interests, whether it be a new stream of income for conservation, or a money-making opportunity for entrepreneurs.

This history of PES provides a clear example of a potentially transformational environmental policy. In place of the traditional reliance on regulation, PES holds the promise that regulatory approaches need not be the primary driver of environmental protection. They can be complemented, perhaps even replaced at times, by contractual payments.

Despite the sincere interest and enthusiasm of its early days, however, it is not at all clear that PES has delivered at the scale its proponents had foreseen. From the vantage point of 2015, PES has not transformed environmental policy and one can honestly ask whether it ever will. This chapter considers how this happened and what lessons can be learned from the hope that the development of PES would be transformational.

Guideline 10.1
The benefits of a transformational reform are easily overestimated by its proponents.

What are payments for ecosystem services?

Ecosystem services have been defined as the conditions and processes through which natural systems make up, sustain and fulfil human life (Myers and Reichert, 1997). A way to think about this more practically is in the financial context of principal and interest. Just as an investment of financial capital yields a stream of revenue income so, too, does the asset of natural capital yield the benefits of ecosystem services.

Despite their undeniable importance, many ecosystem services, ranging from flood control and biodiversity to climate stability, provide public goods characteristics of non-rival and non-excludable benefits. Because these services have no market price, they appear to be free and, as a result, are taken for granted (until their importance is recognized often after their loss).

Through clever design, however, the public goods barrier can be overcome in some instances; this is where PES has emerged. The practice of PES refers to voluntary transactions where a service provider is paid by or on behalf of service beneficiaries for land, coastal, or marine management practices that are expected to result in continued or improved service provision. The payment may be monetary or barter and is intended to compensate the costs of service provision.

The three basic assumptions of a PES perspective are straightforward:

- landscapes provide a stream of services, ranging from water quality and pollination to climate stability and soil fertility, whose economic value can be significant;
- the vast majority of these services are public goods and not exchanged in markets, so landowners have little incentive to provide these positive externalities; and
- therefore *we need to think creatively about creating markets for these services.*

The business potential for PES has been recognized since the late 1990s, catching the interest of a range of investment funds and entrepreneurs. Indeed, the famed investment banking house Goldman Sachs spotted this trend early and created a special group to follow PES. Its first director, Mark Tercek, was headhunted to run the international land trust – The Nature Conservancy. Copying the model of Bloomberg's news service, a dedicated website, www.ecosystemmarketplace.com, was created to provide a centralized source of information about market developments, transactions, and key players.

PES can include many different types of parties – from farmers, communities, and taxpayers to consumers and corporations. PES schemes can occur over very different scales – from pollination of local farms to "shade-grown" coffee beans that are sold half a world from where they are grown. PES also spans a wide range of transaction types, from one-off payments for a biodiversity offset to arm's-length market transactions for carbon credits.[1]

A study by ecosystemmarketplace.com – called The Matrix – analysed the breadth of PES sectors in 2006, 2008 and 2012. There is unquestionably a significant amount of money in PES transactions, on the order of billions of dollars in a few sectors, as well as hundreds of PES schemes around the globe (Landell-Mills and Porras, 2002). These are impressive numbers and indicate that PES has become a credible and accepted business sector.

PES schemes in the field

In the early 1990s, a combination of federal regulation and cost realities drove New York City to develop what is now often referred to as one of the world's first PES. Presented with a choice between provision of clean water through building a filtration plant or managing the watershed, New York City easily concluded that the latter was more cost effective and set up a PES that pays landholders to keep New York's watershed and its water clean. The scheme still operates today and is analysed in detail in Chapter 12 of this book.

Costa Rica's Ministry of Environment and Energy charges 20,000 water consumers near San José a small surcharge on monthly water bills. The funds received are used to pay upper watershed farmers who agree to conserve and manage their forests so as to maintain water quality. Costa Rica has also launched a nationwide scheme of payments for provision of ecosystem services, known as Pagos por Servicios Ambientales. This PES permits the government to enter into binding contracts with landowners for the provision of four services: sequestration of carbon, water quality and quantity (i.e. for drinking, irrigation or hydroelectric power), biodiversity conservation, and aesthetic beauty for ecotourism (Landell-Mills and Porras, 2002).

In Australia, the state of Victoria's Department of Natural Resources and Environment has developed a program, known as BushTender, to conserve native vegetation remnants on private property. In exchange for payments from the state government, the landholders commit to fencing off and managing an agreed amount of their native vegetation for a set period of time (Stoneham et al., 2002). The BushTender program was based on the model of the Conservation Reserve Program in the United States, the largest ecosystem service payment scheme in the world (Farm Service Agency, 2013).

The US Conservation Reserve Program provides annual rental payments to land holders in return for an agreement that they adopt a pre-specified land use practice that makes the adoption of conserving farmland the most cost effective form of land use practice.

There are hundreds of other PES programs that have been set up around the world. Some are business-to-business, such as a bottled water company paying farmers to use organic farming practices that safeguard the groundwater. Others involve payments to offset development harms such as wetlands mitigation banking. Still others take place through government payments, either as direct subsidies or competitive payments. And there are hybrids that combine these approaches. Viewed from this vantage, PES have truly arrived.

What are the key barriers to market development for PES?

While billions of PES dollars is a lot of money, it is tiny by comparison to transactions involving land use or service provision in the larger economy. And it is really tiny by virtually any measure once one leaves out government-funded PES. The fact is, given the size of the global economy and the number of transactions in relevant sectors, there simply are not a lot of PES examples in the real world.

While, in 2006, The Matrix estimated compliant watershed quality trading growing to an impressive US$1 billion by 2020, the 2012 version of The Matrix estimated growth by 2020 at US$43 million. Projections in 2020 for watershed voluntary payments dropped from US$2 billion to US$50 million and compliant carbon forestry from a maximum of US$5 billion to US$470 million. Projections for some sectors have grown, particularly for REDD-Fund carbon financing and government-mediated watershed PES. The fact remains that a number of PES markets are nowhere near where early proponents thought they would be, either in terms of market growth or market penetration.

Guideline 10.2
A transformational reform is more likely to succeed when there is an agency prepared to argue for its continuation as the reform is in the interests of this agency.

So what happened? If PES makes so much sense, why has uptake proven so difficult? As with any complex, recent phenomenon, there is no simple answer or cause. Consider the history of BushTender in Australia. This innovative scheme generated a great deal of interest following its launch at the start of the Millennium. Indeed, over 100 other tender pilots were introduced across Australia over the following decade. The power of reverse auctions to reveal information and drive efficient pricing for conservation was widely recognized and imitated.

A review of Australian attempts to test PES schemes, concluded that "Virtually all appear to be successful, and many have reported cost-effective outcomes relative to other funding approaches" (Rolfe *et al.*, 2014).

This same review, however, found that, from 2009 onwards, no further new reverse auction initiatives were introduced in Australia at either state or federal level. Rolfe *et al.*, (2014) concluded that, despite the undeniable success of BushTender and its progeny, reverse auctions had never been "owned" by a department or agency. When different political parties came to power, there were no institutional interests prepared to push for continued support. Quite the opposite, reverse auctions fly against public agency preference for grants which give them greater direct control and less implementation risk.

One can best understand the trajectory of PES by recognizing the core requirements for successful PES:

- discrete providers;
- discrete beneficiaries;
- perceived scarcity and value of the service;
- mechanism for providers and sellers to agree on price; and
- procedures for implementation, oversight, and dispute resolution.

Inadequate demand

Guideline 10.3
Successful reforms require a clearly identifiable cadre of discrete beneficiaries who are well represented by an identifiable institution. When an identifiable institution is missing, build one.

Unless service beneficiaries can be persuaded that the ecosystem services they receive are both important and scarce or in danger of becoming scarce, then it is unlikely they will be persuaded to pay for service provision.

As described above, we all benefit from the provision of ecosystem services and would be harmed, in some cases irreparably, without them. In that sense, they have enormous value. In many cases, though, we remain ignorant of their value. A basic obstacle to development of PES is that we generally take ecosystem services for granted. We are often oblivious to the natural sources of the goods and services we depend on. Yet, for a market to work there must be demand. If the services are not regarded as valuable – that is, if it is assumed that supply exceeds demand – then there is little reason to be concerned about them, much less pay for their provision.

Hurricane Katrina's devastation of New Orleans provides a poignant example. The flooding was caused by the storm's flood surge in the Gulf, not rainfall. Coastal wetlands could have slowed the floodwaters and reduced damage but they had been degraded over the years, partly from the laying of gas pipelines and partly by Corps of Engineer projects. These occurred because the wetlands were regarded as virtually worthless. Their capacity to buffer floodwaters was essentially ignored in their valuation. This is the case for many services. It is exceedingly hard to persuade an economically rational actor to pay for something they have always gotten for free, particularly if they expect to keep receiving the service for free.

Another aspect of demand in market formation is institutional. Unless there is a class of discrete beneficiaries, collective action problems prevent exchanges. The transaction costs of negotiating, gathering funds from many parties, and paying for services are simply too high. While there may be significant aggregate demand for services, transforming this demand into market action can be difficult. Where there are no pre-existing institutions that can act on behalf of beneficiaries, government may have to step in and act as a monopsony.

It is for this very reason that so many successful examples of PES involve watersheds, where two traits are present:

- water users understand easily the importance of clean water and the threat posed to service provision; and
- there are institutions already in place and able to represent, negotiate and receive payments on behalf of its beneficiaries. This significantly reduces transaction costs.

It should be no surprise, then, that there are very few examples of multiple PES purchasers competing against one another for services provided by the same supplier. It is generally the reverse, where a single purchaser pays for services from multiple providers. Institutions already exist that can act on behalf of large classes of beneficiaries. Water utilities already bill their customers and can add on extra charges for PES with little added cost. The obvious solution when an institution is missing is to build one.

Guideline 10.4
Reforms that rely upon ongoing access to government budgets face much higher risks than reforms that are deeply embedded in market and regulatory processes.

This also explains the role that public funds play in PES for biodiversity. We all benefit from the existence and option values provided by biodiversity. Some discrete beneficiaries create demand by contributing to land trusts but the vast majority of beneficiaries are unwilling to pay for these services. As a result, many PES programs for biodiversity are publicly funded. The obvious implication of this state of affairs is that *demand for these services lies at the mercy of public funding*, which lies at the mercy of government budgets, which are in ever merciful conditions as public expenditures are slashed to reduce deficits. The signals for true demand, in the sense of the value that people derive from many services, are therefore distorted by the need to rely on unsteady public financing for many PES markets.

A last challenge for adequate supply is parallel to that described above for demand. Services are often provided by diffuse suppliers. It may be the case that only a few need to be paid for sufficient service provision. If many suppliers are needed, however, this creates collective action problems. This again explains why *so many examples of successful PES are for watershed services where institutions already exist.* In the well-known example of water for New York City (see Chapter 12), local authorities in the Catskills and Delaware watersheds acted on behalf of their citizens in negotiations with the city government. Farmer cooperatives and soil conservation districts can play similar roles, reducing coordination costs to negotiate payments for farmers who provide services of erosion control, water quality, or pollination.

Measurement capacity

If one pays for any good or service, there is an implicit assumption you are getting value for money. Spend $100 for a bike, and you expect it will get you around the neighbourhood. Spend $1,000 and it had better handle any mountain trail you want. There is an assumption, in other words, that the purchaser desires and can determine quality. In PES, however, this is not always the case.

Measurement capacity can provide a major obstacle. Because many PES schemes operate as one-off transactions and are landscape-specific, understanding how the service is provided *locally* is critical to determining the level of service provision from specific land-use practices. To reassure buyers, at a minimum PES designers must be able to identify services on a local ecological scale – detailing how they are generated and how they are delivered. When service provision is complex, this is by no means a given. Indeed, in most cases our scientific knowledge is still inadequate to undertake meaningful marginal analysis – to predict with any certainty how specific local land management actions will impact the local ecosystem services themselves.

Guideline 10.5
The less expensive and more objective the ongoing quantification of benefits, the more likely it is that a program can be sustained. Surrogate indicators can play an important role in the establishment of low-cost monitoring programs.

This creates a major obstacle to investment. Imagine paying someone $10,000 for a service that you may receive but with no guarantees. You would be hesitant to sign that cheque, to say the least. Yet this is what happens in many PES programs (and what prevents many more PES programs from developing). Due in part to measurement challenges and in part to negotiations over risk allocation, most PES transactions are based on input rather than output. Landowners are paid for particular actions, not for the actual services they provide. Thus farmers are paid to put in riparian fencing, not for improvements in water quality that result. The buyer assumes the risk that services will flow from the adoption of a particular land management regime. The net result is that buyers are paid directly for adopting a pre-specified form of land use not for service provision. This is not a problem if adoption of the preferred land use is a reliable proxy for service provision, but that is often not the case. There has been a running debate within the hydrology community, for example, over whether increased vegetation in a watershed results in improved water quality.[2] This is, at its core, a measurement problem. Investors want to know with a reasonable degree of certainty what they are paying for.

Transaction costs

Guideline 10.6
The probability of successful adoption can be increased by reducing transaction costs.

As with any exchange, the role of transaction costs is fundamental in determining the size and nature of the market. Because most PES schemes are place-based, negotiations must take place between buyers and sellers over their respective obligations. Sellers want assurances they will receive what they have paid for and, in turn, buyers seek assurance that they will receive the compensation they have bargained for. Contracts, then, whether formal or informal, are inescapable elements of PES.

As the contracting costs rise, fewer transactions will take place. This is true, of course, for any market, but merits careful consideration in the context of PES. Because so many PES schemes are place-based, fungibility is rare. Watershed PES, for example, turns on the specific geography and hydrology of an area. Putting in riparian fencing in upper watersheds is a far cry from fungible commodities such as pork-belly futures. This rules out a stock market model of high volume and low fees. Building enough trust among the landowners to enter into contracts takes time and resources for local knowledge.

While PES are often described as "ecosystem services markets", upon reflection this is a misleading phrase. There are precious few markets for ecosystem services, in the sense of multiple buyers and sellers competing over scarce resources. Many PES schemes operate as one-off, arm's-length transactions between a buyer and seller or as government-supported programs. As a result, many of the efficiencies generated by markets are lost, as are the opportunities for easy profits.

Despite the limits on PES growth enforced by high transaction costs, there are a few markets where this general assessment is overly sceptical. The stock market model can work when the goods being exchanged are fungible. This is the case in carbon credits and exchanges such as the European Trading System or voluntary markets. An investment bank model (low volume but high fees) can work where the sums involved are large, as in areas under heavy development pressure. Robust PES markets have emerged in these circumstances – most notably in wetlands mitigation banking, where a credit for an acre of tidal wetland in Virginia can fetch prices from US$400,000–US$653,000 (Ecosystem Marketplace, 2006).

Design flaws and surprises

Guideline 10.7
When developing a proposal for a transformational reform, one should expect to be surprised by the nature of the changes and innovations that will result.

Guideline 10.8
Aspiring policy transformers should expect people to try to rort any regime put in place. Search for ways to minimize the risk that rorting could undermine prospects for success.

The devil lies in the detail. Expect to be surprised. While PES may make perfect sense in theory, effective program design and implementation are critical for market success. The importance of this challenge was clearest in what many believed would become the largest PES market for years to come, carbon trading under the Kyoto Protocol's Clean Development Mechanism (CDM).

CDM was designed specifically to create a market mechanism for Annex I (developed countries) who had agreed to binding greenhouse gas reduction targets and wished to meet their obligations at least in part through engagement with developing countries. Under the CDM mechanism, Annex I countries could pay countries to make investments that would reduce greenhouse gas. At the time of its adoption, many of its proponents thought that CDM would create a huge market for carbon sequestration and inject tens of millions of dollars into tropical forests because trees remove CO_2 from the air. In particular, it was expected that large reforestation and afforestation projects would become more profitable as they would be able to sell the carbon sequestered in the growing trees. This potential PES opportunity generated a great deal of interest among investment and environmental communities.

Highlighting the importance of anticipating innovation and unexpected outcomes, much of the anticipated investment in forestry did not happen. One of the prime reasons for this failure was another feature of the Kyoto Protocol, which sought to give all forms of greenhouse gas reduction equal opportunity. This was achieved by establishing an exchange rate system that allowed credit to be given in proportion to the reduction in global warming achieved – the metric of Global Warming Potential where the climate forcing of CO_2 was set at a value of 1. Among other things, this enabled businesses to receive 11,700 tonnes of credits for the reduction of a tonne of HFC-23s but only one tonne of credit for a tonne of CO_2. For businesses in China and India, this provided a massive opportunity because HFC-23 is a by-product released during the production of the widely used refrigerant HFC-22. The unanticipated surprise came from the fact that, although HFC-23 can be destroyed cheaply and easily, businesses who otherwise would have removed HFC-23 at their own expense changed strategy and decided to do so only if they received support via a CDM. In effect, this design flaw created an opportunity for companies located in developing countries to make far more money creating and destroying HFC-23 than the HFC-22 "product". Carbon dioxide sequestration forest projects simply could not compete in the CDM market (EIA, 2013).[3] The obvious solution is to place a cap on emissions from all countries or from the HFC-22 production process (which later happened), but when the Kyoto Protocol was being negotiated developing countries would not agree to a cap on their emissions.

A glass half empty or a glass half full?

Over the past two decades, we have gained a much better understanding of how PES operates in practice as well as the barriers to market creation and penetration. PES is now broadly accepted in the business community as a viable and credible investment strategy. One can point to examples of PES around the globe as well as emerging initiatives. The growth of PES, however, has not been as rapid as many of its early proponents had hoped. While still popular in policy discussions, it has not proven transformative in the field. In a sense, this should hardly be surprising given the challenges described above. Apart from these observations, though, two particularly useful insights can be taken from the PES experience in regard to transformational change.

First, success in the field may not lead to policy traction and widespread adoption. Despite the strong performance of the BushTender experience on the ground, the inability to create a sense of ownership among the relevant agencies made this policy particularly vulnerable following a change in political parties. In retrospect, PES's survival depended on effective champions in government over an extended period of time. The lack of a powerful supporting interest group proved fatal.

Put simply, it's not just economics and policy: politics and coalition-building matters, and this takes concerted effort over a period of time.

Second, proponents of transformational change can get it wrong. Being innovative and bold is not always a good thing because the unexpected can occur. A group of very smart and accomplished people designed the CDM program. Not one of the environmentalists involved foresaw the extent of the innovations it would induced.

So, think big, but remember that you can't anticipate everything, so start slowly and learn from your mistakes.

As the public and political appreciation of the ecosystem services approach continues to grow, overall PES will surely continue to grow as well. It probably will not, however, prove to be the silver bullet for conservation many had hoped for any more than debt for nature swaps, eco-labeling, or bio-prospecting proved to be. All of these innovative strategies have had a role to play and proven effective in specific settings.

Notes

1   There are three general categories of PES:
    - *Compliance markets* are driven by legal requirements that mandate restoration or reduction of harm in exchange for pollution or development. These include mitigation and pollution-trading programs under the Clean Water Act in the USA.
    - *Voluntary markets* are driven by individual or corporate motivations to promote a particular goal, such as biodiversity conservation. There is no legal requirement for these payments. For corporations, in particular, such payments may also be intended to enhance reputation.

- *Government-mediated markets* spend public funds to change land-use activities. These are generally voluntary, such as payments to farmers to set aside land for conservation.
2 "[I]t is unclear, for example, whether the provision of water will increase (e.g. with native forest conservation) or decrease (e.g. with reforestation) under forest cover" (Pattanayak et al., 2010).
3 The Environmental Investigation Agency (EIA, 2013) reports that "An extreme case is Gujarat Fluorochemicals Limited (GFL), India's largest HCFC producer, that reported revenues from CERs of about US$175 million (about €134 million) in the financial year 2012, compared to revenues from refrigerant sales of only US$14.4 million (approximately €11 million). Therefore, in 2012, a staggering 93.4% of GFL revenues from the fluorochemical business were as a result of selling HFC-23 carbon credits, with just 6.6% of the revenues from the sale of the refrigerants themselves."

References

Dempsey, J. and Robertson, M. (2013) "Ecosystem Services: Tensions and developments within neoliberal environmentalism". *Progress in Human Geography* 36 (6): 758–79.

Ecosystem Marketplace (2006) *Banking on Conservation. Species and Wetland Mitigation Banking*. Available at: http://moderncms.ecosystemmarketplace.com/repository/moderncms_documents/market_insights_banking_on_mitigation.1.pdf (accessed 2 May 2016).

EIA (2013) *Two Billion Tonne Climate Bomb: How to Defuse the HFC-23 Problem*. Environmental Investigation Agency Report, London and Washington DC. Available at: https://eia-international.org/wp-content/uploads/EIA_HFC-23_report_0613_Final1.pdf (accessed 2 May 2016).

Farm Service Agency (2013) "Fact Sheet: Conservation Reserve Program". Available at: www.fsa.usda.gov/Internet/FSA_File/crpfactsheet0213.pdf (accessed 2/May 2016).

Landell-Mills, N. and Porras, I.T. (2002) "Silver bullet or fools' gold? A global review of markets for forest environmental services and their impact on the poor". International Institute for Environment and Development, London.

Myers, J.P. and Reichert, J.S. (1997) "Perspectives on Nature's Services". In G. Daily (ed.) *Societal Dependence on Natural Ecosystems*. Washington, DC: Island Press.

Pattanayak, S.K., Wunder, S. and Ferraro, P.J. (2010) "Show me the money: Do payments supply environmental services in developing countries?" *Review of Environmental Economics and Policy* 4(2): 254–74.

Rolfe, J., Whitten, S. and Windle, J. (2014) "The Australian experience in using tenders for conservation". Paper to be presented at the World Congress on Environmental and Resource Economics, Istanbul, Turkey, 28 June to 2 July. CQUniversity, School of Business and Law Bruce Highway, Rockhampton, QLD, and CSIRO Ecosystem Sciences, Canberra.

Stoneham, G., Chaudhri, V., Ha, A. and Strappazzon, L. (2002) "Auctions for Conservation Contracts: An Empirical Examination of Victoria's BushTender Trial". *Australian Journal of Agricultural and Resource Economics* 47(4): 477–500.

11

ANGLING FOR A SOLUTION

Fisheries management and the individual transferrable quota regime in Aotearoa (New Zealand)

Adam Banasiak

Fisheries have long played a key role in the New Zealand identity. Before colonization, the Maori relied on the sea as a major source of food and developed complex management strategies to help ensure the sustainability of the resource. After the Treaty of Waitangi in 1840, command-and-control management of fisheries eventually displaced traditional methods. By the 1980s, stock collapses and declining catches signalled it was once again time to change the New Zealand approach to fisheries management. Through a transformational series of reforms including the dismantling of command-and-control policies and the introduction of market-based instruments like a quota system, New Zealand was able to turn their fisheries from a marginal component of the economy to one of the top ten export industries while at the same time increasing the health of their fisheries to be recognized as one of the best-managed fisheries globally (Adler, 2010).

Key components of the quota-sharing regime now in place include:

- the definition of entitlements as individually transferable, perpetual fishery shares;
- the annual setting of catch quotas based on share ownership and best available science;
- a requirement for all fishing boats to be licensed and operated in accordance with periodically revised regulations; and
- a catch recording and quota monitoring regime to track compliance.

The stakes: the importance of New Zealand fisheries

Although New Zealand is small (roughly equal to the land area of the United Kingdom or Colorado), its marine resources are extensive thanks to the geologic processes that formed the country. The emergent (land) portions of New Zealand represent only about one-fifteenth of Zealandia, a large continental landmass which separated from present-day Australia during the breakup of Gondwana around 80 million years ago. This resulted in more than 6.5 million square kilometres of continental shelf, about 15 times the land area of the country. These shelf areas support high levels of fish and other marine resources. Most of this shallow shelf area is encompassed in New Zealand's exclusive economic zone (EEZ) (see Figure 11.1), one of the largest in the world by area. EEZ designation gives the state special rights over fisheries, including the ability to restrict access and prescribe or limit the gear used to catch fish.

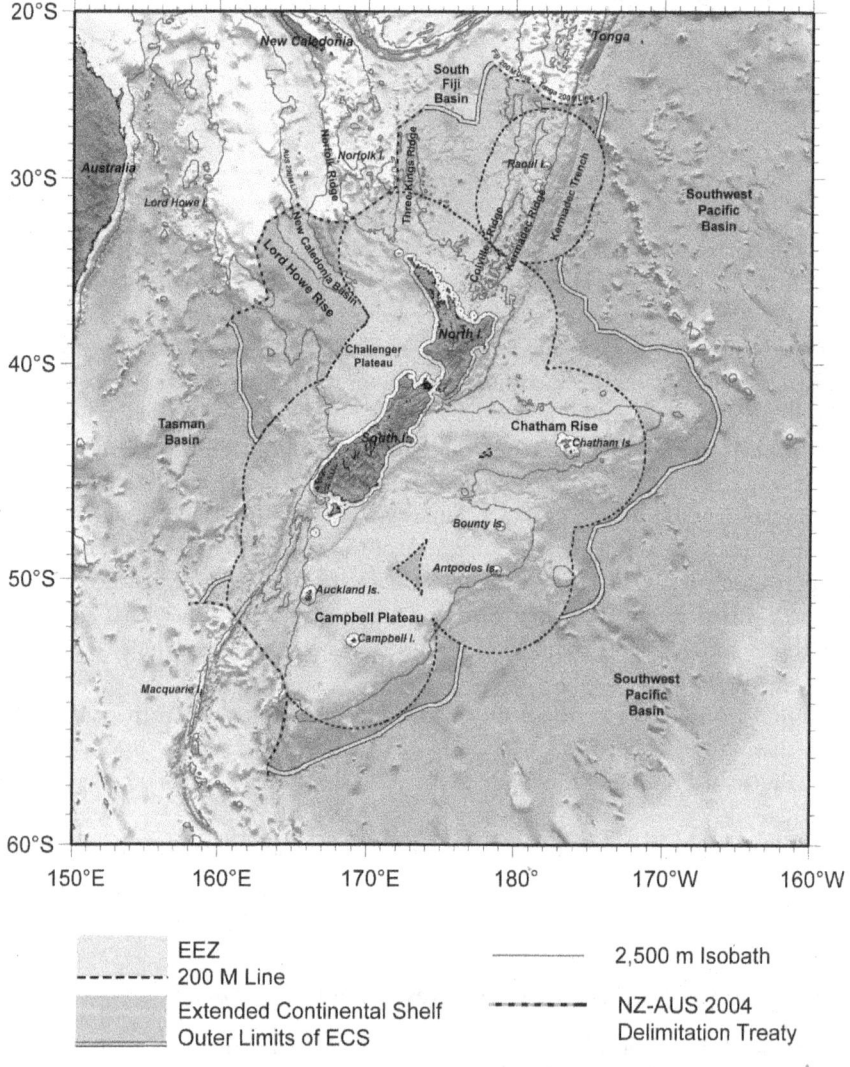

FIGURE 11.1 New Zealand exclusive economic zone established in 1978 (www.linz.govt.nz/hydro/projects-programmes/continental-shelf/undersea-image)

With a population of roughly 4.5 million people, this resource has a large per capita impact. Normalized for population, of the top ten EEZs by area globally, New Zealand has the most EEZ per capita. Since the resource is large, and the population is small, proper management has the potential to have a great effect on welfare of New Zealand citizens.

Getting to the quota management regime

How did New Zealand create one of the world's most innovative fisheries quota management regimes? A key factor was the alignment of government, industry, and civil society behind the need for change, driven to a common goal by a combination of historical and economic causes.

From Maori to Muldoon

Prior to the Treaty of Waitangi in 1840, traditional Maori fisheries management practices governed fisheries access. Maori fisheries management was complex, with a quota regime of nested rights divided among families, sub-tribes, and tribes. Seasonal closures of fisheries and complete closures were also used as management tools (Hersoug, 2000). Although the exact efficacy of such measures is hard to measure, these fisheries had sustained Maori populations for at least 500 years.

After the Treaty of Waitangi was signed in 1840 between the Maori and the British Crown, management of the commercial dimension of fishing was increasingly based on the classic western regulatory framework. In large part, the Maori were left to their own devices. Fishing by Maori groups was viewed in state regulations as falling under a "customary practices" umbrella that did not need to be regulated.

For commercial fishers, state management was largely based on "command and control" arrangements centred on the restriction of access and/or gear. From 1938 to 1963, a quota licensing regime was used as the principal method of control. This regime, however, suffered from the structural weakness that affects nearly all fishery access allocation schemes around the world: under this type of quota control regime, there is limited capacity to reduce the total catch as pressure on the resource increases (Lock and Leslie, 2007). Illustrative of this problem, discovery of crayfish in the Chatham Islands in 1966 turned into a bust by 1973, when stocks failed due to overfishing. Elsewhere across New Zealand, other stocks of other economically significant fisheries also continued to decline.

Pressure to produce: Muldoon's National Party years

Deterioration of the New Zealand economy in the late 1970s and early 1980s began to open the door for a shift in resource management policy. As a former British colony, New Zealand had for much of the twentieth century relied on strong government intervention in the economy as well as secure export markets in the United Kingdom. Guaranteed access to these markets was lost in 1972 when the UK entered the European Community. Prime Minister Robert Muldoon's National Party responded to a growing economic crisis in the late 1970s and 1980s by continuing the command-and-control economic tradition and unsuccessfully attempting to rebalance the economy through wage and price controls coupled with increased use of subsidies to industries such as fishing (Barnett and Pauling, 2005).

These policies exacerbated unsustainable fishing through the 1980s. The National Party attempted to jump start the economy through a series of "Think Big" projects, which promoted large-scale industrial capital investments. The National Party's investments in the fishing sector included hiring foreign expertise to teach new fishing techniques to New Zealand fisherman. Capital investment in new boats and fishing gear were made cheaply by purchasing surplus gear from collapsing northern hemisphere fisheries. The collapse of these northern hemisphere fisheries, such as the Atlantic cod fishery, also created a surge in demand for new sources of fish. These interventions, combined with continued government subsidization of fishing, caused over-investment in the sector as more and more fishers entered the sector (Gibbs, 2008). Instead of jump-starting the sector, these policies had the opposite effect. By 1980, catches were falling for key species, such as snapper, despite increased fishing effort (Gibbs, 2008). In line with experience elsewhere, over-fishing in the search for short-term profits was leading to over-exploitation and failure.

Finding a way to make the fishing sector profitable became an even more important objective for the National Party Government's economic investment efforts after 1982, when NZ territorial waters were extended from 12 to 200 nautical miles from the shore (see Figure 11.1). The change occurred as a result of the ratification of the UN Convention on the Law of the Sea. Recognizing the enhanced economic potential of their fisheries, the government passed the Fisheries Act 1983, which attempted maximize the economic potential of the new off-shore fisheries. The Fisheries Act 1983 provided the first taste of a new approach to fisheries management, using a quota regime which guaranteed fishers a set amount of catch in perpetuity as opposed to restricting how they caught their catch. A trial quota regime was set up for previously undeveloped deep-water fisheries but never fully implemented.

The quota regime appealed to the National Party in part because the guarantee of private rights and future access was viewed as a way to spur private investment in the failing New Zealand economy (Mace et al., 2013) at a time when the government, potentially nearing bankruptcy, could no longer afford to continue with its investments. Heavy borrowing required to finance the Think Big investments at a time of economic stagnation had racked up debt on the government's balance sheet (eventually leading to the loss of the country's AAA credit rating in 1983).

The National Party collapses: the window for wider change opens

Public dissatisfaction with the economy culminated in a snap election in 1984 and the ousting of Muldoon's National Party for the more free-market oriented Labour Government in 1984. With a new government in place, fishing industry leaders sensed that conversion of the existing regulatory fishery quota management regime into a fully market-oriented quota regime might be feasible and offer a solution to the over-fishing problem.

Elsewhere, at the same time outside of the commercial sector, the Maori were becoming increasingly dissatisfied with being shut out of commercial fisheries rights and management. The ability of a new quota management regime to align these stakeholder's interests – for improved stability, economic returns, and recognition of Treaty rights – helped advanced political willingness to consider the merits of transforming the way New Zealand fisheries were managed.

The stage was set for all key players – industry, civil society, and the government – to reshape fisheries management.

Free market solutions for all: the government on board and QMS

From 1984 until the 1990s the newly elected Labour Government radically reoriented the New Zealand economy (Nagel, 1998). This was part of a global shift toward neo-liberalization, marked by deregulation under Margaret Thatcher's Conservative Government in the UK and President Reagan's Reaganomics in the US. Although lesser known, New Zealand's market reforms were far more radical and pervasive than reforms in either the UK or the US. The Labour Government dismantled economic controls, removed subsidies for agriculture, floated the currency, lowered tariffs, removed production and distribution controls for industries, deregulated finance, and cut public expenditures (Barnett and Pauling, 2005).

Turning to its fisheries, the newly elected Labour Party looked for market solutions. Quota share regimes, where certified rights-holders are guaranteed a share of the catch in perpetuity, had long been recognized by economists as an economically efficient potential solution to commons management problems such as fisheries. Essentially a type of cap-and-trade quota regime, instead of facing the incentive to focus on catch volume, fishermen have an incentive to focus on catch quality and minimizing effort because their entitlement to a proportion of the total allowable catch is guaranteed. Additionally, because the shares are tradable, inefficient fishermen have an incentive to sell their share and exit the business, improving the calibre of fishermen and the efficiency of the boats left in the pool.

While small-scale, piecemeal experimentation with such quota regimes had occurred in some fisheries outside of New Zealand, no country had decided to implement a full-scale national share-based quota regime.

The comprehensive quota regime rollout begins

Seizing the opportunity provided by the wave of market-based reforms they were unleashing, in 1986 the Labour Government officially amended the Fisheries Act 1983 to create the world's first comprehensive individual transferrable quota regime (ITQ) (Day, 2004) and admitted the first 26 species to the quota management system.

Maori opposition: avoiding a stalemate

It did not take long for the Maori to oppose the new system when they became aware that they had largely been left out of the new quota regime. From the government's perspective, this was because the new regime was intended to manage commercial fishing activities, whereas Maori fishing had traditionally fallen under customary use definitions, which allowed for fishing for private consumption and cultural (non-commercial) uses.

Many Maori saw the quota regime's distribution of permanent fishing rights as a violation of their rights under the 1840 Treaty of Waitangi, which had guaranteed the Maori "the full, exclusive, and undisturbed possession of their lands and estates, forests, fisheries and other properties which they may collectively or individually possess, so long as it is their wish and desire to retain the same in their possession" (Waitangi Treaty, 1840). Accordingly, if the rights belonged to the Maori people, the government of New Zealand could not grant them to individual owners in the form of a perpetual quota.

Although largely ignored for well over a hundred years, interest in Treaty principles had increased concurrently with the worldwide resurgence of indigenous people's rights in the 1970s, expressed in New Zealand as the passage in New Zealand of the Treaty of Waitangi Act 1975. The Act created a tribunal to redress actions taken by the Crown since 1840. In 1987, the Tribunal sought and was granted an injunction in the High Court of New Zealand to stop further rollout of the quota regime.

The government looked for a solution to the stalemate. Initially, they established a joint working group to recommend how traditional Maori rights and Treaty claims could be reconciled with the new quota regime. The working group failed to come up with a solution and produced two reports: one of these reports advocated the government position and the other advocated the Maori position. In order to avoid a standoff, the 1989 Maori Fisheries Act was passed as an interim measure allowing the quota regime to continue while the Treaty claims were resolved.

As a basis for negotiation, the 1989 Act set out an arrangement whereby the Maori received NZ$10 million and 10 percent of all quotas. There was minimal support for the Act within Maori communities, though it did provide a pathway back to the table and negotiation of a final solution (Hersoug, 2000). Conceptually, Maori leaders were not opposed to a transferable quota regime, but they wanted a larger say in decisions about the commercial use of what they saw as resources under their rightful ownership. Both the Maori and the government were interested in making the new regime work. The problem was finding a way to include the Maori as both customary users and commercial partners (Lock and Leslie, 2007).

An opportunity to resolve the negotiation arose in 1992. Sealord Ltd – then New Zealand's largest seafood firm[1] – was offered for sale. This presented an opportunity to provide the Maori with a substantial stake in the commercial fishing industry. The Maori were offered, and accepted, NZ$150 million dollars in order to purchase half of Sealord Ltd and 20 percent of all existing and future quotas. Formalized through the Treaty of Waitangi Settlement Act 1992, this arrangement officially recognized the Maori as commercial as well as customary fishers. The Maori were left to work out how to divide the resultant fishing assets among themselves.

This internal settlement process among the Maori was contentious and took over a decade to sort out. Initially, the settlement set out in this Treaty did not enjoy widespread support among the Maori. Following failure of an appeal to the New Zealand courts, the Maori regrouped and began to focus on the development of economic opportunities. Through appropriate investments and well-timed buyouts, the Maori were able to successfully leverage their quota and market placement into becoming the single largest owner of quota in New Zealand. Today, they hold around 50 percent of all shares in NZ fisheries and all three key stakeholders – government, industry, and civil society – were aligned behind the quota regime. This success effectively silenced opposition to the agreement.

Design detail

The New Zealand quota regime contained many design features that have allowed it both to endure and to deliver results. Characteristic of many transformational policy reforms, while there was a clear of vision from the Labour Party as to the nature of the reforms that had to be made, much of the detail had to be worked out along the way. In fact, while the core concepts remained the same, virtually all of the details of the New Zealand system changed as the system unfolded and adapted to the environmental realities and governmental conditions at hand.

The overarching quota concept

Guideline 11.1
When separate instruments are used to pursue separate objectives, a dynamically efficient quota management regime can be established and more easily maintained.

Individual transferable quota regimes work on the basic concept that, by giving a property right to an individual, fishers have a direct interest in supporting processes and arrangements that ensure management excellence. By using separate policy instruments to pursue separate policy objectives economically efficient, socially equitable and environmentally sustainable outcomes can be achieved. Provided each component is fully specified in a manner that is consistent with resource performance these outcomes can be maintained in an adaptive manner as conditions change. Resource-wide considerations can be managed at that scale using robust planning and governance processes and markets used to allow adjustment at the individual level. This core kernel of insight has remained the same throughout the system's development.

New Zealand's fishery quota-sharing regime has the same basic structure as many other share management regimes comprising:

- *Total allowable catch limits*: each year, the total allowable catch limit for each quota species is determined based on a scientific assessment of the health of the fishery.
- *Individual shares*: the current resource is split into shares and divided among current resource users. Shares are issued in perpetuity, and are mortgageable and tradable just like any other capital investment. Each share entitles the owner to a percentage of the total annual catch. If any fisher wants a larger share, they have to find someone prepared to transfer some of their shares to them. Once the quota regime is set up, no more shares can be issued.
- *Annual catch entitlements*: the total allowable catch is then distributed to fishers in proportion to the number of shares they hold as annual catch entitlements (ACE). Unitized, ACEs are also tradable. Any shareholder can transfer ACEs to another person or company while still maintaining the permanent right in the form of shares to receive future allocations in proportion to the number of shares held.

Who? Eligibility for quotas

Guideline 11.2

Limit the amount of time between announcement of plans to introduce a new quota policy regime and conversion to that regime so that opportunities to game the transition process are minimised.

The New Zealand Government decided that, in order to be eligible for a quota, fishermen needed to either be subsistence fishers or derive at least 80 percent of their income from fishing. Initially, quotas were allocated to vessel owners, excluding skippers and others (Lock and Leslie, 2007). Recreational and customary users were excluded from the quota regime. Instead, it was agreed that the proportion of the total allowable catch necessary to accommodate these users should first be set aside and the remaining portion divided among quota holders (effectively giving these users a de facto, pre-emptive right).

Initially, standard commercial quotas were distributed based on catch history from the past three fishing years. In order to avoid the incentive to fish excessively, the government moved quickly to assign quotas (Lock and Leslie, 2007). However, since not all fisheries were included initially, fishermen were observed to be increasing their catch of other species in anticipation of quota expansion. From 1992 to 2004, a moratorium was placed on issuing new fishing permits to minimize this unintended side effect (Lock and Leslie, 2007).

These choices reflect the government's view that the quota regime was primarily a management tool for commercial fisheries. They also reflect the idea that the primary objective was the economically efficient use of the fisheries resource. Many of these decisions were designed to reduce transaction and management costs and preserve economic efficiency. As a result, social justice and community considerations were not taken into account when deciding the quota distribution regime. For example, many Maori people were part-time fishermen, who worked at other jobs while supplementing their income with fishing trips. Similarly, it was decided not to allocate quota to crew. As a result, this community was heavily hit by the decision to allot quota only to "commercial" fishermen. Likewise, the decision to allot quota to vessel owners impacted coastal fishing communities and part-timers as wage and other employment conditions were renegotiated.

Many of these decisions were designed to reduce transaction and management costs and preserve economic efficiency. The decision to exclude recreational fishing reduced transaction and management costs. The annual catch entitlements were developed by the Fisheries Act 1996 Amendment Act passed in 1999 as a means to further help reduce transaction costs.

Where? Defining the extent of a quota

Guideline 11.3
Allow for learning. Align management and administrative boundaries with biophysical realities and expect to have to change boundaries and management arrangements as knowledge improves and social expectations change.

The New Zealand Government recognized that the health and population dynamics of fisheries vary from region to region. Accordingly, a countrywide quota regime may not result in the long-term goal of improving fishery health. To address this problem, New Zealand divided its EEZ into ten regions and defined management areas for each quota species based on the available knowledge about each resource, including the pattern of distribution and migration. For sedentary species such as some shellfish, up to ten different management zones were created.

The initial legislation did not allow for changes in management area boundaries. Amendment of the Act in 1996, however, created a process to allow for boundaries to be changed with the consent of 75 percent of the quota holders (Lock and Leslie, 2007). This allowed the government to react to changes in knowledge about the nature and distribution of fisheries stocks. A potential problem with this method was that quota holders were reluctant to agree to a boundary change when it negatively impacted on their profitability. To address this, the Act was amended again in 1999 to give government power to alter boundaries without the consent of quota holders. To date, only one boundary has been altered under this power.

Illustrating the benefits of a degree of pragmatism and the need to curtail administrative costs, some quotas are defined for multiple species. For example, two closely related types of squid, which are typically co-fished, are managed under one quota-sharing regime (Lock and Leslie, 2007). In addition, some species are included on a separate schedule list for species where the maximum sustainable harvest has not been determined, species that have a high degree of migration, and for species to which New Zealand has signed international agreements on catch limits (Lock and Leslie, 2007). Such quotas are determined through different processes.

What? Rights associated with quotas

Guideline 11.4
When setting limits, build into any quota allocation regime a capacity to revise allocations. Regimes that lock in assumptions such as about sustainable yield, etc. can be costly to adjust if conditions change. Expect to pay compensation when fundamental changes in the structure of a quota regime are required.

Initially, the quotas were allotted in absolute terms; that is to say that a quota translated into the right to harvest a fixed tonnage of the resource. The initial fixed tonnage quota scheme was thought to be tenable because it was assumed that better management of fisheries would continually increase the maximum sustainable harvest; therefore the government would not need to ever decrease the quota. It was soon discovered, however, that many fisheries are cyclical and fluctuate with weather patterns and other events. Additionally, the population dynamics of many of the fisheries were not well understood. Within a short time, it was clear that the quota for 21 of the 26 species would have to be reduced.

In an attempt to correct this imbalance, initially the government chose a quota buy-back regime, where users were given compensation for a reduction in their catch. This option was chosen in order to maintain public support (Lock and Leslie, 2007). Originally, an auction-type method was chosen to determine the buy-back price; however, the resulting price was too high. As a result, the quota reduction scheme was revised to include a mix of buy-back and, when required, a proportional reduction of quotas without compensation. By doing this, the cost to the government was limited to NZ$42.4 million (Guerin, 2003; Anderton, 2006). An appeals process for those affected by proportional reduction was also set up.

At the same time, and so as to prevent the re-emergence of this problem, the Fisheries Amendment Act 1990 changed the quota regime design so that quotas were proportional rather than absolute. That is, each fisher's absolute entitlement was redefined as a share on the understanding that, at the start of every fishing season, each shareholder would be issued an annual catch entitlement. To facilitate conversion, it was decided that 100 million shares would be issued for each species.

Guideline 11.5
Build in arrangements that can be expected to increase the value of the new quota regime to each participant and use this to lock in the reform.

At the same time, the Fisheries Amendment Act 1990 also made other modifications to the rules that determine who can hold shares. While shareholdings can be split and sold in smaller volumes, limits were set on the maximum and minimum holding as well as limits of foreign ownership (Guerin, 2003). Shares were also allowed to be leased (Sanchirico and Newell, 2003).

The Fisheries Act of 1996 added further changes to the rights associated with a quota. Starting in 1996, shares were allowed to serve as mortgageable securities (Hartley, 1997). This was a relatively simple change, as shares had already been recorded in a certified, publically accessible government registrar to ensure transparent ownership and bring financial integrity to the quota regime (Lock and Leslie, 2007). Allowing shares to be mortgaged was important because it gives the financial sector a vested interest in seeing the value of shares remain stable or rise. This approach increased the robustness of the quota regime by adding another stakeholder with a vested interest in its success.

Paying for the quota regime

Regardless of the design of the quota regime, creating a self-sustaining regime requires a source of funding. New Zealand has so far failed to create a self-financing quota regime, although this has not been for the lack of trying.

From 1986 to 1992, New Zealand attempted a rent capture regime to finance management of the quota regime. Essentially this was an annual payment to the government that attempted to offset the added value of holding a quota, effectively driving the quota price to zero. In theory as well as in practice this was an impossible undertaking. Additionally, it undermined an important incentive of a quota regime, mainly that if individuals improve the management of their resources they will be able to reap greater benefits. Both industry and government were unhappy with this regime. Industry felt their costs were arbitrary and excessive, while government failed to recoup the expected earnings. Since the payments were made to the New Zealand Treasury, the government also had difficulty accounting for fisheries management funds.

Guideline 11.6
Set up a dedicated structure within government to handle the quota regime that emerges from the reform. This facilitates budget tracking and outcome measurement and increases accountability.

In 1994, New Zealand switched to a cost-recovery quota regime, which lasted until 1999. The major idea behind this regime was that fishers would pay for the costs actually incurred. To provide greater accounting transparency, the Ministry of Fisheries was spun off from the existing Ministry of Agriculture and Forestry, and management services were spun off to the National Institute of Water and Atmospheric Sciences (NIWA). In theory, the government would task NIWA with fisheries management work, such as determining the species-specific total allowable catch (TAC), which would then bill the fishers. However, this regime still ran into difficulties. NIWA maintained a monopoly of services (quantity, quality, and price for services were all governmentally set) and was not accountable to fishers for finishing projects or taking on projects that interested fishers. Acrimony increased between industry and government, until the quota regime was modified again in 1999.

Additional amendments to the Fisheries Act in 1999 changed the cost-recovery quota regime once again. To more fairly distribute costs, the government agreed to pay for public goods related to fisheries management. However, separating out public goods from club goods is not easy, and neither the industry nor the government is satisfied with the current outcome. Further changes are likely.

The impact of the transformational fishery reform on New Zealand

Did the transition from a traditional regulatory quota regime to a quota-sharing regime help improve the health of New Zealand fisheries and the economic efficiency of the fisheries industry? Success was arguably achieved for both objectives.

Quota market operation: economic gains achieved

Introduction of a fishery quota-sharing regime has transformed this industry to a cornerstone component of the New Zealand economy (Hersoug, 2000). Today, fisheries rank as New Zealand's tenth largest export industry (New Zealand Trade & Enterprise, 2016). Although the counterfactual case is not clear, it is hard to ascribe this level of success to purely technological or market innovations that would have occurred in the absence of the transformational reforms that had been put in place.

The ITQ regime has also solved the industry's overcapitalization problem. Analysis of boat registrations indicates that expansion of the inshore fleet in stressed fisheries was first halted and then reversed, while investment in export-oriented deep water fisheries increased (Connor, 2001). This realignment happened through market forces without the need for government buy-outs or other interventions. By allotting proportional quotas (shares) in an overfished regime and then reducing the annual quota to sustainable levels, fishers were incentivized to sell their shares and exit the regime because the value of their shares enabled the market to compensate them for the cost of exiting the industry.

Analysis shows that the majority of the boats which exited were small owner-operated or single-fisher operations (Gibbs, 2008). Additionally, ownership of shares and guaranteeing proportion of the catch allowed for owners or operators to secure funding for larger capital investments, such as larger boats for deep water fishing, further allowing the industry to grow organically.

Trade in quotas and in annual catch entitlements (ACE) has been robust. Prices for shares are advertised in trade magazines and online. While large owners trade shares themselves, smaller owners and exchanges are often carried out using brokers who typically charge between 1 and 3 percent of the value of the transaction. The number of ACE trades in 2000 was 9,300 and the number of shares sold in the same year was 1,500. A notable increase in the percentage of annual allocations that were transferred to another fisher has increased from 9 percent in 1987 to 44 percent in 2000 (Lock and Leslie, 2007).

A potential concern with quota-sharing regimes of the type introduced in New Zealand is that shares are issued in perpetuity in a manner that makes government intervention to prevent centralization and monopolization of quotas difficult. Since the inception of the quota-sharing regime, New Zealand has observed a 37 percent decline in the number of shareholders, which in gross would suggest this fear is valid. Closer inspection of the data, however, suggests this decline has been more benign than malevolent and may suggest a properly functioning market for three reasons:

- The greatest consolidation occurred in fisheries that were known to be stressed or overfished, where quota holders unable to catch fish sold their shares and exited.
- Markets dominated by a small number of holders appear to be markets where there were only a small number of holders at the outset.
- The most common size for quota holders across markets is the minimum quota size in the respective market, suggesting crowding-out of quota holders has not occurred (Lock and Leslie, 2007).

However, considerable vertical consolidation has occurred in some segments. As a result of the reforms put in place, the industry has evolved into a structure where 80 percent of all shares are controlled by ten heavily vertically integrated fisheries companies. This consolidation is strongest in high-value export-oriented species (Hersoug, 2000). It should be noted, however, that the Maori-controlled Sealord company is one of the ten megaholders.

The fishery share market has also proven efficient as a mechanism to bring new species in under this quota regime. By the mid 1990s, over 85 percent of the commercial catch was regulated under New Zealand's fishery quota-share regime (Sanchirico and Newell, 2003). Today, there are more than 275 share quota markets in existence for 45 different species and the net worth of the quota regime is estimated to be US$2.5 billion (Sanchirico and Newell, 2003).

Positive environmental impact? At least by some measures

Current research suggests that, if anything, the effect of the fishery quota-share regime on fish stocks has either been to hold stocks at a constant level or enable a slight increase in the size of the stock. A few select fisheries also show clear signs of recovery (Lock and Leslie, 2007). The largest problem in assessing performance so far is lack of baseline data and the relatively short amount of time that the regime has been in place. Greater evidence of impacts may emerge over time.

The biggest criticism to date has been that, while most fisheries have not decreased in health, many fisheries were operating at approximately 20 percent of their virgin biomass at the time the quota regime was implemented and widespread gains have not been observed in the 25 years since the regime was introduced (Gibbs, 2008), suggesting it is not a complete pathway to full ecosystem restoration. Critics also point to some fisheries, such as Hoki, which have continued to decline since the introduction of the quota regime. Defining the environmental outcome as a "success" or failure depends primarily, therefore, on your choice of reference point for biomass.

Fisher behaviour has also changed. Today, fishers are more likely to target their catches to avoid by-catch and are more likely to avoid spawning aggregations (Gibbs, 2008). By-catch remains a persistent problem, but indications are that it has been reduced. Under the current iteration of the quota regime, fishers must either purchase quotas or pay fines for species caught as by-catch.

As another indication of success, by some measures, New Zealand fisheries have been ranked the most sustainably managed in the world (Alder *et al.*, 2010).

Innovation in the industry

Guideline 11.7
Devolve administrative functions and make costs as transparent and accountable as possible.

Greater cooperation among fishers has emerged as a result of the quota regime. For example, squid trawlers agreed not to trawl for part of the season and lobbied against an increase in the total allowable catch so as to promote larger sizes of squid in their catch. Similarly, fishers have formed new entities to provide a common investment path in their fisheries. Scallop fishers, for example, formed the Challenger Scallop Enhancement Company Ltd in 1994 to consolidate existing scallop seeding and enhancement operations, expand upon existing efforts and reap greater efficiency from scale. Today, Challenger manages the New Zealand scallop fishery for common benefit, employing a full-time staff of over ten people (Arbuckle, 2000). Numerous other fisheries have funded research and management initiatives, including those for orange roughy, rock lobster, and snapper (Anon., 1997). Even more extreme forms of cooperation are possible with a share-based entitlement regime. Current law allows all management responsibilities to be devolved to shareholders provided there is a consensus from all quota holders in a management region and the management plan they produce is approved by the Ministry. This degree of cooperation has only occurred rarely, however, due to the requirement for consensus. Arguably, one of the next experiments to be trialled is a requirement that needs only to be approved by, say, 75 percent of shareholders and the Ministry.

In addition to resource and intellectual property investments, increased confidence in the future of fisheries in New Zealand has led to investment in capital. Port and ships have been upgraded. Additionally, there has been an increase in human capital observable through increased involvement in international fisheries-related certification programs (see Chapter 14). These improvements in technique and physical ability to target and process catch more effectively have led to improvements in fisheries by reducing by-catch.

Improved government–industry relations have also resulted. In particular, New Zealand has witnessed the birth of fishery shareholding companies that invest in government research partnerships to better manage the fishery. Joint research on ways to improve fish stock assessment and processing methods (Sanchirico and Newell, 2003).

Why did fishery management transformation succeed in New Zealand?

Around the world, many attempts to improve fishery management have failed. Why has the New Zealand quota regime endured and succeeded? While the design lessons highlighted above relate to specific aspects of the quota-sharing regime used developed by New Zealand, overarching lessons can be learned from the New Zealand experience:

- *A single policy goal*: the goal was clear from the beginning – to create an economically efficient and sustainable fisheries quota management regime. New Zealand did not fall into the trap of attempting to address the social or cultural impacts with the same instruments it used to ensure efficiency and economic development objectives. As a result, they were able to design a policy that did not need to balance two or more different objectives. This enabled New Zealand policy makers to deliver a quota regime that was relatively simple and streamlined for one purpose only, improving the chances of success.
- *Resilience, flexibility, and the willingness to change*: a feature of many aspects of the New Zealand quota regime is the number of times it has been amended or, in some cases, completely changed. In many respects, the existing quota regime does not resemble the original regime. Quotas became proportional, the annual catch entitlement concept was created, the initial attempt to recover rents was replaced with cost recovery, etc. The final share-based regime was able to endure because the overarching objective was clear. Stakeholders were willing to revisit the design and make changes as they learned how to maximize the value of opportunities.
- *Sustained stakeholder buy-in*: the government, industry, and civil society have consistently supported the idea of share-based ITQ regime from the early stages of its development. The quota regime has even withstood numerous shifts between Labour Party and National Party governments. This may be because the quota regime has, from the viewpoint of the stakeholders, largely delivered. Today, the industry is more profitable, Maori interests have gained

a significant standing in the commercial fisheries sector, and fish export has become an important part of the national economy.
- *New Zealand fisheries are very isolated*: New Zealand is geographically an isolated country. Management decisions have had a direct effect on its fisheries because many of the target species live only in New Zealand's exclusive economic zone and do not migrate into other territorial waters (Hersoug, 2000). As a result, poor fisheries policy in other nations has not diluted the positive impact of the changes made in New Zealand. This experience is not widely shared with other countries that have attempted ITQs, resulting in the need for additional multinational agreements to help transitional quota regimes.
- *Phased rollout*: Testing of a quota-based management regime started out with a change in government in 1985. Success proved to industry that a quota-sharing regime could work in New Zealand. The phased rollout of the quota regime, with more species gradually brought in, allowed all of the stakeholders to gain trust in the regime as well as allowing time for flaws to be addressed before they affected every fishery.

Note

1 Today, Sealord Ltd is the second largest seafood processor in New Zealand.

References

Alder, J., Cullis-Suzuki, S., Karpouzi, V., Kaschner, K., Mondoux, S., Swartz, W., Trujillo, P., Watson, R. and Pauly, D. (2010) "Aggregate performance in managing marine ecoregimes of 53 maritime countries". *Marine Policy* 34(3): 468–76. Available at: www.sciencedirect.com/science/article/pii/S0308597X09001614 (accessed 9 May 2016).

Anderton, J. (2006) "Maori Purposes Bill 1st Reading in the House". New Zealand House of Parliament. Available at: www.beehive.govt.nz/node/26281 (accessed 9 May 2016).

Anon. (1997) The New Zealand Initiative. Conservation Strategies for New Zealand. Available at http://nzinitiative.org.nz/site/nzinitiative/files/publications/publications-1997/conservation-strategies.pdf (accessed 19 August 2016).

Arbuckle, M. (2000) "Fisheries Management Under ITQs: Innovations in New Zealand's Southern Scallop Fishery. IIFET 2000 Proceedings". Available at: http://ir.library.oregonstate.edu/xmlui/bitstream/handle/1957/30694/179.pdf?sequence=1 (accessed 12 May 2016).

Barnett, J. and Pauling, J. (2005) "The Environmental Effects of New Zealand's Free-Market Reforms". *Environment, Development and Sustainability* 7: 271–89.

Connor, R. (2001) "Changes in Fleet Capacity and Ownership of Harvesting Rights in New Zealand. Case studies on the effects of transferable fishing rights on fleet capacity and concentration of quota ownership". FAO Fisheries Technical Paper 412. Food and Agriculture Organization of the United Nations. Available at: www.fao.org/docrep/005/y2498e/y2498e0e.htm (accessed 12 May 2016).

Day, Andrew (2004) *Fisheries in New Zealand: The Maori and the Quota Management Regime*. Prepared for the First Nation Panel on Fisheries. Available at www.fns.bc.ca/pdf/NewZealand.pdf (accessed 12 May 2016).

Fishserve (2014) "Quota Shares". Available at: https://www.fishserve.co.nz/information/quota-shares (accessed 12 May 2016).

Gibbs, M.T. (2008) "The historical development of fisheries in New Zealand with respect to sustainable development principles". *The Electronic Journal of Sustainable Development* 1(2). Available at: http://dlc.dlib.indiana.edu/dlc/bitstream/handle/10535/3254/gibbs.pdf?sequence=1 (4 May 2016).

Guerin, K. (2003) "Property Rights and Environmental Policy: A New Zealand Perspective". New Zealand Treasury Working Paper 03/02.

Hartley, P. (1997) *The New Zealand Initiative: Conservation Strategies for New Zealand*. Available at: http://nzinitiative.org.nz/shop/Library+by+type/Business_Roundtable/Conservation+Strategies+for+New+Zealand.html (accessed 12 May 2016).

Hersoug, B. (2000) "Maori Fishing Rights: Coping with Aboriginal Challenge". *Okonomisk Fiskeriforskning* 10: 2.

Lock, K. and Leslie, S. (2007) "New Zealand's Quota Management Regime: A History of the First 20 Years". Motu Working Paper 07–02. Motu Economic and Public Policy Research.

Mace, P.M., Sullivan, K.J. and Cryer, M. (2013) "The evolution of New Zealand's fisheries science and management under ITQs". *ICES Journal of Marine Science* 71(3). Available at: http://icesjms.oxfordjournals.org/content/early/2013/10/16/icesjms.fst159.full.pdf+html (accessed 12 May 2016).

Nagel, J.H. (1998) "Social Choice in a Pluralitarian Democracy: The Politics of Market Liberalization in New Zealand". *British Journal of Political Science* 28: 223–67.

New Zealand Trade & Enterprise (2016) "Statistics". Available at https://www.nzte.govt.nz/en/invest/statistics/ (accessed 12 May 2016).

Sanchirico, J. and Newell, R. (2003) "Catching Market Efficiencies: Quota-Based Fisheries Management". *Resources* 150, Spring. Available at: www.des.ucdavis.edu/faculty/Sanchirico/projo_fishoped.pdf (accessed 4 May 2016).

Waitangi Treaty (1840) "Treaty of Waitangi", Article 2. Available at: www.nzhistory.net.nz/politics/treaty/read-the-treaty/english-text (accessed 3 May 2016).

12

NEW YORK CITY'S PAYMENT FOR ECOSYSTEM SERVICES

Providing clean water for millions

Tim Purinton and Marina LeGree

Throughout the 1970s and into the 1980s, New York's administrators came under increasing pressure to find a way to improve the quality of the City's water supply. For a long time, New York had relied upon naturally filtered water from upstate watersheds.

Increasing development and farming, however, meant that the quality of water from these sources was under threat and the City was under pressure either to find a way to keep its water supplies clean or make a massive investment in building and maintaining water treatment facilities.

Recognising that heavy-handed land-use restrictions and/or widespread land purchases would be politically unacceptable and that the construction of water treatment plants would be extremely expensive, City administrators began to embrace the idea that it was possible to transform its water supply catchments into ones that both supported viable agriculture and produced clean water. The resultant program has converted these watersheds into viable working agricultural areas, saved rate payers billions of dollars and helped to sustain regional economies.

Celebrated as the first examples of an ecosystem service type payment program in the world, key elements of this transformational shift include creating opportunities for local ownership, the commitment of sufficient resources, the integration of flexible design elements, and a bottom-up approach to implementation. The success of the New York City water supply initiative has helped usher in more refined ecosystem service programs worldwide and underscored the previously underappreciated value of natural infrastructure.

Background

New York City, with an estimated population of 8,336,697 (2012 US Census) gets its potable water from three interconnected watersheds in upstate New York. The

Delaware, Catskill and Croton watersheds lie approximately 15–125 miles northwest from the bustling boroughs (see Figure 12.1). According to the National Research Council, these "watersheds and a complex infrastructure of reservoirs, aqueducts and tunnels encompass 1,970 square miles, contain 600 billion gallons of usage storage, and provide as much as 2 billion gallons of water per day" (NRC, 2000).

As a significant portion of the watershed area is held in private ownership, water quality is at continuous risk. The water supply catchment also contains a number of wastewater treatment plants.

The New York City water supply system is unusual in that its water supplies are unfiltered. There are only a handful of other large United States cities including Boston, San Francisco and Portland (Oregon) that rely largely on primarily unfiltered water.

New York City's water supply infrastructure was created in the 1800s. According to Albert F. Appleton, former Director of New York City Water and Sewer, the system started to fail in the 1980s after 150 years of relatively stable clean water delivery to New York:

> [I]n the 1980s, as the economics of industrialized agriculture transformed American farming and began to undermine the economic vitality of the

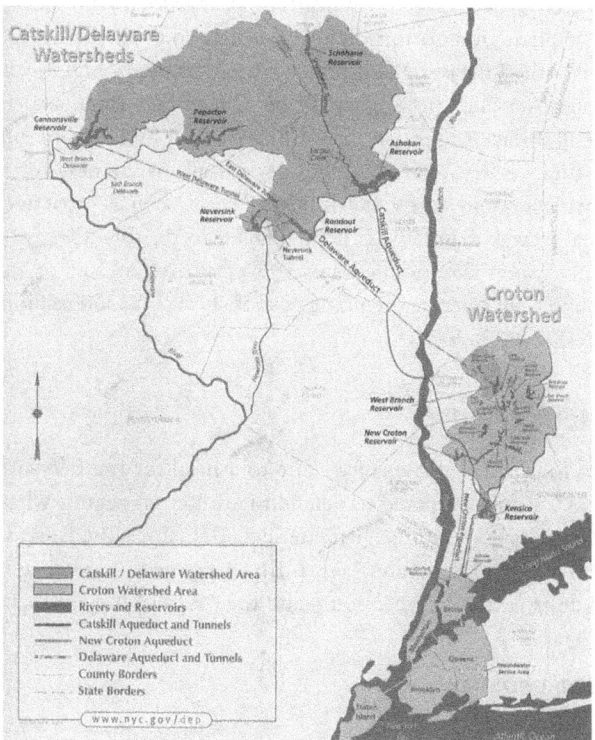

FIGURE 12.1 New York City water supply watersheds (New York City Department of Environmental Protection)

small family farms that dotted the Catskills, things began to change. Catskill farmers, in a desperate attempt to remain economically viable, began industrializing their own farm operations. Nutrient use increased, erosion accelerated, and fears of pathogen contamination began to grow. In a further attempt to maintain economic viability, farmers also began selling off the forested portions of their land for environmentally damaging exurban development.

(Appleton, 2012)

As a result, the quality of water supplied to New York began to decline and public concerns began to rise. In 1969, this issue was highlighted dramatically when pollution fouled the Cuyahoga River in Cleveland to such an extent that it caught on fire. In response the federal government enacted the Clean Water Act in 1972 and the Safe Drinking Water Act in 1974.

Guideline 12.1
Crises create opportunities for the introduction of new legislation with far reaching consequences.

The Clean Water Act established a holistic ecosystem focus and set a "fishable and swimmable" standard for all jurisdictional water bodies and the Safe Drinking Water Act established measurable drinking water standards. Significantly, the Safe Drinking Water Act and the Surface Water Treatment Rule associated with it "requires that all surface water systems treat their water by filtration unless it can be proven to be unnecessary" (NRC, 2000). As a result of the new legislation, New York water managers and state officials needed to be seen as proactive in ensuring that water quality was maintained. If they failed to do this, they would need to install expensive water filtration systems at a construction cost of approximately US$6 billion and then operate them at a cost of about US$300 million per annum (1993 estimates) (NRC, 2000).

Searching for a solution

As pressure to improve water quality came to a head for the City of New York, residents of the Catskills prepared to defend their interests against what they saw as inevitable: the City would use its eminent domain powers and suffocating regulations "to protect" the watershed. If this happened, Catskill residents feared that it would destroy the local economy and their way of life (Soll, 2013).[1]

Who? The stakeholders

Guideline 12.2
Major reforms require a policy entrepreneur with sufficient vision and influence to push for a cooperative solution.

Several key players had a stake in what happened with the watershed: the City of New York, the Environmental Protection Agency (EPA), local residents and farmers, and environmental advocacy groups. Those ultimately signing the Memorandum of Agreement in 1997 (MOA – the document that outlined the provisions of the watershed agreement) included the Governor of New York; the Mayor of New York City; the EPA, the Coalition of Watershed Towns; and the Clean Drinking Water Coalition (comprised of five environmental groups) (NYPIRG, n.d.).

Guideline 12.3
Search early for common goals and develop an understanding of them with key stakeholders.

Albert Appleton emerged as an early key player when he took the helm as Commissioner of the New York City (NYC) Department of Environmental Protection and Director of the NYC Water and Sewer system in 1990. He came from a background in management reform, public finance and environmental policy, and he wanted to move away from the reliance on hard infrastructure to solve water management problems, and to instead design softer land-use and collaborative solutions. A devoted environmentalist (Soll, 2013), his philosophy was based on the idea that a healthy environment would produce clean water, and that it made more sense to protect watersheds rather than allowing for pollution and then cleaning it up at great cost (Appleton, 2012). He believed a paradigm shift was needed: instead of the City being pitted against the Catskills residents, he wanted to demonstrate that they were in fact natural allies. The City and Catskills residents had an interest in the preservation of a rural landscape, and, as a common enemy, industrialized agriculture and suburban sprawl.

Guideline 12.4
Begin by developing a clear, simple vision of the final outcome to be achieved and options for its attainment.

Appleton had articulated a clear vision about the benefits of uniting the Catskills residents and the City around a common goal of an ecologically sustainable rural landscape. But there was a long way to go before there would be sufficient trust from both sides for the residents to be included in the solutions.

In September 1990, the City introduced a new set of regulations to preserve water quality. To Catskills residents new regulations translated as restrictions on land use. The proposed regulations were so restrictive that they made normal farming activities very difficult, and caused locals to wonder if the time had finally come to sell out to developers and end their way of life there (Soll, 2013). Remembering the imperial edicts the City passed down to clear the valleys for the Ashokan reservoir in the early twentieth century, opposition grew and became heated (CWC, 2013).

With the announcement of additional regulations in 1991, Catskills residents, who normally identified with their separate communities, banded together to take on the City, recognizing that individual towns would not have the resources to fight the regulations alone. This group became known as the Coalition of Watershed Towns (CWT) and would remain central to the negotiations and eventual agreement. The Coalition brought together representatives from the thirty-five towns and nine villages in the five counties with land in the watersheds (CWC, 2013). It pledged to protect the rights of local communities and to ensure that the City would compensate locals for the cost of implementing its watershed program.

Impasse and litigation

With the City still pushing top-down controls over land use, the relationship between the Coalition of Watershed Towns and the City reached an impasse (Stave, 1995). Attempts to reach an agreement yielded little progress over several years. The City continued efforts to push the new regulations and the CWT pushed back. Moving all these stakeholders from entrenched (and opposing) positions to a lasting agreement took sustained effort from all sides. Residents and officials central to the negotiations recall that this could not happen and did not happen until the City saw the residents as partners essential to the solution rather than potential spoilers to be managed (CWC, 2013).

Personalities played a significant role. Appleton, the driving force behind the proposed reform, had tremendous influence on behalf of the City, and his vision for a collaborative approach with the farmers to prevent suburban sprawl and pollution should have won support. But his tendency to be condescending to residents, his failure to remove government employees who antagonized locals and his refusal to negotiate seriously with the CWT hindered progress (Soll, 2013). By 1993, the CWT was on a path to litigation, not agreement and, when they filed suit against the City in 1994, a negotiated solution looked impossible (CWC, 2013).

Breakthrough

Guideline 12.5
When the vision is supported by all key stakeholders, but there is a negotiation impasse or lack of trust, be prepared to reduce tension by appointing a new policy entrepreneur with a different style and approach.

State elections ushered Appleton out of his position in that same year, and his replacement, Marilyn Gelber, began her term with a different approach. She deformalized meetings with residents, shifting the tone of communication and made herself readily available to speak to the communities personally. This investment paid off by enabling a more collegial and cooperative exchange (CWC, 2013).

In this case, a change in personalities worked because the right building blocks were in place. When Appleton had taken office in 1991, the City needed a policy entrepreneur to initiate a dramatic change in direction. Appleton's skill set and training enabled him to lay the groundwork for the policy reform, but his implementation approach was an impediment in gaining the community's trust. Gelber came along when the situation was at a tipping point; conditions were set for the reform itself, and her more collaborative approach opened a way around the impasse.

Finding common ground

Guideline 12.6
Early in the development of a transformational reform agenda appoint a policy entrepreneur and give that person responsibility for negotiating the details.

Years earlier, Appleton had begun what would become pivotal discussions with the farmers by turning to Dennis Rapp, Deputy Commissioner for New York State Department of Agriculture, for help. Rapp's background as a rural farmer gave him credibility with locals, and together he and Appleton agreed on a plan for mutual education. The idea was to help both sides better understand the constraints and incentives of the other, and move forward with a joint approach (Soll, 2013).

The new approach worked. Rapp organized a series of forums in which officials thoroughly explained the City's position (the huge costs associated with filtration had it backed into a corner) and farmers described their daily struggles and financial challenges (their incomes had been declining for years and they felt their livelihoods were at stake), making officials understand that the proposed regulations would make farming impossible. The basic trust established through these exchanges formed a foundation that allowed the two sides to create the joint task force that ultimately designed the Whole Farm Planning, which became the centrepiece of the Catskills approach.

Whole Farm Planning

The Whole Farm Planning used a "holistic approach to farm management to identify and prioritize environmental issues on a farm without compromising the farm business" (WAC, n.d.). Whole Farm Planning was first and foremost designed by local farmers. They recognized that their farming practices were ripe for improvement, but lacked the capital to invest in agricultural upgrades. The City made it clear that clean water was paramount, and it would pay for what was necessary to achieve that goal. Thus the Whole Farm Planning was designed to introduce cleaner, more efficient farming practices while the City paid for the upgrades. Under the Memorandum of Agreement a mutually beneficial proposition was put forward: farmers would receive grants to identify and contain sources of polluting run-off such as fertilizer; and the City would get clean water. Participating farmers also received a small stipend for their time and effort. Initially, the farmers wanted the program to be entirely voluntary but the City insisted on a minimum participation rate of 85 percent. Eventually, the farmers agreed to this degree of participation with the understanding that the Agreement would be abandoned if it was not achieved. Reflecting the success of this dimension of the program, more than 93 percent of watershed farmers had chosen to participate by 2013 (Soll, 2013).

Guideline 12.7
Negotiate with stakeholders early while program details are still being developed.

In retrospect, it can be seen that personalities played a key role in negotiating the final outcome. None of the City officials had great rapport with the communities, according to archival interviews (CWC, 2013), but once Rapp led the co-educational process relations went more smoothly. Also contributing to the locally led nature of the reform was the Coalition of Watershed Towns, which gave farmers a forum to organize themselves in a way they had not done previously. Once the joint task force began developing the Whole Farm Planning, momentum grew as more and more Catskills residents saw that the approach could bring benefits for their communities. The consensus around the Whole Farm Planning led both sides to invest in the reforms, and catalysed enthusiasm that paved the way for the Agreement to succeed.

In 1997, after intense negotiation between local, state and federal officials, including the intervention of the Governor of New York, the New York City Watershed Memorandum of Agreement was signed (valid until 2002,) at a cost of US$1.5 billion, which was about 75 percent less than the US$6 billion that water filtration would have cost (NRC, 2000).

What? Components of the agreement

The Memorandum of Agreement had three main components:

- watershed protection and partnership programs;
- watershed rules and regulations; and
- land acquisition.

Watershed protection and partnership programs formed the basis of cooperation between the various stakeholders in the Whole Farm Planning to implement measures that balance economic development with environmental protection. The City budgeted more than US$270 million to fund these programs, and the state contributed US$53 million (between 1997 and 2012) (Stave, 1995).

Watershed rules and regulations outline requirements necessary to control point and nonpoint sources of pollution, including wastewater treatment plants, septic systems, and storm water run-off.

Funding for land acquisition is based on a willing seller/willing buyer premise, meaning the City is obligated to solicit land from private owners, but it may not use compulsory acquisition (eminent domain) powers to acquire land that meets what the Memorandum of Agreement defined as "Natural Features Criteria" relative to parcel size, slope, and watershed protection values. The City also pays property taxes on land that it acquires, which constitutes a significant source of income for upstate communities.

Implementation

Guideline 12.8
When seeking a transformational change, if at all possible, ensure that no significant interest group is made worse off.

The signing of the Memorandum of Agreement in 1997 marked the start of the implementation phase of the transformative reform of New York City water supply and management arrangements. Embodying the sweat and grit of many dedicated stakeholders, the Agreement also satisfied the needs of a suite of diverse interests, not just a privileged few. Significantly, the Agreement was created transparently and endorsed by powerful politicians. As a guiding framework it was visionary and, after 16 years, remains a sturdy document.

The Agreement's success was propelled by the threat that, if the goals of the document were not met, federal regulators could force New York City to choose between a politically unpalatable regulatory solution and a costly engineering solution. This is important to note. Many environmental reforms have a dark shadow lurking behind them that forces stakeholders to do their best to avoid a much more painful alternative.

Given that the consequences of failure were great, early demonstration of success was critical. The participation of farmers in the Whole Farm Planning was a potential stumbling block, but the economic conditions of the area at that time, with the growth of industrialized farming operations increasingly putting pressure on small farms, created incentives for farmers to sign up to the program. It offered a much-needed infusion of capital into their farming operations and allowed their continued way of life.

Strong funding

Guideline 12.9
Don't begin a transformational reform without having secure funding in place that is protected from politics.

One reason that New York City could invest significant resources in the MOA was the decoupling of the water authority from rickety and unpredictable City general finances, as David Soll (2013) describes in his book, *Empire of Water*.

In 1984, the state legislature passed a bill creating two new entities: the New York City Municipal Water Finance Authority and the New York City Water Board. Instead of relying on City coffers to fund its substantial capital expenses, an arrangement that brought most capital construction to a grinding halt during the fiscal crisis, the structure created a self-sustaining water system.

It is important to consider that New York City was in deep fiscal crisis during the 1970s and teetered on bankruptcy during this decade. This crisis came to a head in 1975 when the mayor and governor travelled to Washington DC to plead for a federal bail-out from President Gerald Ford. It took approximately a decade to pull the City out of this recession. During that time period municipal infrastructure was in disrepair and capital needs were overwhelming. A primary goal of this enabling legislation was to create a self-sustaining system that could keep up with and adapt to changing water supply needs and necessary upgrades.

The ability to more freely set rates, leverage a broad base of rate payers, float capital improvement bonds and optimize budget processes meant the City could eventually advance the enormous sum of US$1.5 billion to support the Agreement a dozen years later. Too many ambitious environmental initiatives wither on the vine due to lack of resources or the need to share scant resources with existing, over-burdened organizations.

Diverse staff

Guideline 12.10
Build new administrative structures to bring in new skills and appoint people with appropriate expertise.

Guideline 12.11
When beginning a transformational reform, bring in people with capacity to implement the new regime.

The long history of the expansion of the New York Water System was one that was biased towards hard-structured, engineered solutions. The forerunner to the City's Water Supply Bureau was the Board of Water Supply that mostly comprised engineers. The New York legislature disbanded this Water Supply Bureau in 1978 and over the next two decades hired a slew of new employees with more holistic skills. The new team included foresters, geographic information systems experts and ecologists as well as engineers. Staff diversification was paramount in implementing a more organic plan that relied on balance, flexibility and creativity (Warne, 2014).

Significantly, the lead negotiators, Commissioners Albert Appleton and Marilyn Gelber, brought perspectives that emphasized ecology, planning and partnership building. They were not from the old engineering school (Soll, 2013).

Science and monitoring

Guideline 12.12
Don't guess the outcomes. Invest early and use the best science available to collect robust information early in the development of a reform. Simultaneous investments in staff and new data collection methods empower stakeholders.

According to David Warne, Assistant Commissioner of the current Bureau of Water Supply, heavy frontloaded investment in technical systems and scientific monitoring meant that the implementation phase could proceed on solid technical footing. According to Warne, the "systems they put in place at the beginning are largely still there; it was not dumb luck, but lots of effort to get the science right". He attributes coupling a powerful geographic information system with comprehensive monitoring as the action that put those responsible for implementing the program on the right track (Warne, 2014).

Early on-the-ground success

Guideline 12.13
Design the program so that success can be demonstrated early and used to prevent undermining of the reform. Collect the data needed to ensure that early success can be demonstrated.

One of the most risky innovations in the Agreement was the component that made implementation dependent upon voluntary agreements with farmers. Farmers were not to be coerced into signing whole farm management contracts. The fact that today over 90 percent of basin farmers are in the Whole Farm Planning is a testament to the Agreement's effectiveness. Warne observes that early pilots, based on very simple best management practices, were critical in gaining support. These pilots included payments to fence stream corridors, improve barnyard construction and reduce fertilizer use.

The Watershed Agricultural Council set up by the Agreement was front and centre in this success. According to Soll, "WAC built support by carefully selecting pilot farms to participate, explaining the potential benefits, and positioning itself as an intermediary between the farmers and the City" (Soll, 2013).

Governance

Guideline 12.14
Do not attempt to control all elements of a program centrally. Build structures that allow and encourage innovation.

New York City, given its size, scope and history has dense layers of bureaucracy. This means that the Catskills reform was susceptible to collapse under its own weight. To implement an enormously complex US$1.5 billion watershed planning initiative requires flexibility. This was achieved by establishing two non-profit organisations: the Watershed Agricultural Council and the Catskill Watershed Corporation. These two entities receive block grants from the City and are then responsible for directing the money into on-the-ground projects. From the outset, it was recognized that, if the City were to contract directly with farmers, wastewater treatment operators or private home owners, the governmental procurement process would be overwhelming (Warne, 2014).

The creation of the Watershed Agricultural Council (WAC) and the Catskill Watershed Corporation (CWC), with offices in the watershed, also takes power out of New York City and puts it into local governance structures that are accountable to the residents of the Catskills. Farmers have a sense that they are in control of the continuous search for the best way to deliver the required outcomes.

Morality

In addition to the above major lessons, there were other ingredients for success. For example, the City established some much-needed moral authority early in the process by fixing up its own wastewater treatment plants before asking non-City owned plants to do the same.

Practicality

Soll stresses throughout his book that the Whole Farm Planning approach was built on "low tech" solutions. Fencing streams, buying land and educating landowners is far from cutting edge science, but if done at scale and with oversight and follow-through it can be highly effective.

A remarkable result of the first two decades of implementation has been the lack of need for enforcement. The Agreement established a special adjudicatory process and forum called the Watershed Protection and Partnership Council. According to Warne, although this Council "is not active, it still exists but they have not met in years". There have been "very few disputes" (Warne, 2014).

The lack of disputes illustrates that there were very few losers in the implementation phase. This is in stark contrast to the earlier days when attempts to improve water quality in the catchment had involved the eviction of farmers, the flooding of towns, the conversion of streams into quiescent impoundments and the displacement of the residents (Kenny, 2006).

Transferability

The Catskills program has become the "go-to study" in Payments for Ecosystem (or Environmental) Services (PES) for water supply. The story has inspired countless conference discussions and academic papers and this interest has followed through into political processes. Since 1997, more than 140 cities in the US have considered establishing a similar program rather than building or expanding a filtration plant (Kenny, 2006). Why so few have adopted a whole scale replication of the New York model is probably a function of the fact that suburban land values are prohibitively expensive. Hard engineering, especially during the period of twentieth century urban expansion, was seen as preferable. Moreover, planning at such an ambitious scale requires a unique political environment with steady and supportive leadership willing to commit significant resources to infrastructure. Overall, the transformational reform seen in the Catskills is not truly comparable with other cases of large-scale watershed management. However, some essential elements of the reform can be replicated.

Inclusive approach

Typical of almost all first attempts to adopt a new transformational paradigm, the negotiating process was messy and volatile, and went on for years before an agreement was finally reached. While messy, the benefit of this process is that it allows stakeholders to air their grievances and for those responsible for implementing the reform to develop working relationships with local representatives. To a significant extent, many of the solutions were worked out with local stakeholders and not imposed on them. Farmers wanted to play an active role in designing the interventions that would occur on their farms, but did not want to be told what to do. They were given the opportunity to do this. Whole Farm Planning provided the collaborative process that answered those concerns and convinced farmers that participating would be in their best interests (CWC, 2013).

Community ownership

A decisive factor in reaching negotiations was the change in relationship between the officials and the community. The factor that has given the reform its stickiness is the depth of local ownership in both the design and the ongoing implementation of the reform. A top-down approach was never going to work. City and state officials had to build enough confidence within the community to enable all to negotiate in good faith. Achieving community ownership meant the City had to find a way to align incentives and demonstrate to the residents that the reform was in fact in their own interest. Early successes with funding projects helped, as did "Good Neighbour Payments", but money alone was not sufficient. The formation of the Catskill Watershed Corporation gave residents control over how projects would be designed, approved, and implemented (Soll, 2013).

Payment vehicles and contracting arrangements

A good portion of the community's enthusiasm for the reform has to do with the generosity of funding available to residents and the way the payment vehicles were designed. A mix of instruments is used. Among other things, direct grants are given to community members, municipalities, and local government entities as well as farmers. The Catskill Watershed Corporation also oversees a broad variety of community development programs, small business loans, educational and recreational activities, and much more.

This variety of payment vehicles is seen by the community as one of the key reasons why this reform has been so successful. This approach, however, limits the transferability of this reform to other catchments. Typically, when making payments, government agencies prefer to have more control and involvement – their tolerance for arrangements not directly associated with a community is low (see Salzman's chapter in this book). The Catskills approach is expensive and not easily transferred to cities with fewer resources.

Generous funding

Initial cost–benefit estimates have shown the reform to be a good deal for New York City. According to an audit done in 2009, the City has spent far less on the Catskills watershed protection programs than it would have on building and maintaining a filtration plant (Kenny, 2006). Besides, as Appleton argues, "ecosystem services not only produce superior environmental and social results, it produces them far more cheaply than traditional environmental strategies" (Kenny, 2006).

The budget of the Catskills Watershed Corporation in 2014 was just under US$34 million, a meaningful sum for a rural economy by any measure (CWC, 2014).

Ecosystem services

The New York City water supply approach has been lauded because it reportedly represents one of the most successful Payment for Ecosystem Services (PES) models in the world. The concept is straightforward: users (rate payers) pay for a natural service, such as clean water, not through the operation of a water treatment plant, but by paying for natural filtration (an ecosystem service) that takes place across the vast watershed area. As described by former Commissioner Appleton:

> Ecosystem service payment programs like the one used in New York are a way of capturing the environmental profits from the services rural ecosystems provide urban areas and then funnelling those profits back into the rural landscapes and the rural communities that provide them, creating a righteous cycle of mutually supportive economic and ecological investments between urban and rural areas, leading to a more sustainable future for both.
>
> (Appleton, 2012)

The concept of "ecosystem services" was not explicitly laid out in the 1997 Agreement, nor is "ecosystem" even used in the document. The concept of ecosystem services probably was launched in Gretchen Daily's 1997 book *Nature's Services: Societal Dependence On Natural Ecosystems* in the same year that the

Agreement was finalised (1997), and was mainstreamed a few years later in the Millennium Ecosystem Assessments reports of the 2000s that sought to take stock of the world's ecosystems and the contribution that they make to human well-being (UNEP, 2014). Those who herald the New York Water supply system as a world class example of a PES program are often unaware that it was not explicitly intended to be one.

If you consider the agreement as a means to express fair payment for services rendered, the New York City model is crudely designed. The US$1.5 billion set aside was mostly thought of as a cost avoidance approach. The amount allocated seems to never have been assessed carefully.

By neo-classical economic standards the New York City Water Supply payment for ecosystem services model is highly inefficient. The system is dependent on government intervention as the single payer (representing the rate payers). In Chapter 10 of this book, Salzman describes government sponsored PES arrangements as *"monopsonies*, with only one buyer for multiple service provider sellers" (see also Salzman, 2005).

In the Catskills, some of the payments appear to be completely unrelated to the ecosystem service. Ratepayer funds, for example, have gone to renovating hospitals, purchasing a senior citizen bus, sprucing up main streets and other community capital projects. These "Good Neighbour Payments", as they are called, seem critical in maintaining community support for the program. Justification for payments relies totally upon the political argument that this approach is critical in gaining and retaining community support for the actions that maintain water quality.

Another criticism that highlights the inefficiency of the New York system is that some of the most effective water quality investments have been for waste water treatment plant upgrades in the catchment and septic system replacement. These are hardly Mother Nature's creations. Furthermore, the complex system of dams, 19 reservoirs, dozens of water control structures, and miles of artificial channels relies on a highly manipulated landscape to provide clean water. The Catskill and Delaware Watersheds, especially those areas most directly connected to the water supply, are engineered landscapes of inundated wetlands and physically altered streams. They are not intact, native ecosystems.

In thinking about transformative reforms and the implementation of more effective payment arrangements Salzman (2005) articulates the challenges well:

> Service markets have been difficult to establish, focusing on the obstacles raised by our poor understanding of service provision, the shortcomings of current institutional arrangements, and the economic challenges to private provision of a public good.

To backup Salzman's point land protection parcels are prioritized according to an array of factors including their proximity to stream corridors, but land is not specifically gauged and assessed for how much it would improve water quality and priced according to the service rendered (Salzman, 2005).

It is difficult to gauge whether the current payment system properly reflects the true value of the services provided. Are the payments excessive, in-line or insufficient for the benefits derived? To answer this question one would need a much better understanding of the "service provision". In the absence of this information the default position held by Appleton and others is that the project is successful because of the large costs avoided and the fact that water quality has not declined appreciably since implementation of the program.

To compare the New York program with the more progressive models such as auction-based land conservation programs and land-use carbon sequestration programs based on rigorous accounting methods is problematic. Both of these program types require a full understanding of the true value of ecosystem services and also a more direct relationship between payments made and services rendered. Outcomes for these programs, however, do not require a high degree of targeting. In the case of carbon sequestration, for example, this can occur anywhere in the world. Similarly, it can be argued that it does not matter where species protection occurs. In the case of the Catskills, however, it is critical that nearly all farmers participate in the program.

Note

1 The residents of the Catskills had a long history of disagreement with New York City and its water needs dating back to the 1880s. When the City began to construct water supply reservoirs and aqueducts in the area, using eminent domain powers, the City displaced thousands of people from villages and farms in a process that left lasting bitterness among residents (Appleton, 2012). In later years, this unhappy legacy was exacerbated by the disparity in economic well-being between local residents and City-dwellers ("New York Times weighs in on upstate reservoir battles – but it's not the whole story", *Watershed Post*, 2012). Even in the 1980s, these memories were still fresh for many residents whose parents and grandparents had lived through that turbulent period, reinforced by the fact that final payments to compensate those residents who were moved out during this period were still being settled into the 1990s (CWC, 2013).

References

Appleton, A. (2012) "How New York City Kept Its Drinking Water Pure – And Saved Billions of Dollars". Available at: http://onthecommons.org/magazine/how-new-york-City-kept-its-drinking-water-pure-and-saved-billions-dollars (accessed 4 March 2014).

CWC (2013) "Behind the scenes: The Inside Story of the Watershed Agreement". Catskill Watershed Corporation. Available at: www.cwconline.org/behind_the_scenes.html (accessed 4 March 2014).

CWC (2014) "Corporate Budget, 2014". Catskill Watershed Corporation.

Daily, G. (ed.) (1997) *Nature's services: Societal dependence on natural ecosystems*. Washington, DC: Island Press.

Kenny, A. (2006) "Ecosystem Marketplace – Ecosystem Services in the New York City Watershed". Ecosystem Marketplace. Available at: www.ecosystemmarketplace.com/pages/dynamic/article.page.php?page_id=4130 (accessed 16 February 2014).

NRC (2000) *Watershed management for potable water supply: assessing the New York City strategy*. National Research Council. Washington, DC: National Academy Press.
NYPIRG (n.d.) "Clean Drinking Water Coalition". New York Public Interest Research Group. Available at: www.nypirg.org/enviro/water/about/coalition.html (accessed 4 March 2014).
Salzman, J. (2005) "Creating Markets for Ecosystem Services: Notes From the Field". *New York University Law Review* 80(3): 870–961.
Soll, D. (2013) *Empire of Water: an Environmental and Political History of the New York City Water Supply*. Ithaca. NY: Cornell University Press.
Stave, K. A. (1995) "Resource use conflict in New York City's Catskill watersheds: A case for expanding the scope of water resource management. Water in the 21st Century: Conservation, Demand, and Supply 61–68". Available at: http://digitalscholarship.unlv.edu/sea_fac_articles/231 (accessed 12 May 2016).
UNEP (2014) "History of the Millennium Assessment". United Nations Environment Program. Available at: www.unep.org/maweb/en/History.aspx (accessed 26 April 2014).
Warne, D. (2014) "Telephone Interview with David Warne", 26 March 2014.
Watershed Agricultural Council (WAC) (n.d) "Whole Farm Planning". Available at www.nycwatershed.org/ag_planning.html (accessed 4 March 2014).
Watershed Post (2012) "New York Times weighs in on upstate reservoir battles – but it's not the whole story". Available at: www.watershedpost.com/2012/new-york-times-weighs-upstate-reservoir-battles-its-not-whole-story (accessed 4 March 2014).

13

EMPOWERING CONSUMERS

Forest Stewardship Council leadership in internationally traded product certification

Juliette Gundy and Julia Radice

Introduction

While legislation and regulatory arrangements have struggled to keep pace with public demands for mechanisms that discourage unsustainable forestry practices worldwide, civil society has been able to make demonstrable progress by developing and implementing market-driven certification schemes. One of the best known certification organizations, the Forest Stewardship Council (FSC), emerged in the 1990s and quickly secured worldwide recognition. This case study identifies policy development lessons stemming from the FSC's early years. Our aim is to search for guidelines that can be usefully applied to other transformational policy development processes.

The FSC is an independent, non-profit organization that promotes responsible forestry management practices internationally. Established in 1993 in response to concerns about global deforestation, environmental degradation and social exclusion, the FSC aims to transform forest management by encouraging consumers to "purchase certified wood with confidence" (Espach, 2009).

The FSC was a pioneer in the development of market-driven certification systems, and in a relatively short time frame has established a market-based system that promotes sustainable forest management and eco-consumerism on a global scale (Espach, 2009).

The case for change

In the late 1980s there was new appreciation of the problems associated with the worldwide forestry sector. Forestry management practices around the world had deteriorated rapidly after World War II, with simultaneous pressures created by high consumption and increasing demand for timber. The intensification of logging and management practices (such as the use of heavy machinery), coupled with a decrease in many governments' ability to regulate the forestry sector, were particularly problematic (Synnott, 2005). Changing forestry management practices contributed to deforestation, declining biodiversity, and had negative impacts on communities living in or near forests.

In the 1980s, conservation organizations and communities worldwide became increasingly active in publicizing localized or regional issues, arguing against specific forestry practices (like clear-cutting or burning), denouncing deforestation and habitat destruction, and contesting logging concessions on indigenous land. A sense of crisis grew in academic, expert, and civil society organizations. Publicity campaigns contributed to broad public and political concern about deforestation and forestry management practices, focussed largely on tropical deforestation in developing countries, but also encompassing temperate and boreal forests in developed countries in Europe and North America (Synnott, 2005; Gale and Haward, 2011).

Industry under pressure

Guideline 13.1
Transformational change is rarely linear. Many draft proposals and countless stakeholder interactions may be needed to build the consensus needed to enable implementation.

The international timber industries' public profile was further affected by the International Tropical Timber Organization's (ITTO) 1989 report on tropical forest management in member states, which concluded that deliberate and sustainable management practices for timber production were in place in a negligible proportion of tropical moist forests worldwide: "It was now extremely difficult for any supplier to endorse tropical timber as coming from well-managed forests .... Companies found themselves branded as contributing to forest destruction based on the simple fact of using tropical timber" (Synnott, 2005).

Synnott, the FSC's first Executive Director, also notes that, in the late 1980s, retailers became the targets of campaigns by environmental NGOs and the media. Manufacturers sought to allay concerns by placing labels on their products, noting that there products had come from sustainable sources. These early certification schemes were not connected to independently verifiable processes or norms, but Synnott states that they served to prepare the ground for the FSC (Synnott, 2005).

Initiatives in the European Parliament in 1988 and 1989 to ban tropical timber imports from countries without acceptable social provisions and forest management/conservation plans ultimately failed, but served to further galvanize environmental groups which had also launched campaigns to boycott tropical timber imports. It is significant that disagreements emerged between these environmental groups; more prominent and conservative groups such as the World Wildlife Fund (WWF) and the World Conservation Union argued that boycotts would reduce the value of forests and forestry, thus increasing incentives to clear forests for rubber and palm oil production. This dialogue focused civil society on the goal of ensuring that timber came from well-managed forests, rather than halting its production (Gale and Haward, 2011).

Guideline 13.2
High levels of public awareness and concern tend to create a sense of urgency, help to establish the legitimacy of a proposal and provide access to important actors.

Pressure mounted in the early 1990s for an international forests treaty, but the failure of negotiations at the 1992 United Nations Conference on Environment and Development (the Earth Summit in Rio de Janeiro) to produce such an agreement led environmental groups such as the WWF to conclude that they should exert direct influence and recognize organizations that practiced sustainable forestry (Bernstein and Cashore, 2004).

Learning from earlier attempts

Guideline 13.3
Early failures can be used to learn and, also, to build consensus and provide legitimacy for a proposed reform.

Several initiatives to use certification and labelling systems to address environmental and social issues appeared in the late 1980s, with the first large-scale fair trade certification scheme emerging in the Netherlands in 1988 (the Max Havelaar programme) (Gale and Haward, 2011). In the late 1980s, the UK-based environmental group Friends of the Earth developed (in partnership with Timothy Synnott) a "modest proposal for a feasibility study into whether certification or labelling of tropical timber could improve forest management practices" (Gale and Haward, 2011). With the UK Government's support, this proposal was presented at a 1989 meeting of the ITTO, but was rejected by developing countries and industry as representing a non-tariff barrier to trade.

While the ITTO was thenceforth not a viable route to pursue a certification scheme, a number of proposals continued to be developed, most notably one spearheaded by the UK's Ecological Trading Company (in consultation with the WWF) for an international forest monitoring agency to verify that timber was sourced from well-managed forests. In 1990, this proposal was presented to a meeting of the Woodworkers Alliance for Rainforest Protection (WARP) (composed of "woodworkers, environmentalists, foresters, scientists and importers and dealers of wood products"; Synnott, 2005), which endorsed the concept and set up a Certification Working Group (CWG) (Gale and Haward, 2011).

Establishing the FSC

Guideline 13.4
The broader the coalition of support, the greater the chance of adoption and financial support.

In a 28-month period between 1990 and 1993, the CWG exercised leadership by further developing the original proposal, secured financial support from philanthropic organizations and expanding stakeholder networks. During this period, it secured legitimacy and broad buy-in for the proposed design. Due to these efforts, consensus emerged internationally to create a "global forest management standard based on a set of international principles and criteria" (Gale and Haward, 2011). The system was to be audited by third-party certifying bodies and would include temperate, tropical and boreal forests. It was also agreed that the system would use labelling to leverage market demand for products derived from sustainable sources, which would in turn create an incentive for improved forest management (Synnott, 2005).

While different groups wished to achieve diverse outcomes through the FSC, it was recognized that one of the central purposes of the FSC was to incentivize industry to use good management practices, and that offering companies "positive alternatives to bans and boycotts" (Synnott, 2005) could achieve this. It was also recognized that national chapters would be needed to formulate national standards. Consultations were held in eleven countries before the FSC founding assembly took place (Synnott, 2005).

Agreement to launch the FSC was reached in 1993. The CWG became the FSC's interim board and held the founding assembly in 1993. Initial objections to the inclusion of industry in the FSC were overcome, as institutional arrangements were put in place to ensure balanced participation, and as awareness had grown that industry would need to be involved in policymaking if the FSC was to have an impact. Meanwhile, the WWF had been working with UK industry representatives to establish an initial buyers group "of companies committed to purchasing certified timber" (Gale and Haward, 2011). The WWF and the UK retailer B&Q also contributed resources to establish the FSC, and the WWF chaired the first meeting. The founding assembly agreed to two significant governance elements: open membership, and aggregating individual and organizational members through the formation of "chambers" (Gale and Haward, 2011; Synnott, 2005).

How the FSC was designed

Guideline 13.5
The broader the structure of a governance system, the more legitimacy it will have and the greater its power will be.

The central purpose of the FSC is to provide certificates that identify products derived from forests where good forestry management practices are in place. It is designed to be an organization that can renew itself and adapt to new conditions and imperatives through flexible membership, transparent decision-making processes and opportunities to change even the most fundamental element of the FSC, its principles and criteria. Earlier attempts to institute sector-wide regulations and/or international forestry treaties did not succeed.

The FSC has ensured broad appeal by accepting the existence of different problem definitions and priorities amongst its stakeholders (deforestation, biodiversity, social ills, etc.), and by harnessing potentially divisive contestations to instead create an adaptive and resilient regime.

Forest certification models rely on market forces; this requires that manufacturers, retailers, and consumers prefer and demand sustainably derived products. This in turn creates incentives for the production of these goods by forest owners. Forest owners and businesses internalize the costs of sustainable forestry management practices and certification processes, as they stand to benefit from gaining access to suppliers and consumers, and avoiding boycott campaigns and public censure (Bernstein and Cashore, 2004; Espach, 2009).

Certification processes

The FSC provides two certification processes. *Forest Management Certification* applies to forest managers or owners that can demonstrate that they have met the FSC's principles and criteria. *Chain-of-Custody Certification* is provided to manufacturers, processors and traders to verify that only FSC-certified materials and products are included in their production chain. For a product to receive this certification, every company in the production chain must be able to keep FSC-certified wood separate from other materials, and the final product must contain only (or a stated percentage of) wood from sustainably managed forests. Certificates are valid for five years, and are monitored through annual surveillance audits for Forest Management Certification, or every six months for Chain-of-Custody Certification (Espach, 2009).[1]

If a certification process finds a forest operation is not fully up to FSC standards, a certifying body may grant a Forest Management Certification "with conditions", which obliges a company to make changes within a specific period of time, or "with pre-conditions", where certification only follows once changes have been made (Gale and Haward, 2011).

> **BOX 13.1**
>
> **FSC PRINCIPLES**
>
> The ten FSC Principles require the forest owner or manager to do the following:
>
> 1. **Compliance with laws and FSC Principles** – to comply with all laws, regulations, treaties, conventions and agreements, together with all FSC Principles and Criteria.
> 2. **Tenure and use rights and responsibilities** – to define, document and legally establish long-term tenure and use rights.
> 3. **Indigenous peoples' rights** – to identify and uphold indigenous peoples' rights of ownership and use of land and resources.
> 4. **Community relations and worker's rights** – to maintain or enhance forest workers' and local communities' social and economic well-being.
> 5. **Benefits from the forest** – to maintain or enhance long term economic, social and environmental benefits from the forest.
> 6. **Environmental impact** – to maintain or restore the ecosystem, its biodiversity, resources and landscapes.
> 7. **Management plan** – to have a management plan, implemented, monitored and documented.
> 8. **Monitoring and assessment** – to demonstrate progress towards management objectives.
> 9. **Maintenance of high conservation value forests** – to maintain or enhance the attributes which define such forests.
> 10. **Plantations** – to plan and manage plantations in accordance with FSC Principles and Criteria.
>
> Source: https://ic.fsc.org/en/certification/principles-and-criteria/the-10-principles.

Forest Stewardship principles and criteria

The FSC's ten principles for forest stewardship were first released in 1994, and have been amended and revised four times since, most recently in 2012. These principles form the backbone of the organization, guiding its work in protecting the environment, indigenous peoples' rights, workers' rights and promoting responsible management practices (see Box 13.1).

Each principle is supported by several criteria to ensure that adherence can be measured. Although all ten principles and associated criteria must be met for an FSC certificate to be issued, FSC national or regional working groups (coordinated by national chapters) can develop standards that "provide locally appropriate indicators for each criterion to show compliance can be demonstrated in that national situation".[2] Indicators associated with FSC standards are thus adapted for particular countries or regions as determined by its representative committee members (Gale and Haward, 2011; Espach, 2009).

Governance and membership

Guideline 13.6
Legitimacy can be increased by creating an environment where all stakeholders perceive they will be heard and will be given an equitable say irrespective of the sector or region they represent.

The FSC has a diverse membership and includes individuals and organizations from around the world. Members are drawn from environmental and social civil society organizations; the timber trade; retailers and manufacturers; indigenous peoples' organizations; and forest owners and forestry organizations.[3] Its structure is designed to give all members a voice and vote in decision-making.

The FSC General Assembly meets every three years to debate and makes decisions on issues such as the FSC's operation and structure, the performance of the FSC's international board of directors, and FSC principles and criteria. Members are assigned on the basis of their interests to one of three chambers: an environmental chamber, a social chamber or an economic chamber. Each member is then further assigned to a "north" or "south" sub-chamber. Votes are then weighted so as to give equal voting weight to each chamber and, also to "northern" and "southern" interests. Assignment to the north and south sub-chambers depends upon whether or not the member is "legally registered in a high-income country (North) or non high-income country (South), according to the World Bank definition".[4] This prevents groups from dominating the FSC based on shared interests, economic or political power (Bernstein and Cashore, 2004; Gale and Haward, 2011).[5]

All eligible FSC members have voting rights in relation to policies, standards and principles. Decision-making processes are designed to strive for consensus. Within each North or South sub-chamber, individual members hold 10 percent of votes, while organizational members hold 90 percent of votes (Espach, 2009).[6]

The membership criterion for each chamber is unique. The economic chamber is comprised of members with a vested interest in commercial forestry (i.e. "employees, consultants or representatives of forest product companies, certification bodies, industry Associations – whether for profit or not-for-profit – wholesalers, retailers, traders, end-users, and consulting companies"). This contrasts with the social chamber, which is strictly made up of non-profit NGOs "and assigned individuals with a demonstrated commitment to environmentally appropriate, socially beneficial and economically viable forest management". The environment chamber includes indigenous organizations, individuals, and social movements that promote good forest management based on environmental, social and economic values (see Table 13.1).[7]

Members vote for both national and international boards of directors, and national members directly elect their own national boards.

TABLE 13.1 Structure of the Forest Stewardship Council as at December 2009

Chamber	North	South	Total	% of total
Economic	182	154	336	41%
Environmental	132	210	342	41%
Social	57	94	151	18%
Total	371	458	829	
%	45%	55%		

Source: Gale and Haward, 2011.

The International Board considers "FSC policy and operational matters including those referred to it by its constituent bodies" (Gale and Haward, 2011). Responsibility for FSC operations is delegated to the Director General, who is also responsible for managerial oversight of the FSC's three constituent bodies:

- FSC International Center;
- FSC Global Development; and
- Accreditation Services International.

The FSC International Center in Bonn, Germany is responsible for the day-to-day operation of the organization. Global Development ensures "the appropriate use" of the FSC logo, promotes certification and seeks to increase revenues from use of the logo. Accreditation Services International accredits third-party certifying bodies, undertakes audits of these groups and can propose changes to related policies and standards (Gale and Haward, 2011).[8]

Independent, third-party verification

Guideline 13.7
Market mechanisms can be used to drive transformational change and bring legitimacy to and investment in the mechanisms that underpin a reform.

The FSC does not carry out assessments for certification itself, but rather accredits independent, third-party organizations to do so.[9] Public monitoring and open investigative processes provide oversight of the certification bodies. Owners or companies seeking FSC certification approach an FSC-accredited certification body, and pay a fee to receive a scoping visit; contingent on the subsequent scoping report, owners and companies pay another fee for a full certification audit (Gale and Haward, 2011; Espach, 2009).[10] Of note, if no national FSC standards exist in a country where a certification process is requested, certifying bodies may utilize their own standards, which must be derived from FSC principles and criteria.

Certifying bodies may use different systems to conduct these audits, which led to discrepancies and disputes early in the FSC's history. If a dispute arises following a certification decision, complaints are meant to be resolved at the lowest level possible; complaints that cannot be resolved directly with the forestry company can be brought to the certification body, and subsequently to the national working group and eventually the international level of the FSC (Gale and Haward, 2011).

Group certification is available for both forest management and chain of custody certificates As a general, this is less costly for smaller businesses than each applying for their own certificate. However, if one operation or business does not meet the required standard, all connected businesses would also lose their certification.[11]

A number of factors and players ensured that the FSC's certification scheme took hold. As a market-driven mechanism, the demand-side market needed to be established and willing to engage. Aside from markets, public support and networks were needed to buttress and legitimize the scheme. Focussing on these two aspects at the outset ensured the adoption of FSC's certification scheme at a significant level.

First and foremost, the development of buyer networks was essential for the credibility and adoption of a certification system for forestry products. Companies began investing in the process in 1991 with the support of NGOs involved in the creation of FSC. At the same time individual activists, Friends of the Earth, rainforest action groups and other environmental groups began to develop the buyer market by targeting "do-it-yourself" retailers in the UK (Gulbrandsen, 2010). WWF UK took on a significant role in assisting the FSC to access these markets, and created the first buyer group of retailers, called the WWF 95 Group:

> The name was derived from the members' pledge to support WWF's ambitious goal, set in 1989, for the world's tropical timber trade to be based on sustainable timber sources by the end of 1995. At the time, of the difficult issues for environmental groups was retailers' misuse of claims about wood products sourced from well-managed forests. Because FSC was not yet operational, the original requirements for membership committed retailers to an immediate phase-out of all wood labels and certificates claiming sustainability until "a credible independent certification and labelling system" was established.
>
> (Gulbrandsen, 2010)

Retailers joined the buyers group for various reasons: some joined because they saw the potential value added to their brand. Some were motivated by eliminating the existing constellation of wood labels making unsubstantiated claims to "sustainability" in favour of a more independent system. Some were motivated to join the buyers group due to bad publicity and social pressure resulting from: "direct targeting from more radical environmental groups such as Greenpeace, Earth First and Friends of the Earth, which organized a series of protests at retail outlets and wholesalers' timber distribution centres" (Gulbrandsen, 2010). After gaining initial support from buyers, efforts increased to attract wider engagement, including pulp and paper, construction, and furniture companies. An important early win for the FSC was obtaining support from Sainsbury and Tesco, major supermarket chains in the UK.

FSC and its affiliated NGOs employed a similar strategy to develop buyer groups outside of the UK, in Europe and North America, but it is important to note that "in several countries, support from large retailers was forthcoming only after intensive NGO targeting, threats of boycotts and shaming campaigns" (Gulbrandsen, 2010). In the United States, for example, the Rainforest Action Network (RAN) was instrumental in protesting Home Depot, a retailer that sells home improvement, lawn and garden products.[12] In the span of three years (1997–99), the Rainforest Action Network convinced Home Depot to cease sourcing merchandise from environmentally sensitive forests and to "give preference to wood that is certified as coming from forest managed in a responsible way" (Gulbrandsen, 2010).

Receiving Home Depot's support and its commitment to buy FSC-certified wood products was a significant coup in the American market. Home Depot was the largest home improvement retailer in the United States, and influenced other retailers to buy FSC-certified products including Lowe's, the second largest home improvement retailer in the USA (Gulbrandsen, 2010). Over time, the relationship between FSC-aligned NGOs and large retailers shifted from animosity to alliance, as those retailers applied pressure on their supply chains to also seek FSC certification.

After initial inroads had been made to secure buyer networks, continued efforts from FSC's affiliated NGOs were necessary to achieve and sustain market penetration, thus allowing the FSC scheme to exist and grow. WWF's Global Forest and Trade Network (GFTN) has been an important vehicle to ensure market penetration for FSC.

Originally a demand-side network, as of mid-2009 GFTN included producers and buyers that controlled more than 20 million hectares of certified forest, employed nearly 3 million people, and handled 16 percent of all internationally traded forest products (Gulbrandsen, 2010).

In the early years, after retailer demand networks had been established, a concern arose over whether there would be adequate supply to meet demand. However, FSC-certified large retailers (Home Depot, Lowe's, IKEA, and B&Q) enjoyed an enormous share of the market for wood products, and were able to exert tremendous pressure on their producers and suppliers to certify (Gulbrandsen, 2010).

Another piece of the adoption puzzle was the role of governments. At the outset, governments could not be full members of the FSC, yet their role has been vital. Some governments have supported the FSC, seeing "eco-labelling as a way of circumventing trade rules that hindered them from imposing tropical timber import restrictions to control illegal and irresponsible logging" (Gulbrandsen, 2010). Public procurement of FSC-certified products gave more momentum to the certification scheme; it both augmented demand, and enhanced the perception of the FSC as a valid and trustworthy certification scheme, thus promoting private market adoption (Gulbrandsen, 2010).

How was the system adapted during implementation?

Guideline 13.8
Allow for adaptation during implementation as those involved gain experience and develop an administrative capacity.

The structure and organization of the FSC allows it to continuously revise its principles and criteria, national standards and operating procedures.[13] Such changes can be driven by the FSC's membership, which can raise challenges and propose revisions that keep the system aligned with best practice. Care is taken to maintain an egalitarian and entrepreneurial spirit.

The principles and criteria were originally published in 1994, and have been revised four times: 1996, 1999, 2001 and 2012.[14] Some notable changes include:

- approving a social strategy for forestry in 2002 which streamlined certification procedures for small and low-intensity forests (Liedeker and Spencer, 2005);
- the FSC, following extensive consultations, taking steps to "ensure that forest communities' and indigenous peoples' land tenure and resource use rights are taken fully into account in the elaboration of national forest management standards and the application of FSC Principles & Criteria in the forest" (Liedeker and Spencer, 2005); and
- allowing government forestry departments to join the FSC as Economic Chamber members starting in 2002 (Gale and Haward, 2011).

Emphasis now is placed on providing regions and countries with the autonomy and guidance needed to adapt the FSC principles and criteria to local conditions. National working groups develop and amend national standards and indicators on an ongoing basis. The first national working group to begin work on standards was Sweden in 1997. By 2009, several countries were renegotiating their national standards for a third time.

Given that the FSC's overarching principles and criteria have also been revised several times, it is unsurprising that national standards themselves differ depending on when they were negotiated; by 2000, however, the FSC's International Center had developed a template for national standards, and was monitoring and enforcing this template, which led to greater coherence between national standards (Gale and Haward, 2011).

Impact and behavioural change

Guideline 13.9
With attention to design and an emphasis on the establishment of market-based legitimacy, early detractors can become the biggest supporters.

Despite its success, there are still some distinct and important barriers to FSC adoption. One of the most contentious issues may be the disparity in regional adoption: while FSC certification is common and expanding in Europe and North America, certification is less prevalent in developing countries.[15]

The FSC now has a presence in more than 80 countries and, by October 2013, had certified over 186 million hectares of forest worldwide. Europe accounts for the largest certified areas at 43 percent with North America close behind at 40 percent. The remaining total is drawn from South America and the Caribbean (7 percent), Asia (4 percent), Africa (4 percent), and Oceania (1 percent).[16] Given rigorous requirements for FSC certification, this is an impressive advancement of sustainable forestry practices across the globe.

It is less clear whether the FSC has achieved its original goal to drastically improve forestry practices worldwide. Here, FSC faces a hard reality: effecting change with regard to tropical timber has proved to be a challenge. Thus far, market mechanisms have been unable to bring about large-scale certification in tropical-timber producing nations. There are some indications that, while FSC is making inroads in tropical timber producing countries, increases in certification levels are taking place slowly.

Brazil, for example, has seen an uptake in tropical forest certification. Plantations now represent a large percentage of certified concessions in this country. Brazil has established buyer's groups that include state governments, whose members agree to preferential procurement of certified products. In areas where certification has taken hold, forest management practices and worker conditions have both improved. Thus there is reason to be optimistic about tropical timber producing countries adopting FSC, but with the understanding that it will take time.

The impact of public support for the FSC and other forest certification systems on government procurement policies must also be considered. For example, the state government of Victoria (Australia) has stated that, in order to improve biosecurity for sustainable timber production, it will not allow any Victorian government department or agency "to adopt or endorse any position, including in relation to procurement policies, guides or tools, which does not equally recognise third-party certification from the Australian Forestry Standard, Forest Stewardship Council, or any equivalent scheme" and "Victorian Government funding or endorsement will only be available to organisations administering sustainability or procurement guides that are consistent with this policy".[17]

Conclusion

Challenges notwithstanding, FSC certification has consistently expanded, as evidenced by the increasing area of forest certified each year. The story of its adoption highlights the importance of the FSC's alliances with powerful NGOs, civil society's advocacy work, the strategic decision to target big retailers, and the FSC's ability to leverage both public and private market demand.

The FSC's success has demonstrated the viability of voluntary, market-driven models for environmental management. It was born out of the creativity and relentless determination of group of individuals and organizations from many sectors, considerable demand-side pressures, and the absence of other means to promote global change in forestry management practices. Crucially, the FSC model has demonstrated that ecological, social, political, and economic gains can be made through multi-stakeholder engagement and voluntary processes.

The FSC scheme seems to be effective, as the principles and criteria are relatively robust, there is significant buy-in from stakeholders, and there continues to be strong demand-side support for FSC products. We believe that the FSC would benefit from comprehensive and rigorous impact evaluations, which could produce useful lessons learned and unlock greater demand for FSC certification and products.

The FSC is now closely associated with concepts of ethical resource management. The model has already been replicated in other sectors (most notably through the Marine Stewardship Council in the fisheries sector), which both demonstrates the FSC's success as well as expectations that this same model could plausibly address other resource management challenges.

Notes

1 See also "Types of FSC Certificates", Forest Stewardship Council, https://ic.fsc.org/types-of-certification.35.htm (accessed 22 April 2014) and "FSC Certification", Forest Stewardship Council, https://ic.fsc.org/certification.4.htm (accessed 22 April 2014).
2 "FSC Principles and Criteria," Forest Stewardship Council, https://ic.fsc.org/principles-and-criteria.34.htm (accessed 22 April 2014).
3 "Governance", Forest Stewardship Council, https://ic.fsc.org/governance.14.htm (accessed 16 February 2014).
4 "Frequently Asked Questions about FSC and Membership", Forest Stewardship Council United States, http://us.fsc.org/download.membership-faqs.130.pdf (accessed 22 April 2014).
5 See also "Governance: Members Lead FSC," Forest Stewardship Council United States, https://us.fsc.org/governance.181.htm, (accessed 22 April 2014).
6 See "Governance: Members Lead FSC," Forest Stewardship Council United States, https://us.fsc.org/governance.181.htm (accessed 22 April 2014).
7 "International Bylaws", Forest Stewardship Council, https://us.fsc.org/download.fsc-international-bylaws.114.pdf (accessed 16 February 2014).
8 See also "Governance: Members Lead FSC", Forest Stewardship Council United States, https://us.fsc.org/governance.181.htm (accessed 22 April 2014) and "Governance", Forest Stewardship Council, https://ic.fsc.org/governance.14.htm (accessed 16 February 2014).
9 "Certification Bodies," Accreditation Services International, www.accreditation-services.com/archives/certification_bodies (accessed 22 April 2014).
10 See also "FSC Certification," Forest Stewardship Council, https://ic.fsc.org/certification.4.htm (accessed 22 April 2014) and "Three Steps Towards FSC

Certification", Forest Stewardship Council, https://ic.fsc.org/3-steps-to-certification.36.htm (accessed 22 April 2014).
11 "Group and Multi-site Chain of Custody standards", Forest Stewardship Council, https://ic.fsc.org/group-and-multi-site-chain-of-custody.366.htm (accessed 22 April 2014) and also "Group Certification", Forest Stewardship Council, https://ic.fsc.org/group-certification.312.htm (accessed 22 April 2014).
12 "Home Depot," Forbes, www.forbes.com/companies/home-depot/ (accessed 20 April 2014).
13 "Current consultations", Forest Stewardship Council, https://ic.fsc.org/consultations.106.htm (accessed 22 April 2014).
14 "FSC Principles and Criteria", Forest Stewardship Council, https://ic.fsc.org/principles-and-criteria.34.htm (accessed 22 April 2014).
15 There are various factors contributing to this challenge, and in part this is due to the fact that "forest holdings in tropical countries have had little trouble selling uncertified and even illegally sourced timber in the world market"(Gulbrandsen, 2010). Other factors include the lack of information and awareness in developing countries about certification, the challenges of varied levels of land tenure systems and robustness of government regulation systems (Gulbrandsen, 2010), as well as the costs of certification.
16 "Facts and Figures: February 2014", Forest Stewardship Council, https://ic.fsc.org/facts-figures.19.htm (accessed 22 April 2014).
17 "Timber Industry Action Plan: Priority 2", State Government of Victoria Department of Environment and Primary Industries, www.depi.vic.gov.au/forestry-and-land-use/timber-production/timber-industry-action-plan/priority-2 (accessed 22 April 2014).

References

Bernstein, S. and Cashore, B. (2004) "Non-state Global Governance: Is Forest Certification a Legitimate Alternative?" In J. Kirton and M. Trebilcock (eds.) *Hard Choices, Soft Law*. Ashgate, Burlington.
Espach, R. (2009) *Private Environmental Regimes in Developing Countries*. New York: Palgrave Macmillan.
Gale, F. and Haward, M. (2011) *Global Commodity Governance*. New York: Palgrave Macmillan.
Gulbrandsen, L.H. (2010) *Transnational Environmental Governance: The Emergence and Effects of the Certification of Forests and Fisheries*. Cheltenham: Edward Elgar.
Liedeker, H. and Spencer, M. (2005) "Forest Stewardship Council". In D. Burger; J. Hess and B. Lang (eds.) *Forest Certification: An innovative instrument in the service of sustainable development?* Eschborn: Deutsche Gesellschaft für Technische Zusammenarbeit.
Synnott, T. (2005) "Some notes on the early years of FSC". Forest Stewardship Council, 19 November 2005. Available at https://ic.fsc.org/our-history.17.htm (accessed 22 April 2014).

14

THE ART OF GOOD GOVERNANCE

Analysing water management success in Phnom Penh

Timothy Grant

Background

In the early nineties, the infrastructure of water supply services in the capital of Cambodia, Phnom Penh was truly broken. In terms of distribution, only 20 percent of the city's inhabitants received mains water (Otis, 2013). The system was operational for 10 hours a day and in terms of quality, the supply was inadequate for human consumption. Water loss rates hovered at 70 percent of supply. Poorly maintained pipes and thousands of illegal connections meant the entire system was dysfunctional. Much like the system it ran, the Phnom Penh Water Supply Authority (PPWSA) was a state-run enterprise rife with corruption and inefficiency. Political pressure combined with poor management made coordinated attempts to improve the supply system fruitless. A lack of skilled employees further exacerbated an already deplorable situation.

In a span of ten years of reform, the PPWSA went from one of the poorest performing government utilities in the world to one of the most highly regarded and has became a case study of efficient policy reform. In recognition of this achievement, the PPWSA received the 2004 Asian Development Bank Water Prize for "dramatically overhauling Phnom Penh's water supply system and demonstrating leadership and innovation in project financing and governance". In 2006, PPWSA CEO Ek Sonn Chan was awarded the Ramon Magsaysay Award – the Asian equivalent of the Nobel Prize – for Government Service. In 2010, PPWSA received the Stockholm Industry Water Award.[1]

Although all water management systems are contextual, the reform of Cambodia's capital city water supply utility is an important reference for engendering policy change in water supply mechanisms. Despite major obstacles to reform, the PPWSA restructured successfully due to its systematic targeting of institutional inefficiencies and solid international assistance. A key component of this transformation lies with the resilient, dedicated leadership of the PPWSA during its reform and the steps they took to engender change.

The history of the PPWSA

In order to understand how truly successful reform was in Phnom Penh, it is important to observe the historical context that led to its late nineteenth-century inefficiency. The PPWSA was officially established by royal decree of the Kingdom of Cambodia in 1959 by King Norodom Sihanouk.[2]

From 1959 to 1979, the system was left unattended and became largely inefficient due to the political instability of the country, primarily at the hands of the authoritarian Khmer Rouge regime (Das et al., 2010). This was followed by 11 years of continued mis-management until 1990 by which time the system was running at only 45 percent of its original capacity. Unskilled labour, unmotivated management and corruption were common.

Structural reformation

The transformation of the PPWSA into a prosperous institution began in the 1990s. The combined efforts of various actions to promote this change were as follows:

- appointment of Ek Sonn Chan as the Director General in 1993;
- granting of operational autonomy in 1996;
- metering, monitoring and reduction of non-revenue water;
- implementation of a new tariff policy and volume-based pricing in 1997;
- obtaining financial assistance from international sources;
- independent financing;
- removal of corruption; and
- investment in human capital.

The appointment of Ek Sonn Chan

Guideline 14.1
When commencing a major transformational change, begin by appointing a new leader who is not associated with or responsible for the development of the policies and institutional arrangements that are about to be replaced.

A crucial element of the reform of the authority has been the integrity of leadership Chan provided. In 1993, Ek Sonn Chan was appointed as Director General of the PPWSA (Das et al., 2010). Under Chan's direction, the Authority pushed for higher water quality standards to increase system coverage and increase revenues. Chan's investment in infrastructure and human capital while lowering non-revenue water has resulted in the PPWSA being currently one of the world's few publicly managed water utilities that has continued to net profit since the 1990s (Das *et al.*, 2010). Chan was instrumental in ensuring transparency in the company's actions and increasing public trust in the PPWSA.

The son of a soldier in the Khmer Rouge, Chan was born into a poor, working-class family and started his career in the Cambodian utilities sector in 1979 (Unknown, 2009). His appointment to the PPWSA occurred during a period of international engagement and a culture of transformation throughout Cambodia at a time when it was regarded, according to Transparency International, as one of the most corrupt countries in Asia (Crothers, 2013). National transformation began with the lifting of economic sanctions upon Cambodia and was followed by foreign donor investment. Known for a staunch commitment to hard work and social justice coupled with a familiarity with the international assistance world, Chan's ascension to the PPWSA represented a new direction for the water utility.

The new Director General showed courageous leadership during his early appointment to the PPWSA and set a new standard for the management of public utilities in Cambodia. By way of example, as soon as he was appointed, he insisted that all government agencies should pay for their water services. The action was met with heavy resistance by government agencies, including one incident in which a Cambodian Army official threatened Chan with a gun. The Director General responded by shutting off this depot's water supply until the military paid its bill (Bahree, 2009). Under Chan's direction, and as people began paying their bills to increase water coverage, the increased revenue was used to increase water supply coverage and improve service.

Granting the PPWSA operational autonomy

Guideline 14.2
Prospects for a successful reform can be increased by establishing a strong independent authority whose revenue base is not dependent upon access to government budgets.

In 1996, the Cambodian Government granted the PPWSA administrative autonomy, freeing it from political interference (Biswas and Tortajada, 2010) so that the Authority was able to pursue the changes it needed to make without interference from political agendas. Operational autonomy was achieved by turning the Authority into a corporation with a decentralized structure so that each branch of the PPWSA was responsible for its own monitoring and annual reporting. In its current form, the Authority has five distinct branches:

- planning and technology;
- productions;
- commercial department;
- administration and human resources; and
- finances (Das *et al.*, 2010).

The Board, including its President, comprises five government officials and two PPWSA members. The Authority's Board meets every three months to discuss the general strategic direction of the PPWSA and, also, to approve investment programs and the budget. Subject to direction from the Board, the Director General is responsible for day-to-day management of the company and oversees all operational and organizational decisions.[3]

Metering, monitoring and reduction in non-revenue water

A monumental step forward for the water authority was the introduction of meters and the development of more efficient methods of monitoring. Initially, the Authority was unable to track water and could not account for usage (Unknown, 2009). As the company began to collect data, metering of water mains was introduced to gauge water use more accurately, allowing the PPWSA to see at the street level who was paying for water and who was not. In addition, the PPWSA compiled a consumer database to monitor their clients. These actions led to an improvement in collections for revenues to facilitate greater reform process and reduced non-revenue water to only 6 percent, an amazing number given the original pre-reform rate of over 70 percent (Das et al., 2010).

Implementation of tariff policy and volume based pricing

Guideline 14.3
As a transformational reform is implemented, work hard to secure political support from beneficiaries, especially those who under the old regime were disadvantaged.

In the initial stages of reformation, Ek Sonn Chan instituted a block tariff policy on water for customers to further cover costs, maintenance and planned modifications for the system (Biswas and Tortajada, 2010). In order for the company to instigate such a policy without sparking civil unrest, the PPWSA first made significant improvements to the quality of the Phnom Penh water supply with a view to creating a sense of trust and that the quality of the service provided was worth paying for. As part of this process, they moved from a flat rate pricing plan to a volume-based pricing plan, which was made possible through the metering process (Unknown, 2009). To avoid public backlash, the PPWSA orchestrated the changes slowly, increasing tariffs gradually first in 1993 and then again in 1997.

Aware of the benefits of the provision of water to poor households that previously had not had access, the PPWSA invested in the recruitment of support from these beneficiaries. He saw these people as strong supporters for its restructuring plan. The proposition was simple. Poor households who did not have access to a mains water supply typically paid 5,000 riels for water that the Authority could supply to them for 500 riels. From the PPWSA viewpoint, buy-in to the system by the poor assisted considerably in the reduction of non-revenue water losses and enabled the company to achieve the positive cash flow needed to expand investment.

Foreign assistance

Guideline 14.4
The probability of a successful reform will be greater if any increase in service charges follows rather than precedes improvements in performance.

Financial assistance from other countries and third party organizations was fundamental in the transformation of the PPWSA. Financial assistance included grants, loans, consultations and technical assistance.

With the establishment of the Royal Government of Cambodia in 1993, countries and organizations offered to help the country in its restructuring process. One of the first countries to offer aid was France, which provided two initial grants to the government that enabled the PPWSA to improve Phnom Penh's water distribution network and supply facilities (Biswas and Totajada, 2010).

From the outset, Japan proved to be one the largest support donors and was instrumental in increasing management and service efficiency. In the early 1990s, Cambodia often worked in collaboration with the Japanese International Co-operation Agency (JICA). Major operations involved operations and management training for Cambodian staff through technical assistance. In 1993, the JICA collaborated in the preparation of the plan for the improvement of water management in Phnom Penh (Das *et al.*, 2010). This plan became the established roadmap for reformation of the PPWSA and bedded down the vision that the PPWSA could be an efficient, comprehensive and self-funded water supplier. In the years that followed, JICA provided multiple grants to the PPWSA. In 1993, the Japanese and French governments provided US$5.3 million in aid to Cambodia. By 1997, JICA had provided close to US$47 million to the PPWSA (Biswas and Tortajada, 2010).

Other organizations that provided financial support included the Asian Development Bank, the World Bank and the UNDP. In addition to Japan's efforts, the UNDP and the World Bank also offered technical assistance training in the early 1990s. As a result, the PPWSA met operational costs for the first time in 1997 and, as this happened, assistance from these three organizations moved from the provision of grants to loans. These loans enabled further innovation and capacity building.

Having achieved financial security, World Bank loans were then taken out to enable the rebuilding Phnom Penh's water supply network. These loans were paid back fully in four years (Biswas and Tortajada, 2010). In addition to this financial assistance function, the World Bank also provided advice to the PPWSA on the institutional structure and operation of the company which proved important in enabling it to secure and retain administrative autonomy.

Donor aid in the reformation of the water authority was important because it gave the PPWSA the autonomy needed to enable it to radically change at the same time as the Cambodian Government was re-establishing itself in the early 1990s. Significantly, donor assistance extended well beyond finance to include significant technical assistance and staff training that freed the Authority from political pressures within its own country. This allowed the PPWSA to pursue a much more aggressive reform strategy that otherwise would have been the case.

Independent financing

The PPWSA continuously refined its servicing database and gradually extended the coverage of its water-supply system until it began making revenues to cover its operational cost (see Figure 14.1). With the assistance of foreign aid to meet its budgetary obligations, the company successfully used its increased revenue to fund rapid expansion of its network. As such, the PPWSA has continuously made a profit since the 1993 (Biswas and Tortajada, 2010).

Removal of corruption

One of the most difficult tasks that the PPWSA had to undertake was to find a way to turn their organization from a company filled with corruption and incompetent labour into one that employed effective, honest workers who take pride in their jobs. Initially, many of the bureaucrats in the PPWSA were opposed to the reforms being implemented. Some officials, for example, were adverse to the introduction of meters as this eliminated the ability of workers to make illegal connections for a side payment.

The initial process of routing out corruption involved Ek Sonn Chan firing a significant number of corrupt employees. He also took the opportunity to lay off staff who were considered to be grossly inefficient. When the company gained autonomy in 1996, Chan was able to hire his own staff, resulting in more competent appointments. In addition, bonuses were initiated for honest and hard-working staff.

Transparency was utilized in the initial evaluation process of the system not only to ensure that tasks were performed honestly, but also to generate support from the public and government. Evaluations are still performed by the Director General and are submitted to all employees. The company also encourages auditing (Biswas and Tortajada, 2010).

Investment in human capital

To purge gross inefficiency in the PPWSA, the Authority began investing in its workforce to ensure that the most skilled labourers were employed. The first step was to offer higher wages as a means of instilling pride in workers and encouraging efficiency. Incentives and bonuses were given to staff and rewards offered to those who reported corruption. Employees are now paid for overtime, and interest-free

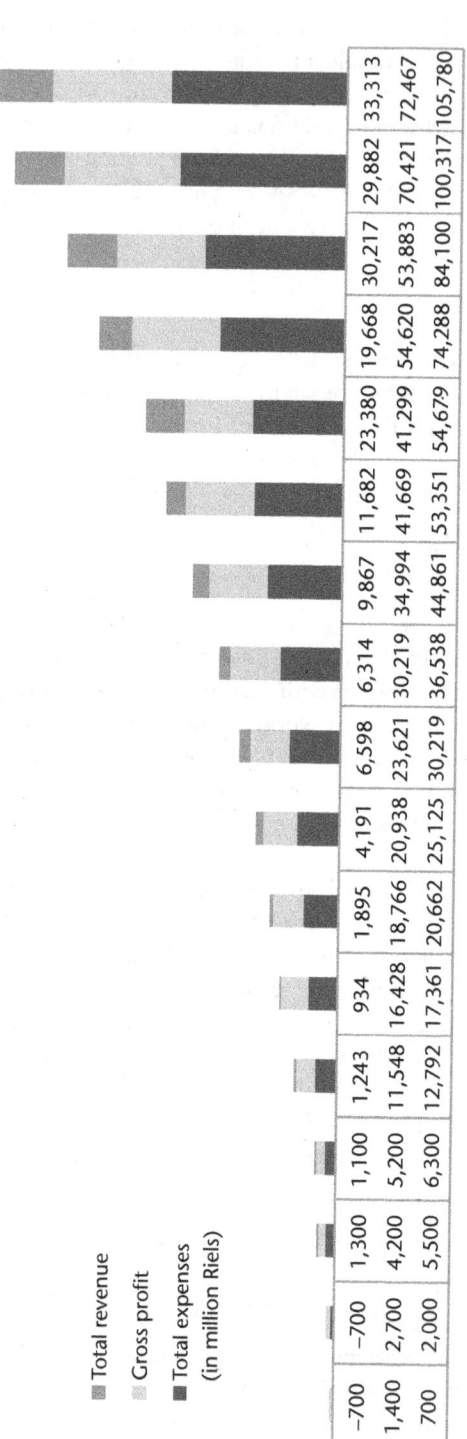

FIGURE 14.1 Changes in PPWSA revenue, expenses and profit (PPWSA records)

loans are offered to low-income workers. In addition to these support structures, the PPWSA now gives high priority to staff training. Members of the PPWSA are required to partake in an annual training program. Throughout the course of their career, workshop training sessions are offered to all staff wanting to develop their skills. The Authority also pays for some staff to attend university. Fair treatment of staff in the workplace is another priority (Biswas and Tortajada, 2010).

Perspective on success

One of the most important aspects in the reform of water supply arrangements in Phnom Penh, and arguably one of the most difficult to objectively quantify, was the entire water sector's inherent desire to change for the better. This was shown in the continual support of the PPWSA's efforts by the Cambodian Government and the public.

Decrees mandated by law for the autonomy of the organization were crucial to the reform, as was the country's international request for technical assistance and the active role the government played in seeking administrative guidance and financial support from the international community.

Coalition of interests

Broad interest was crucial to the adoption of the new Authority. As Director General, one of Ek Sonn Chan's most successful initiatives was to seek political support from the poor to create a large show of support for the Authority's pricing strategy. Keen to link revenue to use, and, as already mentioned, in 1996 Chan proposed a transition to volume-based pricing, which was met initially with strong opposition (Unknown, 2009). Rather than giving up, Chan turned to the poor and convinced them that volume-based charging was decidedly more equitable and that its introduction was in their interests. He then organized for them to petition the government to support this change. Using his initial monitoring staff, Chan took the fingerprints of tens of thousands of poor people who wanted to shift to volumetric pricing. With the support of Chea Sophara, the then Governor of Phnom Penh, Chan then met privately with Cambodian Prime Minister Prince Norodom to show him the depth of the support he had obtained for this reform and convinced him that the PPWSA should be allowed to move to volumetric pricing (Unknown, 2009).

Impact of foreign donors

At the same time that he was attempting to convince the Prime Minister of the need for price reform, Chan was able to secure strong support of the Cambodian Ministry of Finance. This was due largely to pressure from foreign aid organizations such as the Asian Development Bank, which was prepared to offer loans only if the PPWSA shifted to a volumetric pricing regime that would increase revenue as more and more water was supplied to users. Eventually and as a result of Chan's efforts, full political support for a shift to volumetric pricing was secured from the government and opposition to this policy change overcome.

Integrity of the proposal

Guideline 14.5
To sustain a reform program, it is critical to deal quickly with and be seen to deal with maladministration. Evidence of corruption, for example, needs to be dealt with quickly.

An obvious lesson to be learned from the PPWSA experience is that once there is a key understanding of the most appropriate suite of reforms that need to be made, there is a need for flexibility in implementation. With regard to the introduction of meters, for example, the PPWSA began by paying contractors a pre-arranged price for each meter installed. Soon, however, it became clear that considerable price gouging was occurring, with side payments going to a small group of PPWSA staff. Great care was needed as the issue was only discovered when the extent of price gouging became public. As soon as it did, members of the public started to complain that they had been taken advantage of. In response, Chan moved quickly to dismiss the staff involved. Today, the cost of meter installation is around one-fifth of the original charges set for installation. The resiliency of the reform shows in the Authority's ability to adapt to public opinion and quickly deal with problems.

Similar case studies

It is easy to argue that transformational policy reforms tend to be highly contextual and that it is difficult to identify general guidelines. In this case of water supply arrangements for Phnom Penh, for example, it is easy to argue that the reforms were possible only because they occurred at a time when Cambodia was reconnecting with the global community. By assessing like-minded reform policies within their own respective settings and times, however, it is possible to find congruent guidelines that lead to successful change.

The failure of the privatization of Cochabamba water supply arrangements in Bolivia, for example, highlights the importance of engaging with the populace and understanding constituency needs. In 1999, Cochabamba, Bolivia's third largest city, contracted Aguas del Tunari, a consortium owned by the American corporation Bechtel to take over management of its water supply system. As the sole participant in the bidding process, Aguas del Tunari signed a 40-year contract which guaranteed it a 15 percent return on investment (Finnegan, 2002). The aggressive consolidation of control over Cochabamba's municipalities and district water rights by the company coincided with the announcement that the company would begin metering and payment collection on *all* water supply sources, steadily increase tariffs and adopt a zero non-payment tolerance policy.

Initially, small organizations of engineers, environmentalists, and water users were concerned over the proposed restructuring process, but the government largely ignored them. In 2000, however, fees doubled and business owners, middle-class income households and the public at large soon joined the initial protestors (Finnegan, 2002). These protestors soon coalesced into the movement known as La Coordinadora, which was so successful that Bechtel was forced to cancel its contract. Management of the Cochabamba water supply system was returned to a government authority.

There are many lessons from Cochabamba for policy transformation. The role of leadership is an important concept in such change, and a flaw in the case of Bolivia. Reformers for Aguas del Tunari consisted of management experts for the company that were distant from water users. Rather than engage in open dialogue with the public, the leadership opted for a more closed setting. As a result, the public felt largely underrepresented and discussion quickly shifted to fervent opposition.

Relative to Phnom Penh, the role of leadership in Bolivia's transition was much different. Ek Sonn Chan's leadership of the PPWSA was founded not from a purely private, profit mentality, but rather from a commitment to the provision of a high-quality service at a reasonable price. Management continuously re-evaluated the needs of its constituency and could be seen to be seeking to adopt policies that stressed the importance of meeting these needs. This is not to say that private ventures are not capable of this type of direction, but rather to illustrate that it is important to implement a *gradual* movement to profitability, with leadership focusing on the inherent problems in the current system first and to begin recovering full costs only after problems have been fixed.

In Cochabamba's case, failure arose due to a reverse focus that gave high priority to financial gain. In contrast, Phnom Penh focused first on extending its service to include the poor and seeking their support for further reform. As part of this process the PPWSA was particularly careful to communicate the value of the opportunity they were offering. The cost of water from PPWSA was much less than that from other sources.

To better understand the role these aspects play in reform, and to also provide insight into the merits of decentralized control and investment in human capital, it is useful to consider the case of Manila Water in the Philippines.

Manila Water is a water and wastewater concessionaire that oversaw the transformation of the Metropolitan Waterworks and Sewerage System (MWSS) in East Manila under a 25-year concession from the government of the Philippines in 1997 (Rangan et al., 2007). Manila Water is a privately owned and managed company. Before Manila Water was established, the MWSS possessed many of the same issues as the PPWSA: alarmingly high non-revenue water rates, low coverage, an inefficient management system and incompetent staff. Today, coverage is close to 100 percent, non-revenue water rates are low and all users receive access twenty-four hours a day.

Similar to the PPWSA, Manila Water initiated a tariff policy with the intention of using revenues to repair and increase coverage as well as reach profitability.

Tariffs, however, were increased slowly over a 25-year period with mechanisms put in place to reduce adjustment pressures. In particular, 5-year reviews and extraordinary price adjustment mechanisms were put in place to cover unforeseen climate events (Rangan *et al.*, 2007).

Manila Water was also quick to engage the poor, who, like in Phnom Penh, represented a large part of Manila's population. In areas where there were large numbers of informal settlers, for example, the company allowed connections to be paid for in instalments and did not require the communities to possess a land title (Rangan *et al.*, 2007). As a result, it was possible to once again reach out to and gain support from people who previously had been ignored.

To further elaborate on the similarities between the two services, Manila Water credits much of its success to its competent staff who it heavily invested in at the start of the reform process as well as the company's largely decentralized management structure. Like the PPWSA, in the initial stages of reformation, the company focused on employee development, setting new performance indicators and routinely offering exchange and training programs for new employees (Rangan *et al.*, 2007). The company also moved to a compartmentalized largely autonomous territorial zone management structure. This allows for the company to quickly respond to the dynamics of their coverage zone without the difficulties imposed by top down coordination processes.

Things to consider

These two case studies provide much perspective in understanding the various successes in Phnom Penh. Across the three reform attempts, and from a general perspective, there is a case for:

1. *Effective, informed leadership*: the reformation of the PPWSA was enabled by Ek Sonn Chan's sound management practices. His awareness of the company's issues combined with an understanding of the needs of his constituents was critical. He was able to initiate specific changes in the company structure while targeting constituents that could benefit from reformation. In the other case studies presented, the direct impact management practices had on its constituents resulted directly in support or opposition to the transformational reform process.
2. *Decentralized control*: the oversight of the PPWSA by a board structure that granted large control to its various branches circumvented the need for a central decision-making process, allowing for expedient decision making with highly specialized management in control of creating outcomes.
3. *Focusing first on revenue collection*: like Manila, Phnom Penh focused on flexible but firm administrative processes. Positive cash flow was achieved more by improving service and bringing people into the system than by raising prices. Profitability, therefore, was emphasized as a long-term goal, allowing the

policy to adapt to initial problems. In Bolivia's case, the immediate drive for profitability was self-destructive.
4. *Prioritizing the problem first and the gains later:* the PPWSA's objectives for expanding coverage, improving water quality, and eliminating non-revenue water worked in harmony with one another and in a sequence that broadened support. Profitability was the end result and not a concept to be prioritized along with solutions.

Conclusion

Phnom Penh has increased its annual water production by more than 400 percent in fifteen years. The distribution network now covers 92 percent of the city, and ambitiously plans to cover 100 percent of the city by 2020 (Das *et al.*, 2010). Tap water, originally a health issue to citizens, now meets World Health Organization drinking standards (Otis, 2013).

In a world where much policy success has occurred with private–public partnerships and privatization of water supplies, Phnom Penh is important because it showcases the fact that it is possible for a publicly owned water utility to lead a transformational reform. At the same time it needs to be observed that Manila Water was able to lead a similar reform process. Debates about the pros and cons of private versus public management miss much of the detail.

The information presented in this chapter suggests that either approach – public or private – can be successful. Leadership, communication, engagement and astute development and skilling of staff coupled with processes that ensure public support are much more important.

Notes

1 Wikipedia, "Phnom Penh Water Supply Authority". Available at: http://en.wikipedia.org/wiki/Phnom_Penh_Water_Supply_Authority (accessed 12 May 2016).
2 PPWSA, "History". Phnom Penh Water Supply Authority. Available at: www.ppwsa.com.kh/en/index.php?page=history (accessed 12 May 2016).
3 "Country Water Action: Phnom Penh Water Supply Authority: Internal Reforms Fuel Performance Upgrade". Available at: www.adb.org/results/country-water-action-phnom-penh-water-supply-authority-internal-reforms-fuel-performance (accessed 12 May 2016).

References

Bahree, M. (2009) "Pricing Water for the Poor". *Forbes*. Available at: www.forbes.com/forbes/2009/1228/opinions-phnom-penh-water-ideas-opinions.html (accessed 28 March 2014).
Biswas, A.K. and Tortajada, C. (2010) "Water Supply of Phnom Penh: An Example of Good Governance", *International Journal of Water Resources Development* 26(2): 157–72.

Crothers, L. (2013) "Cambodia Drops Further in Corruption Index". *The Cambodia Daily*, 4 December 2013. Available at: www.cambodiadaily.com/archives/cambodia-drops-further-in-corruption-index-48513/ (accessed 30 March 2014).

Das, B., Ek Sonn Chan, Visoth, C., Pangare, G. and Simpson, R. (2010) *Sharing the Reform Process: Learning from the Phnom Penh Water Supply Authority (PPWSA)*. Available at: http://cmsdata.iucn.org/downloads/phnom_penh_waterfinal.pdf (accessed 12 May 2016).

Finnegan, William (2002) "Letter from Bolivia: Leasing the Rain". *The New Yorker*. Available at: www.newyorker.com/archive/2002/04/08/020408fa_FACT1 (accessed 2 March 2014).

Otis, D. (2013) "How Phnom Penh Created a Super-Efficient, Totally Drinkable Water Supply". Next City. Available at: http://nextcity.org/infrastructure/entry/how-phnom-penh-created-a-super-efficient-totally-drinkable-water-supply (accessed 15 February 2014).

PPWSA (No date) "History. The Phnom Penh Water Supply Authority". Available at: www.ppwsa.com.kh/en/index.php?page=history (accessed 17 February 2014).

Rangan, V. Kasturi, Wheeler, D. and Comeault, J. (2007) "Manila Water Company". Case Study, Harvard Business School, 9 August.

Unknown (2009) "Ek Sonn Chan and the Transformation of the Phnom Penh Water Supply Authority". Case Study, Lee Kuan Yew School of Public Policy, National University of Singapore.

15

GUIDELINES FOR TRANSFORMATIONAL CHANGE IN ENVIRONMENTAL AND NATURAL RESOURCE MANAGEMENT

Mike Young and Christine Esau

This chapter provides a summary of the guidelines identified in each chapter, classified according to the seven categories listed in Chapter 1 and which provide a logical sequence for transformational change.

Overview

Guideline 13.7
Market mechanisms can be used to drive a transformational change and bring legitimacy to and investment in the mechanisms that underpin a reform.

Developing the case for change

Guideline 2.1
Define a problem in ways that people in the community, as well as specialists, can comprehend.

Guideline 7.9
The resolution of complex trade-offs requires new optics and indicators and new means of communication. This needs to include arrangements that make the costs and benefits of inaction transparent. Benefits for those that win and costs to those that lose need to be more visible.

Guideline 4.5
Transparency is needed as to what is the policy problem that needs fixing, the evidence for the policy, and what the policy implementation will (and will not) achieve.

Guideline 4.4
Design reforms to be adaptive such that there is timely/regular review of policy as circumstances change and within the "policy cycle" that includes actions that Specify, Identify, Act, Monitor and Update (SIAMU) the policy process.

Guideline 2.3
Establish a simple message and document its complexity.

Guideline 12.2
Major reforms require a policy entrepreneur with sufficient vision and influence to push for a cooperative solution.

Guideline 12.4
Begin by developing a clear, simple vision of the final outcome to be achieved and options for its attainment.

Guideline 3.1
Strengths often become weaknesses. Old ways of seeing make it very difficult to understand that the world is changing.

Guideline 2.2
Establish a mandate for action.

Guideline 4.6
Develop a compelling – envisioned – narrative that guides implementation, that accounts for who loses and who gains, who acts and who is acted upon, and that provides a vision of what the policy is intended to achieve.

Guideline 9.3
Use compelling narratives to build broad acceptance of the case for reform and have strategies to deal with stories likely to impede acceptance.

Guideline 5.7
Conduct extensive information campaigns to explain the rationale for and progression of reform and proposed measures to mitigate negative effects of raising energy prices.

Guideline 5.8
Extensive information and communication campaigns to explain the rationale for and nature of proposed mitigation measures can play an important role in building support for change.

Guideline 8.7
When implementing a transformational reform, begin by sending and repeating messages about the nature of the reform.

Guideline 3.2
New products and new offerings often meet emerging needs. Existing customer preferences may be poor guides to the structure of future demand.

Guideline 3.3
Existing products nearly always appear to be more profitable than new products: but investing in new products may nonetheless be essential to ensure that a firm continues to prosper.

Guideline 3.10
Transformative changes require strong administrative and political support from the very top of the organisation.

Guideline 3.5
Focusing on the major uncertainties that may affect the firm through scenario analysis offers a powerful way to identify opportunities which otherwise might be missed.

Guideline 1.6
Don't blink, public confidence rests on your composure.

Guideline 12.12
Don't guess the outcomes. Invest early and use the best science available to collect robust information early in the development of a reform. Simultaneous investments in staff and new data collection methods empower stakeholders with the best information available.

Guideline 4.2
Contestability is desirable such that decisions are taken with genuine opportunity for consideration of the goals, evidence, alternatives/options and risks.

Guideline 13.1
Transformational change is rarely linear. Many draft proposals and countless stakeholder interactions may be needed to build the consensus needed to enable implementation.

Guideline 13.3
Early failures can be used to learn and build consensus about what is achievable and bring legitimacy to a proposed reform.

Guideline 9.1
Persistence and patience improves the prospects of reform and chances of implementation.

Guideline 10.6
The probability of successful adoption can be increased by reducing transaction costs.

Guideline 10.7
When developing a proposal for a transformational reform, you should expect to be surprised by the nature of the changes and innovations that will result.

Guideline 10.1
The benefits of a transformational reform are easily over estimated by its proponents.

Guideline 1.1
For quality policies, you need quality people.

Securing interest in the proposition

Guideline 12.3
Search early for common goals and develop an understanding of them with key stakeholders.

Guideline 6.8
Build a broad coalition of interests in support of the reform, and try to get engagement from as many different kinds of beneficiaries as possible so that the reform has as many parents/champions/sponsors as possible. Don't assume that people have a sophisticated understanding of their own best interests. Try to ensure that at least one influential group is prepared to "die in a ditch" to protect the reform. Think about polycentric governance and leadership models, and invest heavily in identifying and resourcing leaders and champions at all levels.

Guideline 13.4
The broader the coalition of support the greater the chance of adoption and financial support.

Guideline 5.2
Map stakeholder interests and power in order to design a reform that is closely aligned with the needs of different stakeholder groups.

Guideline 10.3
Successful reforms require a clearly identifiable cadre of discrete beneficiaries who are well represented by an identifiable institution. When an identifiable institution is missing, build one.

Guideline 5.4
Build transformative alliances among key stakeholder groups to support reform implementation.

Guideline 5.6
Investment in the creation of new stakeholder coalitions and the development of new narratives that align stakeholder interests with the reform objectives can be used to speed progress towards the successful development, repackaging and implementation of a reform.

Guideline 4.1
Support reform with evidence that is assembled by with qualified, capable and unbiased analysts and uses the best available data and robust and accepted methods.

Guideline 11.5
Build in arrangements that can be expected to increase the value of the new regime to each participant and use this to lock in the reform.

Guideline 13.9
With attention to design and an emphasis on the establishment of market-based legitimacy, early detractors can become the biggest supporters.

Guideline 3.6
Work hard during the early stages of change to work out why innovation will benefit customers and how the organization can charge enough for these benefits to pay for the change.

Careful design and refinement of the package to be implemented

Guideline 5.9
Transformational policy reform needs to be seen as an ongoing iterative process that benefits from the development of new understandings and adjusts to the changes induced by the reform. Learning during implementation and from experience elsewhere can be critical to success and durability.

Guideline 12.8
When seeking a transformational change, if at all possible, ensure that no significant interest group is made worse off.

Guideline 6.9
Analyse where opposition is likely to come from and work hard to understand its drivers. What values or vested interests (real or perceived) feel threatened? What messages/strategies could be effective in defusing or countering opposition? Could the reform package be recast to capture the interests of potential losers without compromising its intent?

Guideline 2.4
Identify potential economic losers and find a way to ameliorate impacts on people who otherwise would lose during the process of implementation.

Guideline 9.6
Focus early on the development of mechanisms to minimise adverse distributional impacts.

Guideline 5.3
Proposals for compensation can be used to build early support for a reform.

Guideline 8.3
Use pilot tests to demonstrate the extent of the benefits attainable from a transformational reform.

Guideline 9.5
Use pilot tests to demonstrate benefits, build administrative capacity and build confidence about the likelihood of success.

Guideline 8.4
Use pilot tests to find ways to help resolve administrative tensions and build capacity.

Guideline 2.5
Recruit economic winners, or what Gladwell would call "mavens", to take their message to the general media.

Guideline 8.2
When trialling a new policy, if possible begin by working with jurisdictions that have a history of collaborating with one another.

Guideline 14.3
As a transformational reform is implemented, work hard to secure political support from beneficiaries – especially those who under the old regime were disadvantaged.

Guideline 8.1
Before implementing a policy transformational reform, bed down the institutional arrangements necessary to facilitate the change.

Guideline 8.5
Begin by clarifying and formalising existing arrangements. Focus on building the legal institutions and administrative capacity necessary to ensure success.

Guideline 8.6
When pilot testing a reform, make it clear to all involved in the pilot test that they should expect to benefit from it and not be made worse off – even if attempts to expand the reform are abandoned.

Guideline 6.14
Continually recruit new political champions and identify new beneficiaries (while honouring the old ones) and help them to see the importance of sustaining the policy reform, so that the policy itself is reinvented if necessary (while remaining true to its Guidelines) and is never taken for granted. Ensure that decision makers (and wider beneficiaries) are always aware that the costs and risks of unravelling or undermining the policy are much greater than any potential benefit from doing so. BUT, if the evidence is clear that the policy is not working, and it is clearly not a problem of poor implementation, then analyse why and start working on the next major reform. Be prepared to "disrupt yourself" rather than waiting for someone else to demolish your program.

Guideline 7.4
Define the boundaries of the system and its range of historic and potential future variability.

Guideline 11.3
Allow for learning. Align management and administrative boundaries with biophysical realities and expect to have to change boundaries and management arrangements as knowledge improves and social expectations change.

Guideline 11.1
When separate instruments are used to pursue separate objectives, a dynamically efficient management regime can be established and more easily maintained.

Guideline 7.5
Good measurement and information underpin robust entitlement and allocation regimes.

Guideline 11.4
When setting limits, build into any allocation regime a capacity to revise allocations. Regimes that lock in assumptions such as about sustainable yield, etc. can be costly to adjust if conditions change. Expect to pay compensation when fundamental changes in the structure of a regime are required.

Guideline 6.3
Over a long time frame, consider carefully what a new program is likely to do to existing programs.

Guideline 7.6
Policy coherence depends on a "portfolio approach". Crises present opportunities to identify and overcome barriers posed by vested interests affected proposed reforms.

Guideline 7.7
Policy coherence requires accounting for food and energy systems, and the drivers and interactions affecting water supply, demand and allocation during times of crisis.

Guideline 7.10
Policy coherence involves high transaction costs, and planning can identify where the most urgent gaps and trade-offs merit the expense.

Guideline 6.5
The interactions among policy elements are as important as the individual components. Never lose sight of the whole package. Think carefully about how diverse elements work together and how to ensure that they don't undermine previous gains, or each other.

Guideline 10.4
Reforms that rely upon ongoing access to government budgets face much higher risks than reforms that are deeply embedded in market and regulatory processes.

Guideline 9.7
Keep the impetus going. Include in the reform package arrangements that lock in the new regime and make backsliding difficult.

Guideline 1.4
Let the dog see the rabbit.

Guideline 13.5
The broader the structure of a governance system, the more legitimacy it will have and the greater its power will be.

Guideline 13.6
Legitimacy can be increased by creating an environment where all stakeholders perceive that they have a voice, can be heard and will be given an equitable say irrespective of the sector or region they represent.

Guidelines for transformational change

Guideline 7.11
Crises provide the window for change but, when the solution to the crisis is not well understood, also provide the potential for maladaptation and triage-based approaches that exacerbate systemic risks.

Guideline 11.7
Devolve administrative functions and make costs transparent and accountable as much as possible.

Guideline 12.14
Do not attempt to control all elements of a program centrally. Build structures that allow and encourage innovation.

Guideline 7.3
Clarify roles and responsibilities to ensure accountability and provide incentives for local innovation coupled with trans-boundary coordination.

Guideline 5.1
Search for windows of opportunity – critical junctures – to initiate a reform. In the meantime, build knowledge about the nature of the and the case for the policy reform and seek opportunites to communicate the need for change.

Guideline 6.4
Genuine crises often create the possibility for transformational reform and for "creative destruction" of prior constraints. However, it is crucial that such destruction does not extend to the foundations on which long-term gains rely.

Guideline 12.1
Crises create opportunities for the introduction of new legislation with far-reaching consequences.

Guideline 4.3
Proposals for transformational policy reform need to be timely so that evidence and options are available when needed and when decision makers are receptive.

Guideline 13.2
High levels of public awareness and concern tend to establish a sense of urgency, help to establish the legitimacy of a proposal and provide access to important stakeholders.

Guideline 7.1
Systemic failures are most likely to occur during crises when biophysical or economic systems are required to operate under atypical conditions.

Guideline 7.2
Crises create significant opportunities for the introduction of policies that reduce deeply embedded systemic risks.

Guideline 7.8
To remove a systemic failure, it is necessary to redesign significant parts of the policy arrangements used to influence decision making

Guideline 9.2
Be prepared: opportunities to implement a transformational reform tend to emerge quickly and, when the groundwork needed to enable speedy implementation is missing, opportunities to adjust are just as quickly lost.

Negotiating the reform package

Guideline 6.6
Build a strong evidence base. Marshall the evidence and facts to support your case for reform, but never assume that the facts will speak for themselves, or be sufficient. If the policy reform is perceived to threaten powerful interests, then assume that opposition will be well organized, well resourced and politically ruthless.

Guideline 2.6
Identify the ideological or vested-interest opponents to a proposed reform and develop an offensive strategy to deal with them.

Guideline 9.4
Engage early with stakeholders. Use this process to improve and gain acceptance of the proposed reform.

Guideline 12.7
Negotiate early on with stakeholders while program detail is still being developed.

Guideline 6.11
Measure impact systematically from the outset (including impacts on "losers"), and adjust policy and program settings as required. Make sure you have more and better empirical data than anyone else, especially likely opponents of reform. Understand how implementation works and how success is interpreted in terms of the dominant political mores and theories of the day. Communicate benefits as early as possible, without over-reaching or making false claims, and keep communicating and refining the narrative. Never assume that the communication task to mobilise and sustain political support is complete. Reinterpret the burning platform as necessary. Assume that all wins are temporary and the case always needs to be made to claim them.

Guideline 6.10
Plan implementation very carefully. There is often a wide gap between policy intent and program practice. Think hard about allocating responsibility and resources at the right level to motivate successful implementation. Build capacity quickly. Ensure that the right people and agencies have the necessary training, resources and instruments to do the job well, and follow through. Implementation is about relationships at multiple levels. It is critical that the operational system is both technically competent and socially rewarding for all involved in policy delivery.

Guideline 1.7
Get the fundamentals right.

Guideline 6.13
Be clear about the fundamental policy objectives and guidelines, and stay true to them, while being flexible and adaptable in implementation to respond to changing circumstances, improvising practice and tweaking the narrative so that it resonates and legitimisses progress as the "current" political context changes. For slow-moving issues like many environmental problems, driven by ecological or hydrological processes that may operate over multi-decadal timeframes or longer, it is crucial to remember that much policy reform is necessarily incremental, building on previous developments. Often, continued investment is required to ensure that those "old" measures (like community Landcare) remain effective. Stay vigilant in implementing reform that new measures don't undermine the foundations on which long-term progress ultimately depends.

Implementing the reform

Guideline 6.2
As far as possible, lock in long-term funding arrangements and secure bipartisan support that will endure a change in government.

Guideline 12.9
Don't begin a transformational reform without having secure funding in place that is protected from politics.

Guideline 12.13
Design the program so that success can be demonstrated early and used to prevent undermining of the reform. Collect the data needed to ensure that early success can be demonstrated.

Guideline 12.6
Early in the development of a transformational reform agenda appoint a policy entrepreneur and give that person responsibility for negotiating the details.

Guideline 14.1
When commencing a major transformational change, begin by appointing a new leader who is not associated with or responsible for the development of the policies and institutional arrangements that are about to be replaced.

Guideline 1.1
For quality policies, you need quality people.

Guideline 3.9
Sheltering new ideas in a separate organization can be a powerful route to innovation, but these units must be managed with care.

Guideline 11.6
Set up a dedicated structure within government to handle the regime that emerges from the reform. This facilitates budget tracking as well as measuring outcomes and increases accountability for management results by clearly defining governmental stakeholders.

Guideline 12.10
Build new administrative structures to bring in new skills and appoint people with appropriate expertise.

Guideline 12.11
When beginning a transformational reform bring in people with capacity to implement the new regime.

Guideline 3.4
Successful innovation requires generating entrepreneurial energy – but most established organizations are optimized to deliver operational excellence.

Guideline 3.8
Success requires balancing entrepreneurial energy and operational excellence.

Guideline 14.2
Prospects for a successful reform can be increased by establishing a strong independent authority whose revenue base is not dependent upon access to government budgets.

Guideline 10.2
A transformational reform is more likely to succeed when there is an agency prepared to argue for its continuation as the reform is in the interests of this agency.

Guideline 10.8
Aspiring policy transformers should expect people to try to rort any regime put in place. Search for ways to minimise the risk that rorting could undermine prospects for success.

Guideline 11.2
Limit the amount of time between announcement of plans to introduce a new sharing regime and conversion to that regime so that opportunities to game the transition process are minimised.

Guideline 1.2
Speed is essential. It is impossible to go too fast.

Guideline 1.3
Once you start the momentum rolling, never let it stop.

Guideline 14.4
The probability of a successful reform will be greater if any price increase follows rather than precedes improvements in performance.

Guideline 5.5
Sequence reforms to increase prospects for success. Early emphasis on fostering dialogue among different stakeholders is critical to the avoidance of setbacks.

Guideline 2.8
Establish a rolling report card on implementation progress.

Guideline 6.12
Celebrate success (even modest wins) and reward champions at all levels.

Guideline 10.5
The less expensive and more objective the ongoing quantification of benefits, the more likely it is that a program can be sustained. Surrogate indicators can play an important role in the establishment of low-cost monitoring programs.

Guideline 14.5
To sustain a reform program, it is critical to deal quickly with and be seen to deal with maladministration. Evidence of corruption, for example, needs to be dealt with quickly.

Adaptation and ongoing improvement

Guideline 13.8
Allow for adaptation during implementation as those involved gain experience and as administrative capacity develops.

Guideline 3.7
The probability of a transformational change enduring will be greater if it is introduced through a process of ongoing experimentation.

Guideline 2.7
Ensure that there is ongoing, comprehensive oversight of implementation.

Guideline 12.5
When the vision is supported by all key stakeholders, but there is a negotiation impasse or lack of trust, be prepared to reduce tension by appointing a new policy entrepreneur with a different style and approach.

Guideline 2.9
Set a formal date for review of the efficacy and effectiveness of the reform.

Learning

Guideline 2.10
Following the review, explore what further structural reform is needed.

Guideline 6.1
When setting formal policy objectives, expect these same objectives to be used as the basis for subsequent reviews. Beware of aspirational objectives.

Guideline 6.14
If the evidence is clear that the policy is not working, and it is clearly not a problem of poor implementation, then analyse why and start working on the next major reform. Be prepared to "disrupt yourself" rather than waiting for someone else to demolish your program.

Guideline 6.7
Ensure that the "three lenses of knowledge and influence" are all considered, mutually reinforcing and well-aligned with the reform agenda. The three lenses are:

- political judgement (the Minister, their office and party, and preferably the Minister's informal advisers);
- professional practice (the relevant agencies, including central agencies and also think tanks and NGOs); and
- scientific research (policy briefs, refereed literature, professional societies, conferences, learned academies, peak groups).

INDEX

Abbott, Tony 41, 132
abstraction permits 110, 111, 115
acceptance of reform 10, 126–8
accountability 8, 97
Accreditation Services International 187, 192
adaptation and ongoing improvements 12–13, 219–20
adaptive policy 42, 47, 50, 55, 57
adjustment assistance 130, 131–2
agricultural sector: drought policy in Australia 122, 123, 130; drought policy in California 96, 102, 104; water markets in China 112, 115, 116
Aguas del Tunari 202–3
AirBnB 32
air pollution 62, 76
Alder, J. 147, 160
Aldy, J. 62, 76
alliances 5–6, 66–9, 70, 75
Alpert, Mark 20
Althaus, C. 39, 125
ambidextrous management 34, 35–6
Anchukaitis, K.J. 95
Anderton, J. 156
annual catch entitlements (ACE) 154, 156, 158, 159, 161
Aotearoa *see* New Zealand
Appels, D. 122

Apple 22, 24, 32
Appleton, Albert F. 165, 166, 167, 168, 169, 172, 176, 178
"app" market 27, 32
aqueducts 99, 178
aquifers 81, 95
Arab Gas Pipeline 64
Arbuckle, M. 160
architectural knowledge 24, 25
Arze del Granado, J. 62
Ashokan reservoir 167
Asian Development Bank 194, 198, 201
assessment framework for resilient public policy: four assessments of public policy 40–56; Home Insulation Program 48–52; Mineral Resources Rent Tax 52–6; Murray–Darling Basin Plan 44–8; National Competition Policy 40–3; resilient public policy 39–40, 56–7
Australia: BushTender 138, 139–40, 145; centralism and national investment in NRM 86–8; design and refinement of reform package 8, 9; developing the case for change 3, 4; difficulty of sustainable environmental reform 15, 16, 18–19, 20; drought in Australia 120, 121–3, 133; drought policy 120–35; failure to capture synergies in natural resource management 80–94; forestry

certification 191; guidelines for "sticky" NRM policy reform 90–3; Home Insulation Program 48–52; individual water rights allocation 113; Landcare and localism 82–3; lessons for drought policy reform success 123–32; Mineral Resources Rent Tax 52–6; Murray–Darling Basin Plan 44–8; National Competition Policy 40–3; natural resource management 80–2, 93; NRM policy reform in parallel 88–90; payments for ecosystem services 138, 139–40; regional NRM framework 83–6; resilient public policy 38, 39, 40–8, 56–7; successful transformational reform 120–1
Australian Government 84, 127, 128
Australian National Audit Office (ANAO) 49, 51, 83, 87

B&Q 183, 189
backsliding 8, 132
Bahree, M. 196
Banks, G. 120, 121, 123, 131
Bardach, E. 39
Barnett, J. 150, 151
Bartlett, Christopher 27
Beaton, C. 73
Bechtel 202, 203
benefits of reform 6, 7, 8, 12, 31–2
Bernstein, S. 182, 184, 186
biodiversity 137, 138, 141, 181, 184
Biswas, A.K. 196, 197, 198, 199, 201
Blackberry 21
Blatter, D. 65, 66
Blindenbacher, R. 74
Bloomberg 138
Bolivia 202, 205
Boully, L. 46
Brazil 68, 191
Brecht, Bertolt 38
Bridle, R. 64, 65
broad coalition 90–1, 92
budgets 8, 13, 64, 126, 141–2
building transformative alliances 68–9, 70, 75
Bureau of Meteorology 129

Burgelman, Robert 36
"burning platform" 90, 92
bushfires 122, 123, 126
BushTender 138, 139–40, 145
business models 32, 33
Buzzell, Z. 65, 66

California: drought and water-policy reform 95–108; hidden trade-offs in water-policy reform 105–6; ongoing drought 95–6; systemic risks and response in water-policy reform 96–8; water, drought and resource interdependencies 98–105
Cambodia 194, 196, 198, 199, 201, 202
Campbell, A. 82, 86
canals 98, 99, 112
Capoccia, G. 63
carbon credits 138, 143, 144, 146
carbon dioxide 62, 76, 144
carbon pricing 17, 19, 64
Caring for our County program 87, 88
Cashore, B. 182, 184, 186
Catchment Management Authorities 84, 85
CAT scanner 27
Catskills 11, 142, 165–70, 173–8
Catskill Watershed Corporation (CWC) 167, 168, 170, 174–6, 178
CDM *see* Clean Development Mechanism
celebrating success 12, 91, 92
cell phones 21, 23–4
centralism 81, 86–8, 89
Central Valley, California 98, 100, 101, 102
certification processes 184–5, 187–8, 191
Certification Working Group (CWG) 182, 183
Chain-of-Custody Certification 184, 188
Challenger Scallop Enhancement Company Ltd 160
champions 91, 92, 103
Chan, Ek Sonn 2, 12, 194, 195–6, 197, 199, 201–4
change: ambidextrous senior managers 35–6; creating space for innovation 34–5; developing the case for change

2–4, 126–8, 207–10; difficulty of change 16, 21–3; dynamics of successful change 21–37; making money from innovation 31–2; organizing for discontinuous innovation 33–4; seeing the world in new ways 29–31; strategy development as a process of experimentation 32–3; why innovation is so difficult 23–9
Chatham Islands 149
Cheng, Roger 24
Chile 113
China: anatomy of water rights trading 109–11; challenges to development of water markets 114–17; design and refinement of reform package 7; development of water markets 109–19; fossil-fuel subsidies 76; individual short-term trading: Shiyang River Basin 113–14; inter-sectoral transfers: Ningxia and Inner Mongolia 112–13; lessons for transformational environmental policy reform 117–18; payments for ecosystem services 144; three case studies 111–14; transferring water between two cities 111–12; water scarcity 109
Christensen, Clay 25, 26, 33
Christian-Smith, J. 97
Churchill, Winston 24
City of New York 167, 168, 169, 170
Clean Development Mechanism (CDM) 144, 145
Clean Drinking Water Coalition 167
clean water: New York City's PES 164–6, 167, 169, 176, 177; payments for ecosystem services 138, 141, 145, 166
Clean Water Act 145, 166
Clemens, B. 71, 72
climate change: difficulty of sustainable environmental reform 14–15, 16; drought policy in Australia 122, 124, 129, 130; drought policy in California 96, 105, 106; fossil-fuel subsidies 61; policy detail 8
COAG *see* Council of Australian Governments
coal 56, 61, 69, 71, 76, 116

Coalition of Watershed Towns (CWT) 167, 168, 170
coalitions 68–9, 75, 90–1, 92, 103
Cochabamba 202–3
Cody, B.A. 95
Cohen, M.J. 104
Colebatch, H.K. 39
Colorado River 98, 99, 100, 104, 105
Comité du Différé 71
command-and-control policies 147, 149, 150
Commonwealth of Australia 47, 50, 132
communication 3, 16, 71–2, 75, 91
community involvement 14–15, 44, 46, 81–3, 85, 86, 88, 175
community Landcare 86, 91
compelling narratives 126–7, 133, 208
compensation 6–9, 10, 16, 65–6, 72, 73, 131–2
competent implementation 91, 92
competition 27, 28, 42, 43, 66
complementary assets 27, 28
component knowledge 24, 25
Connell, D. 44
Connor, R. 158
consensus building 69
Conservation Reserve Program 138, 139
consultation 10, 128–9
contestability of policy 42, 46, 50, 53, 56, 57, 90
contracting arrangements 143, 175–6
La Coordinadora 203
Corning Glass 22, 33
corruption 12, 66, 195, 196, 199–201, 202
Cortell, A. P. 64
Costa Rica 138
Council of Australian Governments (COAG) 40, 41, 43, 47
crises: design and refinement of reform package 8–9; drought policy in Australia 125–6, 133; drought policy in California 96–8, 105–6; policy reform in parallel 89–90
critical junctures 63–5, 75
Crothers, L. 196
Croton watershed 165
Curran, G. 47

Curtis, A. 83, 85, 86–7
customer needs 25–6, 33
Cuyahoga River 166
CWC *see* Catskill Watershed Corporation

DAFF (Department of Agriculture, Fisheries and Forestry) 123
Daily, Gretchen 176
dams 99, 102, 122, 177
Das, B. 195, 196, 197, 198, 205
Davis, M. 53, 56
Day, Andrew 152
Decade of Landcare 82, 83
"deep dive" process 33
defining the problem 14–15
deforestation 180, 181, 184
degradation processes 62, 83–4, 87
Delaware watershed 142, 165, 177
Dempsey, J. 136
Department of Water Resources 100
design of reform package 3, 6–9, 143–4, 211–16
developing countries 61, 62, 118, 144, 181
developing the case for change 2–4, 207–10
difficulty of sustainable environmental reform 14–20
digital music 27
digital photography 27, 28
disasters 123, 127
discontinuous innovation 33–4, 36
distance learning 30, 31
distributional impacts 130–2, 133
Dongyang 111, 112
donor aid 198–9, 201–2
Douglas, Roger 1, 5, 8, 11, 13
Dovers, S. 39, 84
drought policy in Australia 120–35; developing the case for change 4, 126–8; distributional impacts 130–2; drought in Australia 9, 121–3; lessons for reform success 123–32; Millennium Drought 9, 45, 88, 122, 124, 126; Murray–Darling Basin Plan 44–8; overview 120, 133; persistence 123–4; preparedness 125–6; stakeholder engagement 128–9; successful transformational reform 120–1; using pilot tests 129–30; watching for backsliding 132
drought policy in California 95–108; energy systems 104–5; food systems 104; hidden trade-offs 105–6; ongoing drought 95–6; policy and governance responses 102–4; systemic risks and response 96–8; water, drought and resource interdependencies 98–105; water rights 100–2; water system 98–100
durability of reform 72–3

Earth First 188
Earth Summit 182
Ecological Trading Company 182
Ecosystem Marketplace 138, 143
ecosystem services 13, 136, 137, 176–8 *see also* payments for ecosystem services
education 27, 29–31
Egypt 64, 66, 75
EIA (Environmental Investigation Agency) 144, 146
electoral mandate 15, 89, 126, 126–7
electricity 62, 64, 65, 104, 105, 126
Eli Lilly 33
EMI 27
Energy Efficient Homes Package 48
energy pricing 62–6, 72, 76
energy sector 61, 62–6, 104, 105
engaging stakeholders 10, 125, 128–9, 133
entrepreneurial energy 6, 11, 28–9, 33–4, 35, 36, 137
Environmental Investigation Agency (EIA) 144, 146
Environmental Protection Agency (EPA) 167
environmental reform, difficulty of 14–20
envisioned policy 43, 47, 51, 56, 57
Espach, R. 180, 184, 186, 187
ethical resource management 192
European Trading System 143
European Union 65, 83, 181, 191
evidence-informed policy 39, 42, 46, 50, 53, 57

"exceptional circumstance" (EC) provisions 124, 130
exclusive economic zone (EEZ) 148, 149, 155
experimentation 32–3, 72–4, 75
Expert Social Panel 129
externalities 61, 137

failure to capture synergies in natural resource management 80–94; Australia's regional NRM framework 83–6; centralism and national investment in NRM 86–8; guidelines for "sticky" policy reform 90–3; Landcare and localism in Australia 82–3; overview 80–2, 93; policy reform in parallel 88–90
Famiglietti, J. 100
Farmhand Appeal 127
farming: drought policy in Australia 122, 123, 126, 127–8, 130, 132; drought policy in California 102, 104; natural resource management in Australia 82, 83, 85, 93; New York City's PES for clean water 165–7, 169–71, 173, 175, 178; Whole Farm Planning 169–70, 173–5
Farm Service Agency 138
Faunt, C. 101
Finnegan, William 202, 203
Fisheries Act 150, 152, 155, 156, 157, 158
fisheries management in New Zealand 147–63; design detail 153–8; getting to the quota management regime 149–53; impact of reform in New Zealand 158–61; importance of New Zealand fisheries 147–9; success of reform in New Zealand 161–2
floods 123, 136, 137, 140
fodder subsidies 122, 123
food 97, 104
Ford, Gerald 172
foreign donors 198–9, 201–2
Forest Management Certification 184, 188
forestry 138, 144, 146, 180–2
Forest Stewardship Council (FSC): the case for change 180–2; certification processes 184–5; establishing the FSC 183; Forest Stewardship principles and criteria 185–6; governance and membership 186–7; how the FSC was designed 183–9; how the system was adapted during implementation 190–1; independent verification 187–9; international product certification 180–93; success of FSC scheme 191–2, 193; ten FSC principles 185–6, 190
formal reviews 13, 19
fossil-fuel subsidies 61–79; building transformative alliances 68–72; critical junctures 63–5; information campaigns 71–2; key guidelines learned from reforming fossil-fuel subsidies 63–72; mapping stakeholder interests and power 65–8; overview 74–6; policy learning and experimentation 72–4; relevance of reforming fossil-fuel subsidies 61–2
Friends of the Earth 182, 188
FSC *see* Forest Stewardship Council
funding 8, 86, 87, 141–2, 171–2, 175–6

Gale, F. 181, 182, 183, 184, 186, 187, 188, 190
Gansu Province 113, 115
Gansu Shiyang River Basin Trading Center 114
Gao, E. 110, 111, 113, 114, 115, 116
Garrick, D. E. 102
gas 64, 105
Gelber, Marilyn 168, 169, 172
Germany 61, 69, 71
Get Up 81
Ghana 71–2, 73
Gibbs, M.T. 150, 158, 160
Gillard, Julia 53, 54, 55
Gladwell, M. 17, 20
Glantz, M.H. 133
glass industry 22
Global Forest and Trade Network (GFTN) 189
global warming 76, 105, 144
Goldin, I. 96, 97
Goldman Sachs 137

"Good Neighbour Payments" 175, 177
"gorilla glass" 22
governance issues 8, 96, 102–4, 173–4
government aid: difficulty of sustainable environmental reform 15; drought policy in Australia 126, 127, 128, 132; forestry 189; fossil-fuel subsidies 61, 66; payments for ecosystem services 139, 141–2, 146; policy detail 8
Grafton, R.Q. 44, 47, 48, 95
"grandfathering" 7, 13
grassroots community action 82–3, 85, 86
greenhouse gas emissions 18–19, 144
Greenpeace 188
Griffin, J. 95
groundwater: drought policy in Australia 44, 46, 47, 121, 122; drought policy in California 99, 100, 101, 102, 103; water markets in China 113, 115
groundwork for reform 125–6
Grove, Andy 35
GSI (Global Subsidies Initiative) 62, 70, 71, 72, 76
G20 62
Guerin, K. 156, 157
guidelines for transformational change 207–20; adaptation and ongoing improvement 219–20; careful design and refinement of the package to be implemented 211–16; developing the case for change 2–4, 207–10; guidelines for "sticky" policy reform 90–3; implementing the reform 217–19; learning 220; negotiating the reform package 216–17; overview 207; resilient public policy 39–40, 42–3, 46–7, 50–1, 53–6; securing interest in the proposition 4–6, 210–11; sequence of transformational change guidelines 1–2; summary of guidelines 207–20
Gujarat Fluorochemicals Limited (GFL) 146
Gulbrandsen, L.H. 188, 189, 193
gun control 9, 125

habitat destruction 87, 181
Haggard, S. 64

Hanak, E.L. 98, 99, 100, 102, 106
Hanger, I. 50, 51
Hartley, P. 157
Hassanzadeh, E. 73
Haward, M. 181, 182, 183, 184, 186, 187, 188, 190
Hawke, A. 51
Hawke, Bob 41, 82
Head, B. 13, 90
Hedley, D. 122, 133
Henderson, Rebecca 22, 26, 33
Hennessy, K. 129
Henry, Ken 52, 53
Henry Review 52–3
Herceptin 33
Hersoug, B. 149, 152, 158, 159, 162
HFC-23 carbon credits 144, 146
higher education 29–31
Hilmer, F. 41, 42
Hilmer Review 41, 42, 43
HIP see Home Insulation Program
Hockey, Joe 132
Hogan, J.W. 63
Hoki fishery 160
Holden 132
Hollander, R. 47
Home Depot 189
Home Insulation Program (HIP) 38, 48–52, 57
Horne, J. 48
Howard, John 125, 126
Hundley, N. 98
Hurricane Katrina 140
Hurst, D. 56
Hussey, K. 39

IBM 26, 34
IC see Industry Commission
ICM see integrated catchment management
identifying opponents 17–18
Ideo 33
IEA (International Energy Agency) 61, 62, 64
IEEP (Institute for European Environmental Policy) 76
IKEA 189

IMF (International Monetary Fund) 50, 62, 65, 68, 69, 71, 72, 76
impact measurement 91
implementing the reform 10–12, 18–19, 91–2, 217–19
improvements 12–13, 219–20
Inall, Neil 127–8
incremental reforms 1, 3, 24, 91
India 72, 144, 146
indigenous people's rights 152, 185, 186
individual transferrable quota regime (ITQ) 152, 153–4, 158, 161, 162
Indonesia 66, 73
industrial sector 112, 116
Industry Commission (IC) 42, 43
information campaigns 69–72
Inner Mongolia 112, 113, 115, 116
innovation: creating space for innovation 34–5; crises and opportunities 97; dynamics of successful change 22, 36; forms of innovation 25; implementing the reform 11; innovation in the fishery industry 160–1; innovator's dilemma 26; making money from innovation 31–2; organizing for discontinuous innovation 33–4; strategy development as a process of experimentation 32–3; why innovation is so difficult 23–9
insulation 38, 48–52, 57
integrated catchment management (ICM) 84
Intel 35–6
international product certification: the case for change 180–2; certification processes 184–5; establishing the FSC 183; Forest Stewardship Council 180–93; Forest Stewardship principles and criteria 185–6; governance and membership 186–7; how the FSC was designed 183–9; how the system was adapted during implementation 190–1; independent verification 187–9; success of FSC scheme 191–2, 193; ten FSC principles 185–6, 190
International Tropical Timber Organization (ITTO) 181, 182

investment: dynamics of successful change 21, 31; in knowledge 4; payments for ecosystem services 137, 142, 143; synergies in natural resource management 84–5, 86–8, 88, 91; systemic risks and response 97
iPhone 22, 23
Iran 72, 73
irrigation: drought policy in Australia 88, 122, 123; drought policy in California 102, 104; water markets in China 112–13, 113, 115
ITQ *see* individual transferrable quota regime
iTunes Store 32

Japan 24, 61, 128, 198
Jia, S. 110, 111, 117
Johnson, O. 69
Jordan 64–5, 73, 75

Kanowski, Peter 87
Keane, B. 80, 89
Keating, Paul 40, 41, 43, 127, 128
Kelemen, R. D. 63
Kenny, A. 174, 175, 176
Keogh, M. 129
Kerr, Robert 125, 128
Khmer Rouge 195, 196
"killing arguments" 127
knowledge 4, 24
Kodak 28
Kojima, M. 71
Kyoto Protocol 144

Laan, T. 71, 72
lakes 98, 99, 100
Landcare 81, 82–6, 87, 91–3
land degradation 82, 83, 84, 86, 122
Landell-Mills, N. 138
Lang, K. 62
leadership 6, 8–9, 11
learning 4, 13, 72–4, 75–6, 220
learning spiral 73–4
Lee, T. 46
Lefroy, T. 86–7
Leigh, A. 125

228 Index

Leslie, S. 149, 153, 154, 155, 156, 157, 159
Liedeker, H. 190
"lines on maps" 124, 130
Li, B. 111, 115
localism 81, 82–3, 89
Lock, K. 149, 153, 154, 155, 156, 157, 159
losers 6–9, 10, 16, 18, 65–6, 91
Low Emissions Assistance Plan for Renters (LEAPR) 48
Lower Colorado Basin 104
Lowe's 189
Ludwig, J. 124
Lu, L. 122, 133
Lütkenhorst, W. 73, 74

MacDonald, G.M. 100, 106
Mace, P.M. 150
making money 31–2
management 35–6
mandate for reform 15, 126–7
Manila Water 203–4, 205
Maori people 147, 149, 151, 152–3, 155, 159, 161
mapping stakeholder interests and power 65–8
March in March 81
Marine Stewardship Council 192
Marshall, G. 83, 84, 85, 86
mass shootings 9, 125–6
The Matrix 138, 139
mavens 17, 20
Max Havelaar programme 182
Maywald, K. 46
McColl, J.C. 104, 130, 131
MDBA *see* Murray–Darling Basin Authority
measuring impacts 12, 91, 92
media 3, 12, 17, 126, 127, 128, 181
Medicare 51, 125
Megalogenis, G. 80
Memorandum of Agreement (MOA) 167, 169, 170, 171
message, establishing 15–16
metering water 113, 197, 199, 202
Metropolitan Waterworks and Sewerage System (MWSS) 203

Middle East 62, 76
Millennium Drought 9, 45, 88, 122, 124, 126
Millennium Ecosystem Assessments reports 177
Millett, Allan 24
Mineral Resources Rent Tax (MRRT) 38, 52–6, 57
mining 53, 54, 56
Minter Ellison 50
Minute 319 98
MIT 29, 30, 31
Mitchell, R. K. 67
mobile phones 21, 23–4
modular innovation 25
money 26–8, 31–2
monitoring 12, 173, 197
Moore, Gorden 35
Moore, M. 65, 69
Moore, S. 115, 116, 117, 118
Morocco 66–7, 75
MRRT *see* Mineral Resources Rent Tax
Muldoon, Robert 150, 151
Murray–Darling Basin 3, 16, 38, 44–8, 57, 126
Murray–Darling Basin Authority (MDBA) 44, 46, 47
Murray–Darling Basin Plan 44–8, 57
Murray, Williamson 24
music publishing 27
Myers, J.P. 137

Nagel, J.H. 151
Namibia 71
National Committee on Violence 9, 126
National Competition Policy (NCP) 38, 40–3, 44, 56, 57
National Institute of Water and Atmospheric Sciences (NIWA) 157, 158
National Landcare Program 82, 85
National Plan for Water Security 44, 45, 88
National Research Council (NRC) 165, 166, 170
National Water Commission (NWC) 46, 47

Index   **229**

National Water Initiative 44, 45, 46, 88
Nation Building – Economic Stimulus Plan 48
natural disasters 123, 132
natural gas 64, 105
Natural Heritage Trust (NHT) 84, 86
natural resource management (NRM): Australia's regional NRM framework 83–6; centralism and national investment in NRM 86–8; definition 81; drought policy in Australia 124, 130; failure to capture synergies in NRM 80–94; guidelines for "sticky" policy reform 90–3; Landcare and localism in Australia 82–3; overview 80–2, 93; policy reform in parallel 88–90
The Nature Conservancy 138
NCP *see* National Competition Policy
negotiating the reform package 9–10, 216–17
Neill, C. 125
Nemawashi 128
Newell, R. 157, 159, 160
Newsha, K.A. 105
New South Wales 84, 85, 127
New York City: background 164–6; components of PES agreement 170–1; implementing PES reform 11, 13, 171–4; New York City's PES for clean water 164–79; payments for ecosystem services 138, 141–2; searching for a PES solution 166–70; transferability of PES 174–8
New Zealand (Aotearoa): fisheries design detail 153–8; fisheries management 147–63; fisheries quota management regime 149–53; impact of reform 158–61; importance of fisheries 147–9; insulation installation 50; success of fisheries reform 161–2
NGOs *see* Non-Government Organisations
NHT *see* Natural Heritage Trust
Niger 71
Nigeria 72
Ningxia 112, 113, 115, 116, 117
Nokia 23

Non-Government Organisations (NGOs) 81, 87, 181, 188, 189, 191
Norodom Sihanouk, King 195, 201
NRC *see* National Research Council
NRM *see* natural resource management
NWC *see* National Water Commission
NYPIRG (New York Public Interest Research Group) 167

Obama, Barack 95, 97
objectives 13, 83, 91, 93
OECD (Organisation for Economic Cooperation and Development) 50, 71, 125, 126, 128–9, 131, 133
Ogbu, O. 72
oil 62, 64, 65, 73
O'Meagher, B. 122
ongoing improvements 12–13, 219–20
online education 27
Open Courseware 31
operational excellence 23, 28–9, 32, 33–4, 35, 36
opportunities 8, 96–7, 125–6
opposition to reform: difficulty of sustainable environmental reform 12, 16, 17–18; failure to capture synergies in natural resource management 80, 90, 91; fisheries management 152–3; fossil-fuel subsidies 66, 72, 75; negotiating the reform package 9; resilient public policy 44, 46; resistance to change 23–5, 32; supportive alliances 5–6
O'Reilly, Charles 34, 35
O'Rourke, S. 50
Otis, D. 194
oversight of implementation 18–19
Owens Valley Transfer 98
Oxfam 104

Pagos por Servicios Ambientales 138
Pahl-Wostl, C. 109
palm oil production 182
Passel, Peter 98
Pattanayak, S.K. 146
Pauling, J. 150, 151
payments for ecosystem services (PES) 136–46, 164–79; adaptation and

ongoing improvements - New York water 13; background 164–6; components of agreement 170–1; definition 137–9; design flaws and surprises 143–4; implementing reform 11, 13, 171–4; inadequate demand 140–2; key barriers to market development for PES 139–44; measurement capacity 142; New York City's PES for clean water 164–79; overview 136–7, 145; PES schemes in the field 138–9; searching for a solution 166–70; transaction costs 143; transferability 174–8
payment vehicles 175–6
PC *see* Productivity Commission
Peiffer, C. 69
Perkin Elmer 26
permits 81, 110, 111, 115, 117, 118
persistence 123–4, 133
pest control 83, 84
Peterson, S. 64
pharmaceutical industry 33
Philippines 203–4
Phnom Penh: background 194–5; coalition of interests 201; history of the PPWSA 195; impact of foreign donors 201–2; integrity of the proposal 202; overview 2, 12, 205; perspective on success 201; removal of corruption 199–201; similar case studies 202–5; structural reformation 195–7; tariff policy and volume-based pricing 197–9; water management success 194–206
Phnom Penh Water Supply Authority (PPWSA) 194–8, 199–205
photography 27, 28
Pierson, P. 63
pilot tests: design of reform package 7; drought policy in Australia 129–30, 133; resilient public policy 57; water markets in China 111–14, 115, 116
Plumer, B. 104
policy clarity 91–2, 93
policy coherence 96, 102–4, 106
policy detail 7–8, 153–8
policy entrepreneurs 6, 9, 12, 13, 20, 169

policy learning and experimentation 72–4
political judgement 13, 90
pollution 62, 76, 81, 105, 166, 167, 169, 170
Porras, I.T. 138
Port Arthur Massacre 125, 126, 134
portfolio approach 102, 103
poverty and social impact analysis (PSIA) 71
power of stakeholders 67, 68, 69
private sector 22, 41, 64, 205
problem identification 14–15, 39
productivity 28–9
Productivity Commission (PC) 42, 43, 48, 89, 122–4, 129–31, 133, 134
professional practice 13, 90
profitability 26–8, 204–5
progress of reform 12, 13, 19, 73
public goods 80, 137, 158
public policy: assessment framework for resilient public policy 39–40; dynamics of successful change 22; four assessments of public policy 40–56; Home Insulation Program 48–52; Mineral Resources Rent Tax 52–6; Murray–Darling Basin Plan 44–8; National Competition Policy 40–3; overview 56–7, 57; resilient public policy 38–60
Pyrex® 22

Queensland 50–1, 56, 125, 127, 128
quotas in fisheries management: background 147; defining the extent of a quota 155–6; design detail 153–8; eligibility for quotas 154–5; getting to the quota management regime 149–53; impact of reform in New Zealand 158–61; overarching quota concept 153–4; paying for the quota regime 157–8; rights associated with quotas 156–7; success of fishery management transformation in New Zealand 161–2

Radonic, L. 102
RAG Deutsche Steinkolhe AG 69
rainforest action groups 188, 189
Ramon Magsaysay Award 194

Rangan, V. 203, 204
Rapp, Dennis 169, 170
Raynor, Michael 33
Razer, H. 80, 89
Reagan, Ronald 151
Reavis, Cate 22, 33
REDD-Fund 139
reform: achieving transformational policy reform 1–2; adaptation and ongoing improvements 12–13, 219–20; careful design and refinement of the reform package 6–9, 211–16; definition of transformational reform 120–1; developing the case for change 2–4, 207–10; implementing the reform 10–12, 217–19; learning 13; lessons from reforming fossil-fuel subsidies 63–72; negotiating the reform package 9–10, 216–17; next step 19–20; policy reform in parallel 88–90; securing interest in the proposition 4–6, 210–11
regionalism 81, 83–6, 89
regional NRM model 84, 85, 86
Reichert, J.S. 137
renewable energy 17, 62, 105
research and development (R&D) 81, 88
reservoirs 98, 99, 112, 177, 178
resilient public policy 38–60; assessment framework for resilient public policy 39–40; definition 38; discussion 56–7; four assessments of public policy 40–56; Home Insulation Program 48–52; Mineral Resources Rent Tax 52–6; Murray–Darling Basin Plan 44–8; National Competition Policy 40–3; overview 38–9, 57
Resources Super Profits Tax (RSPT) 53, 54
Restoring the Balance program 47
reviewing progress 13, 19
"ribbon machine" 22
risks 4, 50, 96–8, 124
rivers 44, 98, 99, 126
Robertson, M. 136
Robins, L. 84, 87
robustness 95, 96, 97
Rolfe, J. 139, 140

Ross, K. 102, 104
Royal Commission into the Home Insulation Program 49, 50, 51
Royal Government of Cambodia 198
RSPT *see* Resources Super Profits Tax
Rudd, Kevin 12, 14–20, 48, 52, 53, 54
Rural Adjustment Scheme 124
rural communities 44–5, 82, 130

Sacramento River 100
Safe Drinking Water Act 166
safety issues 49, 50, 51
Sainsbury 189
Salefi-Isfahani, D. 72, 73
Salzman, J. 177
Sanchirico, J. 157, 159, 160
San Joaquin River 100
scanners 26
scenario analysis 3, 29–31, 36
Schwartz, Peter 30
scientific research 13, 90, 173
Sealord Ltd 153, 159, 162
securing interest in the proposition 4–6, 210–11
senior management 35–6
sequencing reforms 12, 68
setbacks 4, 12
severe drought 95, 97, 124, 127
Shaanxi Province 116
Shen, D. 111
Shenoy, B. 72
Shiyang River Basin 113, 114, 115, 117
Skocpol, T. 76
smart phones 21, 24
soil conservation 83, 137, 142
solar energy 48, 105
Solar Hot Water Rebate 48
Soll, D. 166–70, 171–2, 173–5
Sophara, Chea 201
SPC Ardmona 132
specify, identify, act, monitor and update (SIAMU) 40
speed of implementation 11
Spencer, M. 190
stakeholder engagement 10, 125, 128–9, 133
stakeholder interests 65–8, 69, 75, 175

232 Index

Standing Council on Primary Industries 124
State of Environment Reports 83
State Water Project 95
Stave, K.A. 168
Stockholm Industry Water Award 194
Stoneham, G. 138
strategic policy integration 32–3, 116–17
structural solutions 34–5
subsidies 122–4, 139, 150 *see also* fossil-fuel subsidies
supermarkets 189
supportive alliances 5–6
surface water 44, 46, 47, 99, 100, 101, 103, 121, 122
Surface Water Treatment Rule 166
sustainability 61, 83, 92, 106, 182, 188, 191
sustainable diversion limits (SDLs) 47, 48
Sustainable Groundwater Management Act 98, 103, 106
Sustainable Rural Water Use and Infrastructure Program 47
Swan, Wayne 48, 52
Synnott, T. 181, 182, 183
systematic learning 73, 75–6
systemic responses 97, 105
systemic risks 96–8, 105, 106
Syverson, Chad 29

Tanaka, S.K. 106
Tanzania 71
targeted therapeutics 33
tariffs 130, 197–9, 202, 203–4
Tasmania 84, 134
taxation 52–6
telecommunications 21, 22
Tercek, Mark 138
Tesco 189
testing of reform 7, 89
't Hart, P. 120, 126
Thatcher, Margaret 151
"Think Big" projects 150
"three lenses of knowledge and influence" 13, 90, 92, 220
"Three Red Lines" policies 117
timber industry 181, 182, 188, 189, 191
timely policy 42, 46–7, 50, 53, 55, 57, 65

Tortajada, C. 196, 197, 198, 199, 201
total allowable catch (TAC) 154, 157–8
tracking progress 12
trade-offs 105–6
trade unions 66, 69, 71
transferability 174–8
transfer of water 111–14
transformational change: development of water markets in China 109–19; difficulty of sustainable environmental reform 14–20; drought policy in Australia 120–35; drought policy in California 95–108; dynamics of successful change 21–37; failure to capture synergies in natural resource management 80–94; fisheries management in New Zealand 147–63; Forest Stewardship Council certification 180–93; fossil-fuel subsidies 61–79; guidelines for transformational change 207–20; New York City's PES for clean water 164–79; payments for ecosystem services 136–46; resilient public policy 38–60; in search of excellence 1–13; water management success in Phnom Penh 194–206
transformational policy reform: achieving transformational policy reform 1–2; adaptation and ongoing improvements 12–13, 219–20; careful design and refinement of the reform package 6–9, 211–16; definition of transformational reform 120–1; developing the case for change 2–4, 207–10; difficulty of sustainable environmental reform 14–20; guidelines for transformational change 207–20; implementing the reform 10–12, 217–19; learning 13; negotiating the reform package 9–10, 216–17; in search of excellence 1–13; securing interest in the proposition 4–6, 210–11
transformative alliances 66–8, 68–9, 70
transition arrangements 6–9
transparency: fossil-fuel subsidies 69, 75; removal of corruption 199; resilient public policy 42–3, 44, 47, 50, 55, 57

Transparency International 196
Treaty of Waitangi 147, 149, 151, 152, 153
tropical timber 181, 182, 188, 189, 191
Truelove, C. 105
trust 13, 75, 85, 93, 143, 167, 169
Tunisia 66
Turkey 65
Tushman, Michael 34, 35

UN Convention on the Law of the Sea 150
UNDP (United Nations Development Program) 198
UNEP (United Nations Energy Program) 61, 177
uniqueness 27, 28
United Kingdom 76, 83
United Nations Conference on Environment and Development 182
United States 9, 76, 97, 138
US Conservation Reserve Program 138, 139
US Farm Bill 104
US–Mexico Water Treaty 98

van Djik, A.I.J.M. 126
Vest, Charles 31
vested interests: difficulty of sustainable environmental reform 17–18, 19; failure to capture synergies in natural resource management 80, 81, 90, 91; fossil-fuel subsidies 65, 65–8, 68, 75
Victor, D. 62, 65
Vidican, G. 73
vision 3, 32, 47, 51, 56
Vogel, T. 96, 97
volume-based pricing 197–9, 201–2
voluntary action 85, 86, 145
von Hippel, Eric 33

Waitangi Treaty 147, 149, 151, 152, 153
Walquist, A. 127, 128
Wang, Y. 110, 112, 115
war 24
Warne, D. 172, 173, 174
wastewater 105, 165, 170, 174, 177

Water Act 2007 44, 45, 46, 47
water allocation 97, 110, 117, 121–2
Water Bond 98
water conservation 105, 112–13, 115
Water for the Future 45
Water Law 110
water management success in Phnom Penh 194–206; background 194–5; coalition of interests 201; impact of foreign donors 201–2; integrity of the proposal 202; overview 205; perspective on success 201; removal of corruption 199–201; similar case studies 202–5; structural reformation 195–7; tariff policy and volume based pricing 197–9
water markets in China 109–19; anatomy of water rights trading in China 109–11; challenges to the development of water markets 114–17; lessons for transformational environmental policy reform 117–18; three case studies 111–14; water scarcity 109
water metering 113, 197, 199, 202
water permits 110, 111, 115
water-policy reform: developing the case for change 3; difficulty of sustainable environmental reform 16, 17; drought policy in Australia 120–35; drought policy in California 95–108; implementing the reform 11; policy detail 8; policy reform in parallel 88; resilient public policy 38
water quality: Australia 84, 122; New York City's PES for clean water 164–79; payments for ecosystem services 136, 137, 138, 142; water management in Phnom Penh 195
water rights 100–2, 103
water rights trading 109–12, 113–14, 116, 117–18, 123, 131
water scarcity 88, 103, 106, 109, 111–13, 116, 117
Watershed Agricultural Council (WAC) 169, 173, 174
Watershed Post 178
Watershed Protection and Partnership Council 174

...ls 136, 138–9, 141–3, 164–7, 170,
    -5, 177
  supply 2, 97, 100, 164–5, 194, 201,
    202–3
  ...ter Supply Bureau 172
Webber, M. 110
wells 113, 115, 117
Wen Jiabao 114
Wentworth Group of Concerned Scientists
    48
West Wit 105
wetlands 100, 136, 139, 140, 143, 177
Whole Farm Planning 169–70, 173–5
Wilhite, D.A. 133
WITW (Water in the West) 105
Woodworkers Alliance for Rainforest
    Protection (WARP) 182
workers' rights 50, 185
World Bank 73, 198

World Conservation Union 181
World Economic Forum (WEF) 97
World Health Organization 205
World Wildlife Fund (WWF) 181, 182,
    183, 188, 189

Xia, C. 109

Yan, H. 117
Yellow River Conservancy Commission
    112
Yi, M. 112
Yiwu 111, 112
Yong, J. 109
Young, M. 8, 48, 103, 104, 113, 130, 131

Zhang, L. 110, 111, 112, 113, 115
Zhejiang Province 111
Zipcar 32